ACTS

OF THE

ALMIGHTY

$106

ACTS
OF THE
ALMIGHTY

MEDITATIONS *on the* STORY OF GOD

for EVERY DAY OF THE YEAR

WALTER WANGERIN JR.

ZONDERVAN

Acts of the Almighty
Copyright © 2019 by Walter Wangerin Jr.

Requests for information should be addressed to:
Zondervan, *3900 Sparks Dr. SE, Grand Rapids, Michigan 49546*

ISBN 978-0-310-35688-2 (softcover)

ISBN 978-0-310-35690-5 (audio)

ISBN 978-0-310-35689-9 (ebook)

Cover design: Studio Gearbox
Cover illustration: visuallanguage
Interior design: Denise Froehlich

Printed in the United States of America

19 20 21 22 23 /LSC/ 10 9 8 7 6 5 4 3 2 1

O Lord my God, when I in awesome wonder
Consider all the works thy hand hath made,
I see the stars, I hear the rolling thunder,
Thy power throughout the universe displayed,
Then sings my soul, my Savior God to thee,
How great thou art. How great thou art.

Contents

Introduction

You might think of yourself as reading these daily devotions in your kitchen or your living room or in your bedroom or wherever and whenever you choose a regular and consistent time. But in a sense, I am with you as a friend. We are partners.

This book contains 366 devotions (because I have included leap year).

From January 1 to December 31, we will work through the highlights of the Bible, Genesis to Revelation, in a storylike sequence. Therefore, I suggest that you read these devotions *as* a continual story. Some of you may have dipped into other devotional books here and there as you pleased. If you do the same with *Acts of the Almighty*, you might be baffled by a devotion that is separated from the others.

Whenever a prayer at the end of a devotion says "I," it refers to both of us.

Before I began to write each page, I prayed this prayer, "May these words of my mouth and this meditation of my heart be pleasing in your sight, LORD, my Rock and my Redeemer (Psalm 19:14).

Be at peace, my friend. Christ has guided me. He loves you. All is well, and everything very well.

Walter Wangerin Jr.

BOOK 1

THE
OLD
TESTAMENT

PART I

CREATION and the FALL

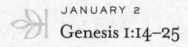

Genesis 1:1–15

In the beginning there is God and . . . nothing. The "void." I can't imagine a nothing-ness, no space no time, because *I'm* always there, a some-thing that fills the nothing.

The Hebrew word for *deep* can mean "a roaring, surging, limitless water."

God says, "Light," and that word *was* light issuing from his mouth. He names the light "Day" and the darkness "Night." An evening and a morning make the first day, and God has created time.

Then he calls into being a hard, blue dome to divide the raging waters above from the raging waters below, and God has created space. He names that blue dome "Sky" and names the land below "Earth." God has created space, a place for every other thing he will create.

And God says, "Good." But "good" isn't a mere observation. It is a shout, the way *we* shout and pump our fists when our team has won the game.

PRAYER

Lord, your hands created a world. All glory to you, and thanksgiving for-evermore! Amen.

Genesis 1:14–25

These verses explain how to tell time.

God puts two lights in the sky, a greater one and a lesser one, and scatters stars in it. He doesn't name them because pagans will name them and worship them, the sun and the moon and the constellations. But there is only one true God.

The big light rules the day, and the lesser light rules the night. The moon marks the months. The sun marks the days and the four seasons.

God says, "Swarm," and birds swarm the skies. Again he says, "Swarm," and schools of fish swim in the seas. Wheat flourishes in spring and summer and is harvested in the fall. Creeping things come to life, the four-footed beasts that roam the earth and feed on green things and those that roam on two feet and those that live in trees.

Good!

PRAYER

Step by step, good God, you created the round globe, this earth we walk on and the air we breathe and the soil we sow today. We delight in your handiwork and do our best to preserve it. Amen.

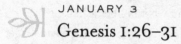

JANUARY 3
Genesis 1:26–31

God creates humankind in his image. He creates them male and female. Sometimes a man will consider himself to be the image of God, or sometimes a woman will think the same.

In fact, the image resides in them both when they are conjoined. "Male and female he created them," the two together. God's image resides in their mutual needs and their love.

God's gift is a blessing and not a command. Those who are blessed must bless. "Fill the earth and subdue it," says the Lord. But *subdue* emphatically does not mean that humankind gets to do with creation whatever it wants to do: take charge, dominate, act as if it were the world's taskmaster. It means to do best by God's creation, to take care of it, to keep the earth as though people were farmers working for God.

PRAYER

Lord, I have loved my wife through the past fifty years. People love their children, their friends, their partners, and their neighbors. We might think love springs from our own hearts. But you first loved us, and our ability to love comes from you. Amen.

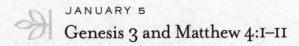

Genesis 2:7–25

Now God rolls a hunk of red, wet clay into a ball, and then, as if it were modeling clay, he shapes it into the human form. The Lord God leans down as if to kiss the man and blows life-giving breath into his nostrils.

In Hebrew and Greek and Latin, the word for *breath* also means "wind" and "spirit." Every baby is the clay. God's wind expands its lungs, and the spirit sparks life in the infant's body.

God gives thought to the man, Adam, and says, "No one should have to live lonely and alone." But the beasts can't be good company. God named his creations—the sky, the earth, and the seas. But human beings cannot create by naming. They can name only the things that have already been created. "Here's a cow, here's a hawk. But where's a being like *me*?"

So God creates that being. Adam's sleep is not like the sleep we get in our beds at night. It is deep. It is so deep that Adam has nothing to do with the woman's creation. God chooses. God remains the true creator. And here she is. Adam wakes and sees his companion and shouts a sort of whoop-de-do! "Bone of my bone and flesh of my flesh!" he cries, delighted, then he makes a pun on their separate genders. The pun is the same in both Hebrew and English: "She shall be called a wo*man* because she was formed from a *man*."

And she is help*mate* for him, his equal because they are each a perfect fit for the other.

PRAYER
Father, we don't have the words to thank you enough for our lives. Because of you, we are. Continue to bind us together in your image of love. Amen.

Genesis 3 and Matthew 4:1–11

The serpent tempts Eve, then both she and Adam fall into sin. Satan tempts Jesus and he does not fall.

The serpent starts by causing Eve to doubt the words of God. "Did God *say*," he says, "that you can't eat of any tree in the garden?" At first Eve answers rightly, but then she whines like a child: "We can't even *touch* it." Satan starts the same way: "If you really *are* God's son, prove it." But in the previous passage, God's words were: "This is my Son." Jesus doesn't answer with his own words but with the words of Scripture.

Next the serpent tempts Eve with an outrageous lie: She won't die. She will be like God. Pride wants that power. Satan also tempts Jesus with scriptural words. But Jesus tells him that he is tempting *God*.

Eve falls for the serpent's lie. The tree is beautiful, its fruit will be delicious, and it'll make her clever in the ways of the world. She eats. But the fruit tastes like ashes, for she has put her foot on the long path to death.

Satan says to Jesus, "Worship me and I'll give you the world." Jesus rejects the tempter's lies and defeats him. He will worship none but the one true God.

PRAYER

More times than I want to admit, I have fallen into temptation. To rule like you, my Lord. To be so proud that I think I'm superior to other people. I have prayed for you to lift me out of the swamp of my sins, and you have, and now I mount up as on the wings of angels. Amen.

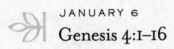

JANUARY 6
Genesis 4:1–16

Cain's story shows and sharpens the consequence of his parents' disobedience. Cain becomes a farmer, and Abel a shepherd—two occupations opposed to one another because sheep will often graze in gardens.

The two brothers offer sacrifices to the Lord (the first sacrifices ever to be brought). Cain burns the fruit of his garden. Abel sends up the sweet fragrance of a lamb. There is no need to ask why God accepts the one and not the other. Simply, the Creator chooses to do what he will.

Cain resents the choice. His face twists with anger. But God has not *rejected* Cain. He says, "Master yourself and I will accept you. Otherwise, sin coils like a serpent at the door of your heart."

But Cain stokes his anger to a white heat and commits the first murder. "Brother," he says, "let's settle matters. Join me in the field." Fratricide! Cain (his name means "spear") kills Abel. God was present when Adam and Eve sinned. He's here now too. His question in Eden was, "Adam, where are you?" Now his question is, "Where is your brother?" Cain answers sarcastically, "What? Should I shepherd the shepherd?" Life is in the blood, and blood belongs to God. God curses Cain more horribly than he did Adam and Eve. He will turn his face away from this murderer. The soil he sowed will deny him. Since Cain's identity is in his farming, he will lose his very self. God doesn't punish him with death. But since Cain will be a fugitive wandering restlessly across the wilderness, anyone who meets him will kill him.

Yet God performs one final act of mercy. He puts a mark (a tattoo?) on Cain so that anyone who sees it won't hurt him at all. Note: This is not a mark of shame. It is a mark of protection.

PRAYER
Lord Jesus, I am more like Cain than Abel. You are Abel. I am the sinner. You are the one who died. Mark me, my God, with the sign of your mercy. Mark me with your blood. Amen.

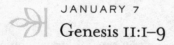

JANUARY 7
Genesis 11:1–9

To be like God. To be like the gods.

The Babylonians built massive towers called ziggurats. They were four-sided structures that resembled the shape of a pyramid and could rise as high as 160 feet into the air. The priest would climb the ziggurat's countless steps to a small shrine on the top to worship their god.

The people who were once God's people now build a tower according to the blueprint of the Babylonians, and they could because they all spoke the same language. They said, "Our tower will reach as high as heaven, and we will demand that God give us a portion of his power." Don't we want the same? Don't some politicians want to climb up to impose their authority on their cities or districts or states? Don't certain people climb the tower to reach the wealthy 1 percent? Don't we step on the heads of those who want what we want?

But God won't have it. He divides the races from other races, and countries from other countries. We grow jealous of those who have what we don't have.

Yet God loves the world, the whole world, and all its people, without distinction.

PRAYER

In you, O Lord, we put our trust. The only tower between heaven and earth is the one you descended. You took our form and lived among us, and now we are one body in the Spirit, confessing one faith. And we all speak one spiritual language. Thank you. Amen.

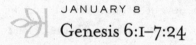

JANUARY 8
Genesis 6:1–7:24

The entire human race has broken the Creator's heart. Like parents who love their children, God grieves—not so much for their individual sins as for the general wickedness of all humanity. There is no help for it, then, but to wipe it from the face of the earth.

The Lord throws open the windows of heaven that the wild waters may gush down. He cracks the earth open that the wild waters may fountain up. In other words, he could destroy the space he created at the beginning. But he can't bring himself to drown *everyone*. He will save a few—Noah and his family and every kind of animal so that they may once again be fruitful and multiply. Noah's righteousness is in this: that he will trust the Lord's outrageous command to build a boat where there is no water to float it.

And so he does, and so the salvation of one family.

PRAYER

> All people that on earth do dwell,
> Sing to the Lord with cheerful voice.
> Him serve with mirth, his praise forth-tell—
> Come ye before him and rejoice. Amen.

—"ALL PEOPLE THAT ON EARTH DO DWELL"

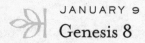

JANUARY 9
Genesis 8

Remember the wind that God blew over the primeval waters? He blows it again on another sort of water. He closes the windows of heaven and shuts the fountains of the deep—and he remembers Noah. The flood begins to subside. The ark comes to rest on a mountain, and Noah tests the waters to know if there's some dry land on the earth.

He sends out a raven (like the raven that will feed the prophet Elijah) which flies over the horizon and over the world but returns with nothing to show for its labors.

Then he releases a dove (like the dove of the Spirit that will one day perch on Jesus's shoulder). This dove too doesn't find a place to land. But after its second flight, the dove returns with an olive leaf in its bill. A wonderful sign!—not only that the waters have subsided, but also because olive branches are a sign of peace. "Peace be with you, Noah!"

Noah builds a stone altar and sacrifices a burnt offering to God which pleases him with the scent that proves Noah's righteousness. Then the Lord makes a timeless and worldwide promise never again to destroy humanity in spite of its future evil. The earth will endure. It shall never again be brought to ruin.

PRAYER

Let our prayers come unto you, our Lord, as a sweet scent in your nostrils. Mornings and evenings, we lift our prayers to you. Mornings and evenings, you listen to us, and year after year, by your righteousness, you save us alive. Amen.

PART 2

The

PATRIARCHS

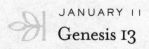

Genesis 12:1–9

Biblical history starts with Abraham.

He has lived for seventy-five years when suddenly, out of the blue, God appears to him, and asks him to pull up stakes and to travel in a foreign land—a place and a people he knows nothing about—as if he were stepping out into the dark.

But Abraham puts his faith in God and goes with his wife and a nephew and his cattle and all his possessions.

The land God takes him to is Canaan, populated by pagans.

When he arrives at the sacred oak tree called "Moreh," Abraham builds a rude altar of stones and offers sacrifices to God.

My first call was to be the pastor of an inner-city, African American congregation. I didn't have the faith of Abraham. The inner city scared me, and I hadn't ever lived among black people.

But Grace Lutheran Church took me and my family to its bosom. It was a helpful beginning. Then I forced myself to walk the inner-city streets, passing by young men on corners, smoking and shooting the bull. I nodded to women rocking on their porches. I learned their names and slowly was accepted in the neighborhood. My faith became a faith like Abraham's.

Is God calling you to serve in a new place with people different from yourself?

PRAYER

I am trusting you, Lord Jesus, trusting only you. Amen.

JANUARY 11

Genesis 13

Abraham has sojourned in Egypt, accumulating riches and larger herds of livestock. Now he travels north across the Negev desert to Bethel, where his men pitch tents to accommodate Abraham's and Lot's families. They are nomads. The citizens nearby allow them to drink from their wells and to graze their herds on harvested fields. After that the nomads will wander on to other places.

But Lot's and Abraham's cattle are too many to find fodder in the region. It's the better part of wisdom, then, to separate. Abraham offers Lot first choice. From Bethel, Lot sees the entire Jordan valley as far as the southern tip of the Dead Sea. He has no trouble choosing. He points to a territory as beautiful as a garden (of Eden?). But the city of Sodom will be no garden in the end.

The Lord God promises to give Abraham all the lands to the north, the south, the east, and the west. And though the man is very old, God promises that his children and their children's children will be as countless as the stars.

God is steadfast yesterday and today. Jesus promises, "Blessed are those who are persecuted because of righteousness, for theirs is the kingdom of heaven." Why, then, should we fear death? He promises to be with us even to the end of the world. Why, then, should we feel alone and lonely or depressed?

PRAYER

Lord Jesus, I've pitched my tent among those who are strangers to my faith. There is no garden here. But you promised me, "Today you will be with me in paradise." I believe your promise. Amen.

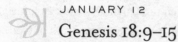

JANUARY 12

Genesis 18:9–15

Three angels of God appear to Abraham in the form of common men. When he sees the men coming toward him, he leaps up and offers them his hospitality. "Wait here," he says, then rushes into his tent. "Sarah! Bake honey cakes!" While she does, Abraham roasts a lamb and rushes out again with the food and wine.

One of the angels says, "Where is your wife?"

Abraham answers, "In the tent." Right, she's in the tent and listening at the door.

The angel says, "In nine months Sarah will bear a baby boy." Sarah laughs. "Me? With a dried-up womb? And my husband a hundred years old?"

The angel says, "Why did she laugh?" Uh-oh. Sarah tries to cover her embarrassment. "I didn't laugh."

The angel says, "With God nothing is impossible."

As old as they are, Abraham and Sarah bear a son. This time Sarah laughs with joy. "Who can believe it? I'm nursing my own baby!" They name the baby Isaac.

When Gabriel tells the Virgin Mary that she will bear a little boy, she murmurs, "Impossible. I have never lain with a man." And Gabriel says, "Nothing is impossible for God."

Impossible promises? Can an alcoholic get sober for the rest of his life? Can a troubled marriage be saved? Can we make friends with our enemies? Can we care for a dear one suffering with Alzheimer's disease?

PRAYER

My hands are yours, my God. My will is yours. My heart is yours. You ask me to do impossible things, then give me the power to do them. Amen.

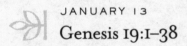

JANUARY 13
Genesis 19:1–38

Lot was a decent man—until now, when radical events work a change in him. Two men (whom he doesn't suspect are messengers of God) come to Sodom. Lot shows them hospitality. He insists that they enter his house. "Eat. Drink. Spend the night." The strangers accept his offer. During the night Sodom's men bang on Lot's door. "Open up! Give us your visitors!" There's no doubt about their intentions. It will be a gang rape! Lot goes out. He shuts the door to protect his guests. Changing, changing, Lot says to the lecherous Sodomites, "I have two daughters, virgins...." But they roar, "Get out of the way! Who do you think you are to judge us?" They would have beaten Lot, but the Lord's angels snatch him inside and strike those outside blind.

The angels tell Lot to pack up. "Get ready to leave—you, your wife, and your daughters. God is going to destroy Sodom." But when the sun begins to rise, Lot hesitates. Why should he leave such a well-built city? The angels of the Lord drag his family out. The Dead Sea erupts with asphalt. Brimstone and fire fall from heaven, igniting the asphalt. The blaze consumes the city and the people and the land. Henceforth the land will be a crabbed, unforthcoming desert.

Lot's wife looks back, sad for her loss. But God wants this family to break from wickedness and to lead a whole new life. Pillars of salt are formed by the erosion of the sea, then crumble quickly.

PRAYER
Save us, Lord. Save us from ourselves. Amen.

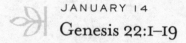

JANUARY 14
Genesis 22:1–19

Sarah's doubt turned to joy when she bore baby Isaac. Abraham brushed his tiny boy's cheek with the back of his hand, overcome with love. And this too: God is keeping his promise. Abraham will be the father of countless generations.

But when Isaac reaches his adolescence, God seems to renege on that promise. "Sacrifice your son, your only son," he says, "to me." What? Then Abraham would have no male heir to carry his name down the ages. Worse than that, how can he kill the boy of his heart? It would be the same as driving the sacrificial sword through his own beating heart. He'd live out the rest of his days hollow and unhappy.

But faith is bound to obey. Abraham carries a smoking fire-coal while he and his son climb the hill of God's choosing. Isaac doesn't understand. "Here's wood, here's fire, and here's a knife. But where's the lamb?" Abraham says, "God will provide." Isaac asks nothing else. He puts his trust in his father.

Abraham obeys *his* Father. He builds a stone altar. He lays the fire-wood on it. He ties Isaac's hands and ankles with tough cords, then lays the lad on the wood. Who knows what Isaac is thinking? His father takes in two hands the handle of the knife and lifts it up, ready to drive it into his son's heart.

Suddenly, things are reversed. "Abraham!" says an angel. "Put your knife away! You've been tested and found completely obedient to the Lord. Your children *will* be as many as sands on the seashore."

The Lord says to us, "Give me what you love most of all. Sacrifice your very hearts on my altar. Name yourselves by my name. O my children, empty yourselves of yourselves, and I will be the ram that dies that you may live."

PRAYER

What terrible things you ask of me, to live my days as if each will be my last. But you wake me every morning, and every night I pray,

> Now I lay me down to sleep.
> I pray the Lord my soul to keep.
> If I should die before I wake,
> I pray the Lord my soul to take. Amen.

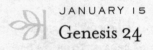

JANUARY 15
Genesis 24

Three times in the Old Testament, men meet women at wells, and marriages follow. Jacob met Rachel at a well and married her. Moses met Zipporah at a well. Now Abraham sends his most senior servant, Eliezer, to find a wife for Isaac.

Abraham is living the last days of his life. It is surely time for his son to bear children. With a caravan of ten camels and wealth enough to pay a dowry, Eliezer rides east to Harran. It's been a very long journey, so he pauses at a well to water the camels. Then here comes a young and lovely woman with a water jar. Eliezer asks for a drink. Gathering more than a drink for the servant, Rebekah walks down the steps to the flowing stream, and carries the jar up again and again till the camels have drunk their fill. Eliezer sees this as a sign from the Lord: Rebekah is to be Isaac's bride. She runs to her mother's house to tell her father (her brother?), Laban, and her grandfather, Bethuel, what just happened. And behold! The man she met gives a robe with a dazzling brooch and jewels and golden bracelets—more than enough for a bride-price. Laban's eyes pop. Eliezer negotiates with Rebekah's family until he persuades them to release her.

Isaac, delighted by the woman, marries her.

PRAYER

Jesus, you've given us more than water—water mixed with blood that sprang from the wells of your wounds, and now we drink the wine of eternal life. All praise and glory be to you. Amen.

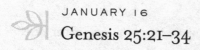

JANUARY 16
Genesis 25:21–34

Isaac is sixty years old when his wife conceives. By Rebekah's eighth month, her womb bulks larger and heavier than it ought to—and so painfully that she would rather die than live. "O God, why is this happening to me?" The Lord answers, saying, "Two boys are wrestling in your womb. The firstborn will be strong, and your second-born so nimble-witted that he'll cheat his twin of his birthright and his blessing."

The first of Rebekah's boys is born ruddy and covered with a thick, reddish hair. The second comes out holding his brother's heel, as if he were taking a ride. The first his parents name Esau, and the second, Jacob, which means the "usurper," one who "grasps the heel," one who displaces another. Isaac favors Esau, a hunter who brings home savory meat. Rebekah favors Jacob, pampers him as a baby, and indulges him as an adult.

One day Esau returns from the forest, famished. A three days' hunt, and he's caught nothing. When he sees Jacob sitting outside his mother's tent and stirring a pot of stew, Esau says, "Jacob, I'm starving! Give me a bowl of your red porridge." Jacob says, "I will sell it to you, Esau, for the price of your birthright." With a birthright goes all a father's possessions when he dies.

It's not much different today. Family conflicts still ruin family relationships. We argue about politics and religion and our parents' last wills and testaments. And our children may take sides, and what then?

PRAYER

When we were young, my brother and I fought. I hit his shoulder bone with my knuckle, hard enough to knock him to the floor. He threw a barbeque fork which stuck in my pant waist. But by your mercy, we reconciled and have been close friends ever since. Amen.

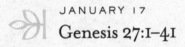

JANUARY 17
Genesis 27:1–41

If we lie to others to get what we want, their truer wants are perverted.

Isaac is old and blind. He says to his elder son, "Esau, prepare to receive my blessing." So Esau goes into the forest with his bow and a quiver of arrows.

Tents sewn of goatskin aren't soundproof. Rebekah overhears her husband's request. "Quick, Jacob," she says. "Put your brother's clothes on." "Why?" "To smell like Esau, to receive his blessing." Jacob hesitates. "Father will know I'm not Esau." "But he'll *think* you are." "My arms are smooth." "No matter," Rebekah says. She covers his arms and neck with goatskins, then gives him a plate of roasted goat. "Go," she says, and he goes.

Isaac asks, "Who are you?" Jacob tells the first of his lies. "Esau," he says. "Here, eat the food you like so much, then bless me." The old man says, "But how did you come back so soon?" Jacob's second lie is worse than the first because it involves the Lord. "God sped my arrow." Isaac isn't convinced. "Let me touch your arm." The hairy pelt is Jacob's third deception. And that his clothes smell of the forest is his fourth. Isaac says, "It's Jacob's voice but Esau's arms. Give me the food." After he's eaten, Isaac remains uncertain. "Come here and kiss me"—not so much to kiss as to sniff Jacob's clothes. The deception works, and Isaac blesses his second son. "You will have dominion over your family and over many kingdoms."

Jacob withdraws, and Esau rushes in. "Father!" he cries. "Enjoy the game I've caught, then bless me." Poor Isaac. "Who are you?" he asks. "Esau, your son." "Then who did I . . . ?" The old man lifts his voice and wails. "I have already blessed your brother." "Revoke it! Give it to me!" But what was done before the Lord can't be undone. "Come here," says Isaac miserably. "I have a second blessing." But it must be lesser than the first. "You will live by your sword and serve your brother." Esau howls in a purple rage. Isaac continues, "But in time you will break the yoke on your neck." Esau hisses, "I am going to *kill* him!"

Rebekah urges her son to flee.

PRAYER

I've lied to my parents in order to do what I want to do. Forgive me, that they might forgive me too. Amen.

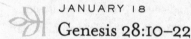

JANUARY 18
Genesis 28:10–22

Jacob's pillow-stone is so marvelously huge (seven feet high when stood on end) that the man must be seen as heroically strong. Night falls. The stone is as much for sleeping as it is for protection. In the starry darkness of his dream, Jacob sees a stairway with angels descending to earth and ascending to heaven again. Hush, Jacob! Your vision is holy! God himself is present!

God says, "Jacob?" Jacob answers, "Here I am." "I am the God who promised your grandfather and your father land and so many offspring that they will rule nations, and I've come to make the same promise to you. I will be with you wherever you go." Jacob wakes, trembling with wonder. Dreams are real. God was—is!—here. Jacob heaves the stone up as a pillar and a sign for all who pass by to bow down and worship in this place. *Bethel:* the house of God, and *gate:* the stairway into heaven.

O Lord, you made a promise to the patriarchs. Jesus, you fulfilled that promise for our sakes. God's love has been "poured into my heart by the Holy Spirit." I bow before your altar and I worship you. Amen.

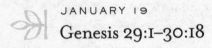

JANUARY 19
Genesis 29:1–30:18

Laban proves to be as cunning as Jacob. What goes around comes around.

Abraham's servant met Rebekah at a well. Jacob meets Rachel at a well. After a journey of more than four hundred miles, he comes upon three shepherds lying around a well, waiting to water their flocks. This irritates Jacob. "You're wasting time! Get up. Push the stone off the well. Let your sheep drink and go." "Yeah, right," they say. "Rule is, the shepherds of Harran don't move the lid till we're all here. Fairness. Besides, it takes four men to move that stone."

"Harran?" Jacob asks. "Yup. Laban lives a mile that-a-way." Jacob glances in the way they're pointing and sees a pretty girl-child coming with her flocks. A shepherd scoffs, "Turn tail, Rachel! Females ain't wanted here." But Jacob has leaped up. He shifts the stone himself, then says to the girl, "You first."

While she waters her flock, Jacob thinks, "Rachel?—my kinswoman!" He helps her finish, then kisses her and weeps. Rachel runs home to her father. Jacob isn't far behind. Laban greets him and invites him in. Since Esau's fury will last a long time, Jacob will work for his relative for at least seven years, after which he will marry his beloved Rachel. Well, another seven years after the cunning Laban substitutes his older daughter for his younger. Finally, Jacob's given the woman of his heart. In the years that follow, Jacob's wives beget eleven children while he tricks the trickster. His ewes beget so many sheep that his flock grows huger than Laban's. What goes around comes around. Time to go home.

How good, Lord, that you are merciful to the imperfect. We play (some-times nasty) tricks on our siblings, our schoolmates, whether they're friends or people we don't like; on our colleagues at the office or in the factory. Good works mean nothing next to bad works. Be thou the Perfect One who undoes our imperfections. Amen.

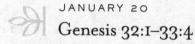

JANUARY 20

Genesis 32:1–33:4

A wadi is a streambed. During the dry season (early May through September), it is hard, cracked clay. During the rainy season (October through April), the wadi can become a torrent.

Jacob encamps along the Wadi Jabbok, east of the Jordan River—he and his wives and children and the drovers of his vast livestock. His servants report that Esau is coming. Jacob doesn't know if it's to reconcile or to attack. He has never ceased to fear Esau. His next trick is very serious—to save his life. Jacob sends his servants across the Jordan, with herds totaling 550 animals. "Tell my brother that these gifts come from me and that I will follow to find forgiveness with him." In the evening he sends his family across and is left alone in the moonless dark by the rocks beside the Jabbok.

A night spirit comes and wrestles mightily with Jacob. Jacob strains and holds his own. Near dawn the night spirit strikes Jacob's hip. Jacob cries, "What's your name?" To know the name of the spirit of the night is to control him. But the spirit says, "It is not for you to know my name. Tell me yours."

Jacob has lost the advantage. He answers, "Jacob." "Your name," says the spirit, "shall no longer be the Usurper, but Israel, for you have wrestled with God and with the men in your life and have prevailed." *With* God can mean "on God's side" or else "against God."

When the sun rises, Jacob is quivering with awe. What he saw dimly in the twilight was the face of God. When he and Esau meet, they are true brothers again, with no strife between them.

Infinite, almighty, and holy Father in heaven, your glory blinds me. But by your love you've shown me your face in the face of your Son. How I love you in return. Amen.

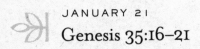

JANUARY 21
Genesis 35:16–21

Rachel is still Jacob's most beloved, still his most delicate, small-boned woman. She survived the torment when she delivered her firstborn son, Joseph, in Harran. Now, near Bethlehem, Rachel is pregnant again. She and Jacob rejoice in the prospect of a second child. But her labor and delivery cause her unendurable agony. The boy's birth tears her flesh. The midwife can't stanch the waterfall of blood. Rachel's face grows ashen. With her last breath, she names the tiny baby Ben-Oni, the "son of my sorrow."

A name contains the identity and the fate of the one so named. Jacob fears that his son's future will be black with sorrows. Rachel has died, so he changes the child's name to Benjamin, "son of my right hand," conferring on his son a quieter, more beautiful life, a lad he will love in his old age more deeply than all his eleven other children.

Today our names are devoid of such meaning. They may indicate our relationships with our parents (I am the Wangerin of my forebears). A first name might refer to a biblical figure or else might commemorate a beloved grandparent or else be taken from a movie star or else be chosen for merely its unique sound. Would that they contained the *who we are*, as the Lakota Indians used to wait to name their children until they'd learned the character of their son or daughter.

PRAYER

Jesus, your name contains yourself: "He will save his people from their sins." When the time comes for you to utter my name, then I will be one of your people. Amen.

PART 3

God Sets

ISRAEL'S CHILDREN

Free

Exodus 2:11–25

Moses is a hotheaded youth, burning with righteousness for his people.

Pharaoh is crushing the Hebrews by forcing them to do hard labor.

One day Moses goes out and sees an Egyptian taskmaster beating a Hebrew senseless. He glances around. Seeing no one, he breaks the Egyptian's skull and lays him dead on the ground, then covers the body under a layer of sand. But someone did witness his act after all.

The next morning, he sees two Hebrews fighting. Filled with fear, they turn to Moses and scold him. "You're going to get us all killed!"

For his own sake, Moses escapes Egypt and runs to Midian. He's resting beside a well when seven sisters come to water their flocks. "Who are you?" he asks, and they answer, "The daughters of Jethro"— Jethro, a priest in Midian. One sister seems quieter and more reserved than the others, a good balance to Moses's impetuous nature. He focuses on her and says, "What's your name?" She blushes. "My name is Zipporah." It isn't long before Moses has asked Jethro for his daughter's hand in marriage.

Moses doesn't expect ever to return to Egypt—not until he hears that the old pharaoh has died, that a new pharaoh has taken his place, and that this pharaoh is more brutal than the first.

The Hebrew slaves cry out, "How long, O Lord? Will you forget us forever?"

God gives ear to their travails and sends Moses back to set his people free.

PRAYER

We are like the Hebrews, Lord, sometimes beaten down by hopeless desolation. Our guilt whips our souls. But guilt also drives us to you. O Lord Jesus, break our chains and set us free. Amen.

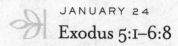

Exodus 3:1–4:15

In the Old Testament, God appears to his people in fire and thunder and thick clouds and a whirlwind. And this is how he appears to Moses too—in a blazing, unquenchable fire. The hotheaded Moses is reduced to fear by a flaming bush and a thundering voice: "Moses! Take off your shoes. Stand before me barefoot. This is holy ground! I am the God of your ancestors, Abraham, Isaac, and Jacob." Moses hides his eyes in his robe. But God eases him by saying, "I have brought you here to deliver my people from the horrors of Pharaoh. I appoint you to be my voice and my messenger and to lead my people out of Egypt."

Moses murmurs, "I can't." God answers, "Yes, you can and you will because I will go with you." Moses tries to excuse himself. "When they ask who sent me and by what authority I have come, what'll I tell them? I don't even know your name."

"My name is Yahweh. Tell them I AM WHO I AM has sent you."

Another excuse: "But what if they do not believe me?"

God says, "Throw your staff on the ground." Moses does. The staff becomes a winding snake. "Now pick it up by the tail." Moses does that too, and the snake stiffens into a staff, and God says, "Do not doubt me, but believe."

PRAYER

We can't hide our fears from you. You see our inward parts—that we're scared, Lord, a raggedy, incapable bunch. Teach us to believe that our voice is yours and that we really can be your messengers after all. Amen.

Exodus 5:1–6:8

Maybe Moses felt he was right when he told God he wasn't the guy to go, that the people wouldn't listen to him.

When he and Aaron try to talk to the people, they get angry. "God's going to judge you! You've made us wretched and more hateful in Pharaoh's eyes than ever before! Bricks without straw? And then to go out and find our own stubble? And then to make not one brick less than our quota?"

Moses turns to God and says, "See? You *knew* I didn't want to come. And your people are being killed all the day long, yet you haven't lifted a finger to deliver them!"

God says, "Who sent you? Don't you still trust my word? Say what I *told* you to say! Say, I WILL BE WHAT I WILL BE sent you. I choose what I choose. I do what *I* will do. I *am*! There is no other. Say my name and they will listen."

PRAYER

What you said to Moses, you say to us: "Trust." And then you send us into a scornful, spiteful world, and then we come whining to you. We come blaming you. We are Peter, who blamed you for your prediction of suffering and death. But you forgave Peter. Forgive us too. Amen.

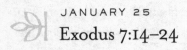

JANUARY 25
Exodus 7:14–24

The Nile is the longest river in the world. Every year it overflows its banks to nourish and enrich the land. So abundant are Egypt's crops that they ship boatloads of grain to neighboring kingdoms and in return are paid a pretty price.

When Aaron whacks the waters with his staff as God commanded, the Nile becomes a blood vein. Its tributaries, its deltas, its lakes, and even its puddles are thick with blood. Egypt stinks to high heaven. The Egyptians can't drink blood, can't cook with it, can't wash their children without smearing their faces with blood.

"Hear, O Israel, and tremble, O Egypt, for the Lord our God is one God! There are no other gods. The Lord, our Lord—he alone is God!"

The plague of blood is God's opening salvo for all the plagues to come. But Pharaoh's magicians are able to do what God did. Therefore, Pharaoh snaps his fingers at the Hebrews' petty God. But that's all right.

God will step-by-step diminish the king's gods and beat Pharaoh and prove that he alone is the master of the universe.

PRAYER

When you descend the second time, O Lord, King of Kings, you will come on clouds of glory, accompanied by flights of angels. All the nations will be gathered before you to be judged by you. Christ, when you divide the sheep from the goats, let us be your sheep. Amen.

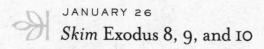

JANUARY 26
Skim Exodus 8, 9, and 10

"Let my people go!"

Frogs follow blood. An Egyptian can't take a step without squishing a frog. Pharaoh can't lie down on his ivory bed without the company of a hundred frogs. The miller opens a sack of flour, and frogs fall out. The whole land squirms green. Pharaoh wavers—until his magicians repeat the plague.

Aaron whacks the ground with his staff. A cloud of dust blows up, but it isn't dust. Clouds of gnats swarm Egypt, stick to the sweat on everyone's faces. They breathe and cough out gnats. This time Pharaoh's magicians are helpless. "King," they say, "the Hebrews' God is in this thing." "What? The God of gnats?"

Hordes of flies darken the sun. They land on eyelids to drink the tears. They crawl into the ears of the children. "Go!" cries Pharaoh. "Worship your God in the wilderness!" But Moses says, "We are hundreds of thousands. Three days to go, three days to make our sacrifice, and three days back again." Pharaoh rages, "Too long! Too long by half! I will not stop the work on my pyramid!"

Next God afflicts Egypt's cattle. The fur falls out of their hides. Their bare skin ruptures and scabs. Pharaoh's herds begin to die, while the Hebrews' cattle remain healthy. Then the Egyptians themselves—taskmasters, magicians, farmers, the lowliest servants—break out in painful boils. Step-by-step the Lord is demonstrating his power over Pharaoh's gods.

Thunder, then, and hail. Locusts. A darkness so black that it can be *felt*. "Let my people go." "Yes," then "*No!*" Well, then the tenth plague will cut the king of Egypt's heart.

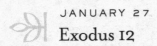

JANUARY 27
Exodus 12

God says to Moses, "I am going to strike down every firstborn son in Egypt—Pharaoh's son and the sons of all the Egyptians, even the male issues of their cattle. Prepare my people for a midnight of destruction."

Moses obeys and prepares them. At sunset each Hebrew household slaughters a year-old lamb without a spot or a blemish. They catch the blood in basins, then smear it on their lintels and doorposts with brushes made of hyssop. Each family roasts its lamb and eats dressed to travel.

Midnight! The destroying angel swoops down over the entire land of Egypt, killing its beloved sons. Fathers and mothers howl, wail in grief. But the angel passes over every house whose door is marked with blood.

PRAYER

Christ, you were the lamb that was smeared with blood. Your blood, not ours—the blood that flowed from your side. We drink the wine you called your blood. We eat the bread you called your body. We receive you in faith, and the angel of death passes over us. Lamb of God, we kneel before you and sing your praises. Amen.

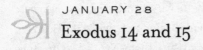

JANUARY 28
Exodus 14 and 15

The children of Israel, numbering more than a million (Exodus 12:37), have led their flocks and herds out of Egypt, together with that kingdom's wealth—and they are free! They pitch their tents on the west side of the Red Sea, eat a good meal, and fall asleep.

At dawn a mighty rumbling wakes them. They crawl out of their tents and are horrified by what they see: streams of dust blowing up behind six hundred rampaging chariots! Horses at a headlong gallop! Riders armed for war! The people yell, "Moses! We *told* you we wanted to stay in Egypt!"

Moses thunders, "Where's your faith? Trust the Lord! See what he can do!"

Ah, what the Lord can do! He blows up a whirlwind. An archangel, wrapped in a pillar of cloud, conceals the people from Pharaoh's armies. At God's command, Moses raises his staff over the sea, and the wind drives the waters left and right, and Moses cries, "Go!" And the Israelites creep forward between two walls of water. But the seabed is dry, and the walls don't topple. So they run in a wild celebration.

When the pillar of cloud evaporates in the morning, Pharaoh sees the Israelites on the far side of the sea and the dry path that lies between him and them. "Up!" he cries. "Attack!" Swords flash. Spears are raised. Pharaoh's horses and chariots charge across the dry ground. Moses lifts his hand. The two walls of water collapse, and Egypt drowns.

Oh, see what the Lord can do!

PRAYER

"Sing ye to the Lord, for he hath triumphed gloriously; the horse and his rider he hath thrown into the sea!" Amen. (Exodus 15:1 KJV)

JANUARY 29
Exodus 20:1–21

Don't worship false gods. Worship the God who is God.

Don't make images of God (as Aaron did when he melted jewelry to make the golden calf). God is the invisible mystery.

Don't misuse the name of the Lord.

The Sabbath is a holy day. Devote it to the Lord.

Honor your father and your mother. *Honor* doesn't mean "obey." Rather, it acknowledges that our parents are weighty with importance. As they decline into old age or dementia or Alzheimer's and cannot do for themselves, bathe them, feed them, dress them, read to them, sing hymns with them, help them to the toilet, and wipe them when they're finished.

Don't murder. Life belongs to God. Vengeance is not *ours*.

Sexuality is one of God's most marvelous gifts. Adultery or abuse kills the goodness of that gift.

Don't steal. God owns everything he created. To steal from another is to steal from God.

A false witness tells lies about our neighbors. Gossip can kill a reputation and isolate a neighbor from her community. Loneliness.

Don't covet. If we yearn to possess what belongs to our neighbor (his wife, her husband, their social status, their superior salaries, their "natural" beauty or athletic prowess or intelligence), we will ruin our own lives, always reaching for what we cannot have.

PRAYER

Lord, it is because you love us that you've given us your commandments. They are meant to keep us on the path of righteousness. Yet we fall short. Renew a right spirit within us. Lift us out of our miry pits, and take us to yourself. Amen.

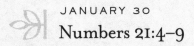

JANUARY 30
Numbers 21:4–9

Complaints upon complaints and short memories to boot! Israel has been complaining that things were better in Egypt. God's been feeding them with his miraculous morning manna, yet the people whine, "We loathe this miserable food!" Miserable? Well, then let them know what true misery really can be—the misery that follows faithlessness.

God sends serpents with fiery bites. Whoever is bitten dies. Now the people's complaining turns into begging. "Moses! Pray for us!"

Moses prays, and the forgiving Lord God says, "Make a brass serpent. Wind it on a pole. Tell the people that whoever looks at that serpent with faith will live."

What was God's sign for Israel has become Jesus's sign for us today, for he says, "Just as Moses lifted up the snake in the wilderness, so the Son of Man must be lifted up, that everyone who believes may have eternal life in him."

PRAYER

We will not die, but we will live, for your death on the post, Lord, was the beginning of our resurrection. Amen.

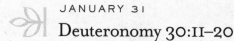

JANUARY 31
Deuteronomy 30:11–20

Moses stands on a small hill above the children of Israel, preaching his last sermon. The man is white-haired and 120 years old. The people, on the other hand, are young. Their parents died in the wilderness. These were born in the wilderness.

Moses is a mother teaching her children how to survive a daunting future, teaching them right from wrong.

He says, "I set before you life and death, blessings and curses. Choose life and live."

Several years ago, I was diagnosed with inoperable lung cancer. Since then my lungs have been slowly closing by fibrosis. Year by year the amount of lung tissue that can't accept oxygen grows. When my wife and I first told our children about my cancer, I said I was about to go on an adventure, that I was looking forward to experiencing things I'd never experienced before. I'm a writer and a poet, always observing, always interested in my interior feelings: baldness, a deep exhaustion, a loss of weight, and even my pain.

While I lay in a hospital bed last Easter, I had the wonderful opportunity to express my faith to my children and my grandchildren, that I had made peace with death.

> Jesus, I live to thee,
> The loveliest and best.
> My life in thee, thy life in me,
> In thy blest love I rest.
>
> Jesus, I die to thee,
> Whenever death shall come.
> To die in thee is life to me
> In thy eternal home.
>
> —"JESUS, I LIVE TO THEE"

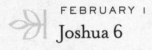

FEBRUARY I
Joshua 6

Seven thousand years ago, Jericho was a small gathering of huts. Another thousand years or so later, it became a village of mud-brick houses. Then Jericho surrounded itself with a wall, and then a second wall.

When Israel is ready to cross the Jordan, God appears to Joshua, saying, "I have given Jericho into your hands. Obey the strategy I give you, and you will not fail."

There will be no weapons. Joshua tells Israel that Jericho will be theirs by means of a God-given holy ritual.

So Israel marches around Jericho, carrying the ark of the covenant, which signifies God's presence. Seven priests blow their ram's-horn trumpets. This is the first day. For Israel *seven* is a sacred number. God rested on the seventh day. His people rest on every seventh day of the week. *Seven* marks the fullness, the completion of some important thing. While Israel marches, Jericho prepares for a war. But this enemy does not attack. After marching around, it returns to its tents. Well, then it will attack tomorrow. But it doesn't. Again Joshua leads the people around the city walls. As he does the next day and the next. Jericho grows anxious.

On the seventh day, they circle Jericho seven times. Then Joshua raises his hand, and the priests make their trumpets scream. God's people fill their lungs and shout. They bellow like outraged bulls. Their roaring shatters the air—and the walls of Jericho fall.

PRAYER

Lord, we want to live every day as a sacred ritual unto you. Whatever troubles block our way, whatever enemies prepare to defeat us, you are with us. O my God, we trust in you. We needn't shout or bellow our prayers. You hear our hearts. Amen.

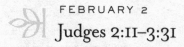

FEBRUARY 2
Judges 2:11–3:31

In the book of Judges, a four-part cycle keeps repeating itself: The children of Israel sin against God. Then God allows an enemy to rule over them. They cry to God. And God sends them a judge to deliver them.

Don't think that the Bible never laughs. Judge Ehud's story is a whopper.

The king of Moab is crushing Israel. Israel cries to God, and God gives them a judge named Ehud—a cunning little man. He travels to King Eglon's palace. The palace guard sees no threat in this little fellow. He *is* little, after all, and he comes alone, with no sword against his left thigh. Warriors strap their sword on the left in order to draw it with their right hand. No sword on the left means they've come in peace. But Ehud is left-handed. He straps his sword against his *right* thigh.

He says to the palace guards, "I'm an undercover spy. I have a secret to tell your king. He will rule not only Israel but also kingdoms and nations abroad." Ehud gives coins to each of the guards and is sent to King Eglon's privy room, which in those days wasn't always private.

Ehud enters and closes the door. The king, groaning over his business, is a grossly fat man. He thinks a servant has come to wipe his behinder. "Soon," he says, "soon." Ehud comes close, saying, "I have a secret," draws his sword, and plunges it into Eglon's guts. The fat closes over the blade and hilt and Ehud's hand. When he pulls out the sword, a fearful stink engulfs the room.

But the deed is done, and God's victory won—grace upon his people.

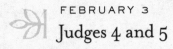

FEBRUARY 3
Judges 4 and 5

A woman has always been as capable as any man.

King Jabin is tyrannizing Israel. His general, Sisera, commands an army of ten thousand troops and nine hundred chariots—so many that the men of Israel have gone and hidden themselves in caves.

While the prophet Deborah, the judge of Israel, sits on a ridge above the Jezreel Valley, she sees Sisera's preparations for war. She summons Captain Barak and says, "The Lord commands you to lead his army into the valley to fight the Canaanites." Barak shakes his head. Finally, he says, "I'll go if you go with me." She will. He calls forth the hiding warriors and leads them into the valley.

Sisera rides at the head of Jabin's massed forces. The stars in the heavens are the hosts of God's warring angels. God thunder-storms the valley. The stars hail the earth with their spears. The wheels mire in the mud. When Sisera realizes that all is lost, he leaps from his chariot and runs and runs until he reaches the tent of a young woman named Jael. He falls faint and begs for a drink of water.

Watch what a woman can do.

Jael invites him in and gives him a drink. All sweetness and innocence, then, she tells Sisera to hide from Israel under her rug. Once he's fallen asleep, she puts the sharp point of a tent peg to the rug above Sisera's temple, then hammers it into his brain.

Does it trouble us that a woman has done what Ehud did before her?

God bless our mothers and our daughters, teachers and physicians, corporate lawyers and housekeepers, women intelligent and bold and self-controlled. Amen.

FEBRUARY 4
Judges 13 and 14

Samson is a Nazarite (see Numbers 6:1–21), which means he's never taken a strong drink or cut his hair or touched a human corpse.

Samson the Israelite decides to take a wife from among the Philistines. He travels to the Philistine village of Timnah. When he's halfway there, a roaring lion leaps out of the bushes and charges Samson. But the spirit of God descends on him. He grabs the lion's jaws and rips them apart. In Timnah, Samson's eyes light on a darkly beautiful maiden. "This is she," he thinks, "the lass I'm going to marry." Samson and the woman's father settle the dowry price, and Samson travels home again.

A few months later Samson returns with joy to celebrate his wedding day. Again he sees the lion, and bees making honey in its carcass. During the week of the wedding feast, Samson calls out, "A riddle, boys! Answer it and I'll dole out thirty purple robes. A good game, one and all!" "What's your riddle?" "Out of the eater, something to eat. Out of a beast, something sweet."

The Philistine lords pummel their brains, growing ever more frustrated, and then downright angry. They approach Samson's wife, saying, "Make that man of yours explain his riddle or else we'll burn you *and* your father's house!"

Samson's wife finds him sitting outside in the sunlight, and pouts. "I think you hate me," she says. "Why haven't you told me the meaning of your riddle?" Samson only smiles. But when he sees that his wife is terrified, he takes pity on her and tells her about lions and bees. She runs straight to the Philistine lords and tells them the answer. They who were angry at Samson now revile him. They shoot out their lips and spit on him. "Israelite! You are filth under our feet!" Well, then anger meets with anger. Samson slaughters thirty men and leaves Timnah to itself. In the end, the woman's father marries her to a good Philistine boy.

PRAYER

O Lord Jesus, when I'm angry at someone or angered by someone, according to your mercy and your forgiveness, let my anger find peace in you. Amen.

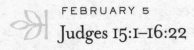

FEBRUARY 5
Judges 15:1–16:22

This pattern of vengeance for vengeance for vengeance—how long can it last? Consider the length of the back-and-forth wars of our present world. For Samson: a lifetime.

(1) He loves his wife still. Therefore, he returns to Timnah. (2) But his wife has married another man. (3) Samson ties three hundred foxes tail to tail with a flaming torch between each pair and sets them free in a Philistine field, burning all the wheat.

The Philistines retaliate by killing the woman and her father. (4) Samson slaughters a thousand Philistines. (5) The Philistine army marches into the lands of Judah. "Bind Samson. Give him to us, or we'll wipe your tribe from the face of the earth!" To everyone's surprise, Samson allows himself to be bound by ropes. (6), Samson smiles, swells his muscles, and snaps the ropes as if they were mere thread. (7) Samson takes another wife, whose name is Delilah. (8) Still hateful, the Philistine lords threaten Delilah as they did the first wife. "Tell us the source of Samson's strength, or we will kill you."

Delilah goes to him in their house, falls on her knees in tears, and says, "I need to know what makes you so strong." (9) Samson smiles. "Tie me up with seven fresh bowstrings, and I'll babble like a baby." It's a trick. He pretends to sleep. Delilah ties him up. Samson pretends to sneeze, and the bowstrings break. Delilah says, "You're laughing at me." Samson answers, "Okay. Weave seven locks of my long hair." Again he lies back and closes his eyes. Delilah weaves seven locks of his hair and pins them tight. As if his scalp were itching, he scratches at the weaves. The pins pop out, and his hair falls long and loose. As with the first wife, Delilah shows her terror: "The lords have sworn to kill me." Samson's heart is moved. He tells her the truth: "Cut off all my hair." This time the man truly sleeps. Delilah sheers him bald. When he wakes, he's no stronger than any other man. The lords come and (10) gouge out Samson's eyes and force him to labor like an ox with a yoke on its shoulders.

PRAYER

Lord, not my eyes but my soul has been blind to your laws. Teach me to see you, and I shall live. Amen.

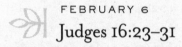

FEBRUARY 6
Judges 16:23–31

The Philistines, now jam-packed in their temple, have just completed sacrificing to their god and are filled with merriment. "Hey! Let's drag Samson here and have a little fun."

A seeing lad leads the sightless Samson into the temple and walks him to the space between the two central pillars that bear up the heavy roof.

"Our god," they shout, "is the lion! Yours is the lamb!"

Samson asks the lad to put his hands on either pillar, then cries out, "O God, let me be your sacrifice." The Philistines laugh at that.

But Samson bows his head and strains against the pillars. They crack. The pagans scream. The pillars shatter. The roof caves in. The people are crushed, and Samson has accomplished his sacrifice.

PRAYER

Jesus, be my Samson. I've dwelt too long in temples, worshipping the idol that is me. My pillars are named Greed and Pride. Tear them down. Batter my heart. Strengthen me with your strength, and my faith will grow strong. Amen.

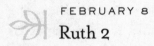

Ruth 1

Tell me, Ruth, you Moabite, how did it feel when your foreign husband died in Moab?

Ruth answers, "I took to my bed and grieved and couldn't get up for a month. He was mine and I was his."

Your husband, Ruth, and your sister's husband too, and Naomi's all perished, and Naomi became a bitter, old woman.

"She comforted me."

When your mother-in-law looked to Bethlehem across the Jordan River, yearning to go home again, and when she traveled thither, why did you follow her?

"I loved her."

Truly you did. But she kept telling you and your sister-in-law to stay in Moab with your mothers.

"Naomi was my mother. How could I separate myself from her?"

Yes, and the lovely poem you sang for her changed her mind.

PRAYER

Keep me ever with you, O Lord my God.
Where you are, let me be there with you.
Let neither life nor death nor life again
separate us one from the other. Amen.

Ruth 2

Your mother-in-law was penniless and too old to work. You supported her by gleaning grain from the edges of the fields owned by a man named Boaz.

He saw you and admired your patience, your shy quietness, and your steady, uncomplaining work. He spoke to you, inviting you to follow his reapers, and told them to leave extra wheat behind themselves that you might gather it up.

"I am a plain, unlovely woman. Feet too big. Hands too calloused, and nothing to recommend me. Yet Boaz paid attention to me, I don't know why. He was and is a noble and gracious man."

Yes, and he praised you for serving Naomi.

Yes, and it sweetened her bitterness when she saw your apron heavy with grain.

PRAYER

Naomi was now childless, as were both Sarah and Rachel for far too long. O Lord, what loving wonders you perform for those who lack the dearest things in life. We praise you and adore you. Amen.

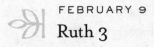

FEBRUARY 9
Ruth 3

In the Bible *feet* is a euphemism for nakedness. And though the Bible doesn't give us specific details, the details below are implied. We must remember that the Old Testament is often very earthy.

Naomi told you to dress in a clean linen garment, to walk through the night to Boaz's threshing floor, and then to spread your garment over him. She said, "Let Boaz know that you're willing to marry him."

So you went and found the man sleeping beside a heap of winnowed grain. You sat down and waited.

Boaz woke at midnight, startled to find that a female was sitting by a male on his threshing floor—and startled the more when she spread her garment over his feet. "Ruth," he said, "why did you come here?"

Shyly you lowered your eyes and said, "I've come with expectations."

The handsome man gazed at you until he understood your

expectations. And he would dearly have fulfilled them, except that he had a kinsman who had first rights to marry you.

Boaz said, "There's something I have to do, Ruth, before we can make a marriage, you and I."

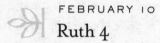

FEBRUARY 10
Ruth 4

In those days, when a husband died, the law required his nearest kinsman to take the widow as his own wife, no matter how many wives he may have already had—and Boaz is not the first kinsman to Ruth's expired husband. Yet he loves her with all his heart.

So he asks this closer kinsman to trade one thing for another. Boaz will give him a plot of Naomi's land in exchange for the right to marry Ruth.

Well, this kinsman had no need for other children. And so the bargain was struck.

Ruth, how was your wedding?

"Joyful."

And Naomi?

"Her bitterness turned into honey. And when Boaz and I bore a son and placed him in her arms, honey learned how to laugh again."

And you suckled the infant. What did you name him?

"Obed."

Ah, yes, and Obed will become the father of Jesse, and Jesse will become the father of David, and David will become the king of Israel. O Ruth, you will become the mother of a kingdom.

PRAYER

Ruth's story ends happily. And so shall ours end happily, for we will eat a wedding feast at your tables in heaven. Amen.

PART 4

The

KINGS

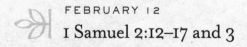

I Samuel 1:1–2:10

Think of Sarah, who bore no children because she and Abraham were far too old, yet God opened her womb. Think of Rachel, who had no children, while her sister was having one after another. Now it's Hannah—childless, while Elkanah's other wife is giving birth to sons and daughters.

Hannah raises her hands in the temple and begs God for a baby of her own.

The old priest Eli watches the woman whose mouth moves, but soundlessly. Though he thinks she's been drinking, he speaks kindly to her, and Hannah opens her heart. Finally, Eli says, "Go home, and may the Lord grant you your petition."

In time God does indeed grant her petition. Hannah conceives and bears a son and calls him Samuel, which means "heard by God."

After this mother has weaned her little boy, she takes him to the tent of the Lord in Shiloh and gives him over to the Lord, leaving Samuel behind with Eli.

I was my parents' firstborn son. My father went out and bought a baby book entitled *Life Begins*. On the flyleaf he wrote Hannah's words in black, bold ink: "For this child I prayed. As long as he lives, he is lent to the Lord." This was his expression that I would follow in his footsteps and become a pastor too. Hannah got her wish. For a long time, my father was disappointed because he didn't get his.

PRAYER

We are the children of our parents. But you are our spiritual Father. They gave us an earthly life. You have given us heaven, and we love you for it. Amen.

I Samuel 2:12–17 and 3

Eli's sons are priests, but iniquitous priests.

Young Samuel is serving God when the Lord calls him by name: "Samuel, Samuel." Thinking it was Eli who called, the boy goes to him. Eli says, "I didn't call you." Again the Lord calls, and again Samuel thinks it's Eli. Eli says, "Not me."

Finally, the Lord says, "Tell Eli that I am about to punish his sons with death."

Eli doesn't raise his voice in anguish. Rather, he accepts the words of the prophecy. Eli knows the wrong as well as he knows God's righteousness. The old man sighs and closes his eyes and waits.

When the words of the Lord come to pass, all Israel learns that the Lord has raised up a new prophet, and his name is Samuel.

PRAYER

O Lord Jesus, we pray that you won't curse us for our sins. The house of Eli perished under God's heavy punishment. But it was you who perished for us. We fall before you in misery. But then we leap up and sing because you have forgiven us. Amen.

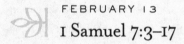

FEBRUARY 13
1 Samuel 7:3–17

How often will Israel repeat the cycle of (1) sinning, then (2) suffering under the armies of their enemies, then (3) crying out to the Lord, after which (4) his mercy raises up a judge who will lead them to victory over their enemies? So it was in the book of Judges. And so it is again.

The children of Israel have begun to worship the pagan Baal. Samuel calls them to Mizpah to account for their sins. There they fast and confess their sins. When the lords of the Philistines hear that Israel has gathered at Mizpah, they attack them right in the middle of their ceremony.

"Samuel! Samuel!" the Israelites cry. "Beg God to save us!"

Samuel then sacrifices a burnt offering to the Lord, and the Lord, with a voice so thunderous that the mountains tremble, throws the

Philistines into a panic. Now it is Israel who attacks *them* and drives them out of the land.

Long ago Jacob erected a stone and called it Bethel, "the house of God." Now Samuel erects another stone and calls it Ebenezer—"the stone of help."

PRAYER

We are on a wheel that rolls from iniquity to salvation, then iniquity, and then salvation again. We've read the book of Judges. We should have learned from it. Here and now we cry out to you, Lord Jesus, "Who will save us from ourselves?" Amen.

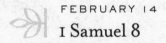

FEBRUARY 14
1 Samuel 8

Israel doesn't pray for, nor ask for, a king. Israel *demands* a king. God selected Israel to be his own people. Now the people want to be like the pagan nations surrounding them. Samuel warns them that kings exert their power for themselves and not for their subjects, but Israel refuses to listen. They don't know that to be ruled by an earthly king is to reject the rule of the Lord, the one true king.

Yet God tells Samuel to listen to the people. We should hear his words as a sigh. This isn't what he wants. God doesn't tell Samuel that his warnings are wrong. It is as if God says, "Give them their king, and we will see what we will see."

PRAYER

We might not say it. We might not even be aware of it. Perhaps it's an unconscious attitude. But we have allowed ourselves to be ruled by kings who are not the King of Kings, such as corporations that pay us good salaries; advertisements and department stores that invite us to buy things we may not need; preachers who preach what we want to hear: condemnations of those who are different from us, that hell waits for sinners—never confessing that we are sinners too. From these false kings, good Lord, deliver us. Amen.

I Samuel 9:1–10:8

Saul and his lad ask the young women who are drawing water from a well where they might find the prophet Samuel.

I wonder about the many wells in the Old Testament. Perhaps they mean that life needs water to live and that God gives life (see John 4:13–14). Again, water flows from the grace of the Creator—a stark reminder that we don't belong to ourselves but to God. When the children of Israel craved drink, God turned a bitter, undrinkable water into a water drinkable and sweet (Exodus 15:25). It's also possible to think of the water in which a tiny infant sleeps before it is born.

God chooses a man named Saul to be Israel's king. He's tall, broadshouldered, and handsome, a man who looks every bit a king. God knows the sins that Saul will sin. Yet for now he sends his Spirit upon the man. In the same manner, God will send his spirit on David and Solomon.

Samuel anoints Saul's head with oil, and Israel shouts, "Long live the king!"

And God will anoint his only begotten Son with the Holy Spirit (*Messiah* means "the Anointed One"), the Spirit who will come down in the form of a dove. All the Old Testament's anointments will be fulfilled in Christ, the King *of* Kings.

PRAYER

> Jesus shall reign where'er the sun
> Doth its successive journeys run;
> His kingdom stretch from shore to shore
> Till moons shall wax and wane no more. Amen.
>
> —"JESUS SHALL REIGN WHERE'ER THE SUN"

I Samuel 13:1–15; 14:24–30; and 15:26

God made Saul the king of Israel, but Saul abuses his kingship. He becomes bold enough to sacrifice in the place of Samuel. God rejects his sacrifice. Though Saul has his reasons, they can't excuse him. Samuel promised to arrive and to make the sacrifice in God's good time. Saul should have trusted in the Lord, whose mighty arm delivered Israel from Egypt. In those days a king passed his kingdom to his son, and that son to *his* son, establishing his descendants as kings forever. But Samuel now prophesizes that Saul's reign will be clean cut off. It will not pass to his son Jonathan.

Later Saul proves himself to be an unreliable king. He swears the rash oath that his troops must not eat until he has avenged himself on the Philistines. Consequently, the Israelite army grows too famished to put up a good fight, and many scatter and hide in the hills. But his son Jonathan hasn't heard of his father's oath. He eats honey, and his eyes "brighten." Instead of Saul, Jonathan becomes a brilliant leader and a wise strategist, and Samuel prophesizes that Saul will live the rest of his life a nervous and anxious man.

PRAYER

We may not be like Jonathan, and we surely don't want to be like Saul. Lamb of God, you who take away the sins of the world, have mercy on us. Amen.

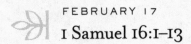

FEBRUARY 17
1 Samuel 16:1–13

David is a ruddy boy—that is, his hair is reddish. He has soft and lovely eyes—that is, he doesn't seem to have the makings of a king. But God doesn't look on outward appearances. He looks into the heart. He says to Samuel, who is now in his old age, "This is the one I want. This shepherd boy, I choose him."

Samuel obeys. Then the Spirit of the Lord, the power of the Lord, fills David's heart from that day forward. David's descendants will be kings for a thousand years until his last and greatest Son, Jesus, receives the Holy Spirit and reigns forever and ever.

It was at my baptism that you named me Child of God. The pastor anointed me three times with water: "In the name of the Father and the Son and the Holy Spirit." Christ, it is your Spirit that fills my heart. I have never been a king, but I have been a king of sinners. From the cross you said, "Father, forgive them, for they do not know what they are doing." Hanging beside you on my own cross, I pray, "Remember me when you come into your kingdom." And you have already answered, "Today you will be with me in paradise." Amen.

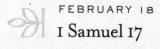

FEBRUARY 18
1 Samuel 17

Saul has failed. The Philistines are back, and it's David who will do what Saul's armies can't, even though he's too young to swing a sword.

David's father sends him to the front with food for his brothers. As so many oldest brothers get angry when their puny little brother butts in, so now Eliab scolds David: "You want to get killed?" Then a thunderous shout rises in the camp of the Philistines, for a monumental giant has stood up and is taunting Israel. He towers nine feet nine inches tall, is armored throat to knees, and carries an iron-headed spear as big as a weaver's beam. Saul's warriors crouch in fear.

But David realizes that the true battle is not fought with flesh and blood but with the Spirit of the living God. He says to Saul, "Send me. Let me fight Goliath." Saul says, "You're only a boy." David answers with a stubborn conviction, "I have already killed lions." Seeing that there's no arguing with David, Saul offers him his armor, which is too heavy for a boy.

So the red-haired shepherd goes forward, taking only a sling and five river stones.

Goliath roars with laughter. David says, "Yours is an iron spear. Mine is the name of the Lord of Hosts." He puts a stone in the sling's soft leather pouch and whirls it around his head, then releases it. It strikes the only spot where the giant is unprotected by armor: his forehead. The stone breaks through Goliath's skull bone. The giant slumps and hits the earth with an almighty *whump*! David has turned the tables, doing what the giant promised to do.

PRAYER

Lord God, everlasting Father, hungry people cry out to you. The impoverished, who don't have a safety net to catch them when they fall, people rejected by society, people oppressed by the mindless giants of this world cry out to you: "Give us a David!" Where are the Davids today? We are the Davids. And you are the glorious son of David. By your love for us, teach us to love the abandoned and the broken. Amen.

FEBRUARY 19
1 Samuel 18:1–16 and *skim* 1 Samuel 20

Israel may continue to respect Saul, but it is David whom they love. Even Saul's son Jonathan loves David with his whole heart. Saul has begun to bristle with such a hatred for David that he tries to kill him. David escapes, yet even now admires the king.

Jonathan's love for David is so deeply personal that he separates himself from the house of his father and casts his lot with his friend, and their hearts are bound in a lifelong, unbreakable bond.

Saul's paranoia increases. He refuses even to say David's name. So the two companions hatch a plan to save David's life. If Saul's rage gets out of control, Jonathan will signal this by shooting three arrows high and far and into the field where David waits. As it happens, the arrows must be shot. David will have to escape. The two friends fall on each other's necks and kiss and bid sad farewells. David and Jonathan will never meet again.

PRAYER

How dearly I love my wife. Throughout our years of marriage, Ruthanne and I have seldom been apart, and when we were, I've always come home again. But one day we will part, and I won't come home, because it's likely I'll be the first to die. Then, O Lord, hold her in your love until she dies too, and we meet in the air. Amen.

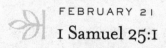

I Samuel 24

Saul is crazy. No, Saul is a madman obsessed by his desire to murder David.

En Gedi is an oasis on the western side of the Dead Sea. Saul's armies march down from the north and set up camp. David and his men have hidden themselves deep inside a nearby cave. Saul feels an urge to relieve himself. He enters that same cave, removes his robe, and squats. David's men whisper, "Kill him." But David has a different idea. He sneaks through the darkness. Rather than killing the king, he cuts off a swatch of Saul's robe, then slips to the mouth of the cave and calls, "Saul, look at what I have in my hand, and know that I could have killed you."

For a moment the madman is jolted into lucidity. "Is that you, David?" David answers, "It's me," and Saul starts to weep. "You're a better man than I am," he sobs, "and now I know that God has anointed you to be the king of Israel."

But if rage isn't extinguished, it waits like a banked fire. Even so today do many nations wait, and neighbors and church denominations who hold angrily to different rules and doctrines. And even the political parties of today.

PRAYER

Violence begets violence. But that cycle can be broken by forgiveness, and things are set aright. O Lord God, as in this case David befriended Saul, help us by your merciful friendship also to strive to make friends of our enemies. Amen.

I Samuel 25:1

When he was a child, Samuel served Eli in the house of the Lord. Now the old man lays himself down and turns his face to the wall and breathes his last breath.

Samuel lived a long, tumultuous life. He obeyed God in everything God asked of him. He was a prophet. He judged Israel with wisdom and courage, never wavering, ever aware of what was evil and what was righteous.

I wonder: have we been blessed with our own Samuels? Perhaps you can think of someone who has both wisdom and the courage to (as they say) speak truth to power. My grandpa Storck knew right from wrong. He taught me to be right, and he pitied those who were wrong. And he didn't hesitate to speak of their sins to them. He wore an explosion of white mustache under his nose. And he died in a good old age.

PRAYER

We serve only one king—you, Lord Jesus Christ. Help our hands to obey you and our minds to know you and our hearts to love you. Amen.

With this devotion we've come to an important transition, the end of one era and the beginning of another. Hereafter, we will study the successions of the kings of Israel and of Judah.

 FEBRUARY 22

Skim 1 Samuel 31 and *read* 2 Samuel 1

To "fall on one's sword" is to be taken literally. A warrior puts the butt of his sword on the ground and falls on its blade. This was considered an honorable way to take leave of this life.

David grieves for his dear friend Jonathan and also for Saul, even though he was his enemy.

He laments his loss with a remarkably beautiful song. (This should be read out loud.) "How the mighty have fallen!" Let the fields be blasted into a wilderness. Let the dead be eulogized. Saul and his son Jonathan, Jonathan and his father Saul, were as swift as eagles and as powerful as lions. "How the mighty have fallen!"

2 Samuel 5:1–16

Saul was a rough-hewn, inexperienced king who didn't understand the ways of a king when he was anointed. David, on the other hand, is a natural. He doesn't have to rule by force; Israel is devoted to him, and his armies admire his leadership. The king has a political mind and a persuasive, rhetorical voice. He rules with a light hand and confidence. And now he recognizes the need for a capital city. He chooses Jerusalem because it belongs to no tribe but sits between the ten tribes to the north and the two tribes to the south. Thus, he unifies all the tribes into a single kingdom.

Right now the Jebusites control the city. Instead of attacking its walls head-on, David plans a sly maneuver to throw the Jebusites into confusion. He'll pop out of the ground inside the city. A narrow shaft tunnels up from the Gihon Spring outside Jerusalem in order to water the people inside. David tells Joab, the commander of his armies, to climb the shaft and tells a small military unit to follow after with their swords bound to their thighs. Joab erupts from the ground. The Jebusites are unprepared—no armor, no weapons with which to meet the attack. One of Joab's men throws open the city gates. David's whole army rushes into the city and captures every last Jebusite. In this manner David has his capital. He names it "the City of David."

PRAYER

We live as citizens of the golden city, Jerusalem. The City of David has become the City of Jesus Christ. He was circumcised there. As a boy twelve years old, he taught in the temple. With thousands of Israelites, he made pilgrimages to Jerusalem to keep the Passover. Jesus died there. He died there and rose to life again. You, Lord, are our Messiah, our "Anointed One." Anoint us too with the fire of your Holy Spirit. Amen.

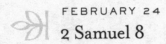

FEBRUARY 24

2 Samuel 8

David is a warrior king and a canny strategist.

In one war after another, God grants him the victory. He's able, then, to expand a small kingdom into a small empire. His territories stretch north to Zobah, east as far as Damascus, down the shores of the Mediterranean Sea, and south to the boundaries of Egypt.

David can be righteous before the Lord. Yet from time to time, he exerts an ungodly savagery. After defeating the Moabites, he commands its warriors to lie flat on the ground, then he measures them arbitrarily, some to be executed and some to become slaves. The high-minded king can sometimes act low-down and cruel. No, David is not always God's golden boy. Remember Jacob, who usurped Esau's birthright and his blessing? David is like his ancestor. And we are like David.

PRAYER

Lord Jesus Christ, save us from ourselves. Amen.

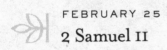

FEBRUARY 25

2 Samuel 11

No, not always God's golden boy.

Long ago the Israelites demanded a king like the kings over other nations. Samuel said to them, "A king will take your daughters." That prophecy rings all down the years until it describes the deeds of King David. The kingdom is at war. Joab's army has laid siege to the city of Rabbah while David remains idle in Jerusalem. While he's pacing the roof of his palace, he glances down into a courtyard where a beautiful young woman is bathing in a copper tub. The sight arouses the king. He asks a servant, "Who is she?" The servant replies, "Bathsheba, the wife of Uriah the Hittite." "And Uriah?" "Fighting at Rabbah." David says, "Go down. Bring that woman to me." No one disobeys the command of a king. Bathsheba enters David's chamber, and David has his way with her. The seed is planted. Bathsheba is pregnant.

Now the cover-up. David sends a message to Uriah: "Friend, come home for a little R & R. Your wife yearns for you." But Uriah is so profoundly loyal to his king that he says that he will not go home until the battle is through.

The cover-up takes a terrible turn. In another message David commands Joab to put Uriah in the forefront of the battle, where he is sure to be, and is, killed. To make Bathsheba's child legitimate, David marries her.

PRAYER

We too cover up our sins. We're too ashamed to confess them aloud, even in God's church. But you, Lord, know our hearts, that they can be evil. Oh, let your merciful tears fall on us and wash us clean through and through. Amen.

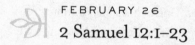

FEBRUARY 26
2 Samuel 12:1–23

David thinks the matter has been put to bed and that he's God's golden boy again.

But God thinks otherwise.

The Lord sends the prophet Nathan to King David. Nathan tells the king a parable about a poor man who has but one ewe lamb and a rich man who has flocks of sheep and herds of cattle yet who seizes the poor man's lamb and roasts it for a guest. David explodes. "Where is he? I'll have his head!" Nathan says, *"You are that man."*

As soon as a baby is born—at first sight—parents are in love with it. Even so does David love his son immediately. But the boy falls sick unto death. David repents. He refuses food. He lies on the ground for six days and six nights, pleading for the life of the boy. On the seventh day the king hears his servants whispering with anxiety, wringing their hands and looking at him where he lies. Has the war been lost? David says, "Don't whisper. Why are you whispering?" One of the servants says, "Your little boy is dead."

Commonly, mourning lasted for a month, but David astonishes his household by standing up, going into his palace, bathing, and putting on a clean, well-brushed royal robe. God gave and God has taken away. Accept the acts of the Almighty.

God takes away and God gives again. David and Bathsheba give birth to a second son whom they name Solomon.

PRAYER

Have mercy on us, O God, according to your steadfast love. According to your abundant mercy, blot out our transgressions. Wash us through and through, and we shall be clean. Amen.

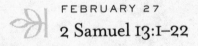

FEBRUARY 27

2 Samuel 13:1–22

David bore other sons by other wives. One of his sons, Amnon, grows as tall and as handsome as Absalom. Amnon has a lovely young sister named Tamar. As she grows, so does his desire for her. It's a man's world. Men dominate women. Tamar is a virgin.

In order to draw his sister into his chamber, Amnon pretends to be sick. "There is nothing for it," he says, "but that Tamar comes to me bringing sweet cakes and honey." Because Tamar loves her brother, she comes.

Amnon is not sick. He's deceived her. He throws her onto his bed. "No!" she cries. "Please, *no*!" But "no" is not no for Amnon. He rapes his sister and then loathes the very sight of her. He flings her clothes to her and cries, "Get out!" Tamar accuses Amnon, saying, "This sin is worse than rape!" Indeed. No man will marry a shamed woman. No one will protect her or support her. Tamar will have to do for herself what she can, scorned and alone.

Still today people will dismiss the claims of an abused woman. "She exaggerates." Or "She wore suggestive clothes." Or "She has herself to blame, walking alone where she doesn't belong." Or "She smeared too much makeup on her face."

PRAYER

O Lord, let your Holy Spirit be an advocate for women wronged by men. As though the world were a courtroom, let the Holy Spirit confront those who bear false witness against women. Let justice prevail. Amen.

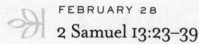

FEBRUARY 28

2 Samuel 13:23–39

Tamar has a brother named Absalom, who invites his father and all his other brothers to attend the feast he'll spread some miles north of Jerusalem. David says that his royal entourage would eat Absalom out of house and home. But the brothers go.

It isn't for friendship that Absalom throws this banquet, but for revenge. He instructs an archer to wait outside the door: "When you hear me cry, 'Shoot!' come in and shoot." With a winsome smile he says to Amnon, "Be my honored guest. Come and sit at the head of the table." Midway through the meal, Absalom cries, "Shoot!" The archer enters and sends an arrow through Amnon's heart. Guests rush here and there to get out of harm's way.

PRAYER

My sins, my Lord, have made me like Amnon. You had every right to pierce my heart. But you didn't. For my sake you chose to be pierced in your heart, and to die that I may live. And then you rose that I might live eternally. Amen.

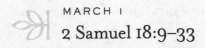

2 Samuel 15:1–6

Absalom has high ambitions. He wants to usurp David's kingdom, to rule in his father's place.

To that end Absalom rides a king's chariot with magnificent, deep-chested horses and fifty courtiers to run ahead of him, crying, "Make way for Prince Absalom!"

He is a comely man, Absalom, with a rich fall of abundant hair and a natural charm. Who *wouldn't* be fond of him? Moreover, he begins to prove himself equal to or even better than the king. When people come to Jerusalem to plead their cases before David, Absalom meets them at the gate. With winsome words he says, "State your case to me. The king can be a cruel judge. I am kinder than he."

Indeed, the Israelites find him kinder and love him more than they love David. Therefore, Absalom plans to mount an army of his own and dethrone David, the king of Israel.

But the seventy-second Psalm (verses 1–4 and 12–15) praises *God* as the only source of truth and perfect justice.

PRAYER
As long as the sun endures, O Lord, reign as the king of all the nations. Let your dominion stretch from sea to sea. Deliver us when we call to you. Amen.

MARCH 1

2 Samuel 18:9–33

A king will often execute a rebel. But a father loves his son. These are the tensions that pull David's heart in two opposite directions.

Two hundred warriors have defected from David's army to join Absalom's. Absalom is battling his way to Jerusalem to seize his father's crown. David escapes with his army to a land east of Jerusalem and tells his captain, Joab, to prepare a counterattack. "But," he says, "deal gently with my son." By hundreds and thousands, then, David's warriors fell Absalom's army. The war is a rout. Absalom's army retreats. Absalom mounts his mule and kicks it into a gallop. But while he speeds through an oak forest, his hair catches in the branches of an oak. The mule races on, and the man is left hanging between earth and heaven.

A foot soldier races to tell Joab. "Absalom's hanging by his hair in a tree!" Joab says, "You killed him, right?" "But he's King David's son." "You fool!" Joab rides to Absalom and pierces him with three spears. Blood gushes out, and Absalom's corpse is left swinging in the wind.

Who grieves more deeply than the father whose son has died before him? When David learns of Absalom's death, he climbs the stairs of the watchman's tower. He looks out over the mown fields and groans, "O my son, Absalom, Absalom. Would God that I had died instead of you. O Absalom, my son, my son."

PRAYER

> In my trials, Lord, walk with me.
> In my trials, Lord, walk with me.
>
> —"I WANT JESUS TO WALK WITH ME"

MARCH 2
1 Kings 1

King David has fought all his fights. He's seventy years old. He takes to his bed, sick unto death, his bones quaking and his teeth chattering. A virgin named Abishag is brought into his chamber. She pulls the blankets over them both so that her warm body can warm his too. The end is near. It's time for David to name his successor.

His son Adonijah seizes the opportunity, announcing that he shall be—that he *is*—the king of Israel. As Absalom did before him, Adonijah performs the rituals to make himself king, sacrificing herds and riding in a gilded chariot with fifty courtiers running ahead and crying, "Make way for the king!"

Bathsheba is older now and no longer shy. She has become the mother who fiercely protects her son. She appears before David and says, "You swore an oath that my son Solomon would be next to rule Israel. But Adonijah has already declared himself the king of Israel even before you've taken leave of this world."

David calls Bathsheba to his side and says, "I bequeath my kingdom to our son."

David commands Zadok, his priest, and the prophet Nathan to anoint Solomon's head with oil. The trumpets blow the news abroad, and the people shout, "Long live King Solomon!"

Adonijah doesn't live long after his attempted coup d'état. Solomon has him executed.

PRAYER

Long live King Jesus! You died, but now your kingdom is everlasting. So shall we die. But when you take us into heaven, we will live eternally. Amen.

MARCH 3

1 Kings 2:10–12

In those days people were buried in little grottos hollowed out of a sheer limestone wall. The body was laid on a narrow stone platform until it became dry bones. There was something like a basin in the grotto's floor, where the bones of a person's ancestors were deposited. To "rest with one's ancestors" meant that the dead one's bones were also gathered in that basin.

Once the dead body lay on its "bed," a heavy flat stone was rolled down a groove to cover the door so that wild animals couldn't get in to feed on the flesh of the deceased.

Today our customs are different, though dead is still dead. We bury loved ones underground, or their ashes are scattered on God's good earth. As Saint Paul wrote in his first letter to the Thessalonians (4:13–18), we need not grieve as those who have no hope. Our deaths are but a sleep until we hear the trumpet of God. His angel will descend, and we will be caught up in the clouds to meet the Lord in the air.

PRAYER

Blessed be God, the Father of our Lord Jesus Christ, the God of all mercies, for he loves us and has given us his everlasting consolation. Amen.

MARCH 4
1 Kings 3

Just as David wasn't always God's golden boy, neither is his son.

Before they entered the promised land, Moses had told the Israelites to have nothing to do with the pagan nations (Deuteronomy 7:1–4) and especially not to give their daughters in marriage to foreign men. Yet young King Solomon marries an Egyptian woman. David worshipped the true and the only God in Jerusalem. Solomon builds altars to other gods.

Nevertheless, the Lord is with him. He appears to Solomon in a dream. "Ask whatever you want, and I'll give it to you." Solomon asks for wisdom, a hearing ear, and a discerning eye. The Lord answers, "Because you didn't ask for wealth or a long life or the death of your enemies, I will give you what you've asked for as well as what you *didn't* ask for. And if you walk in my ways, I will be with you, and you will deal justly with my people."

There follows an example of Solomon's wisdom and his keen understanding of human nature: two women approach him with one baby between them, each one claiming to be its mother. "So," says Solomon, "cut the baby in two." The woman whose baby is not her own says, "Do it." The other woman says, "Don't! Give it to her." Solomon doesn't, but gives the baby to the rightful woman.

PRAYER

Teach us, Lord, to walk in your ways. We don't pray for fat wallets or worldly praise or long lives or the embarrassment of those who wrong us. We pray for a living and lasting faith. Amen.

I Kings 6

When God said to David, "I will build you a house," he meant a long lineage of sons and daughters. It is Solomon whom he appoints to build a real, stone-hewn house, a temple in which the Lord will dwell.

Construction begins in the four hundred and eightieth year after Israel escaped Egypt. In seven years, the house of God is standing high in Jerusalem.

But in order to build it, Solomon imposed the corvée on his people. The corvée is a sort of tax-in-kind. The king demands his laborers to work for him one day every week without pay.

The temple is large and stunning with its storerooms and its multitude of side chambers. Its interior is divided into three rooms: a forecourt, a sanctuary large enough to accommodate many people, and the Most Holy Place, a dark, perfect cube where the ark of the covenant sits under the wings of two mighty cherubim.

When the priest stands in front of the temple's entrance and looks toward the Mount of Olives east of Jerusalem, he will witness God's glorious sunrise.

And the Lord has promised to be present in his temple. Yet his promise is conditional: "If you obey my commandments and walk in my ways, I will not abandon my children."

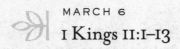

PRAYER

God himself is present, let us now adore him
And with awe bow down before him.

—"GOD HIMSELF IS WITH US"

I Kings 11:1–13

"But if you turn aside and do not keep my commandments, I will cut Israel off from the land and cast them out of my sight." The Lord God has a long memory, for when Israel *does* go astray in the days of the prophet Jeremiah, Solomon's Temple will be destroyed and Jerusalem ruined and the Israelites exiled.

Two thousand years after Solomon's reign, European Christians launched a crusade against Muslims in the Middle East. They marched out in the name of Christ, but they returned in shame because they had run riot in Jerusalem, had slaughtered and walked through the blood of their enemies. During the First and the Second World Wars, Germany fought bitter battles in order to govern Europe and every nation within its reach. In the end the German armies were defeated and paid for its aggression. As for us, we are fighting wars that may never end.

But Jesus said, "Blessed are the peacemakers, for they will be called children of God." And again, "Peace I leave with you, my peace." And again, "You have heard that it was said, 'Love your neighbor and hate your enemy.' But I tell you, love your enemies and pray for those who persecute you."

PRAYER

We love you, Lord, because your love turns our self-love into the love that loves even our enemies. Amen.

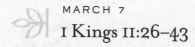

MARCH 7

I Kings 11:26–43

Solomon, Solomon—for one transgression and for two, the Lord makes good on his promise. By the visible sign of tearing a robe into twelve parts and by giving ten to Jeroboam and two to you, your kingdom will be torn into two pieces.

Jeroboam, the young son of Nebat, is one of Solomon's high officials before the break occurs. He sees and he is troubled by the way Solomon deals with his subjects.

A handsome man is Jeroboam, savvy, intelligent, and full of himself. There will come the day. . . .

After reigning over Israel for a full forty years, Solomon dies and is buried with his ancestors, with his father in the City of David, and Rehoboam, Solomon's son, prepares to take the throne.

Our days are not yet finished. But we wonder, don't we? How our children will fare once we are gone? Will they follow the Lord? Will they act wisely? Piously? Will they be able to save our small, ailing island, the earth?

PRAYER

Jesus, we devote our children to you. Lead them. Take care of them. Give them hearing ears and discerning eyes. And this we pray: save the earth, save the world, that their children can live on a healthy and peaceful planet. Amen.

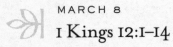

MARCH 8

1 Kings 12:1–14

Now Rehoboam travels to Shechem to be crowned king. The leaders of the northern ten tribes of Israel attend the coronation. Jeroboam comes too. They ask Rehoboam an important question regarding the manner in which he plans to reign over them. "Your father burdened us with yokes almost too heavy to bear. If you lift the corvée from our shoulders, we will serve you willingly."

Rehoboam says, "Give me time to think," then goes to the elders for advice. "Serve your people like a servant. Deal gently with them, and they will obey you." Rehoboam thinks that theirs is the advice of doddering old men, so he goes to his young friends, and they say, "Strength is the ticket." So Rehoboam returns to the tribal leaders and says, "Did my father yoke you with wooden oaks? I will yoke you with iron! Did my father whip you with whips? I will whip you with scorpions!"

Thus is the kingdom of David and Solomon torn in two, for the leaders return to their tribes and sever themselves from Rehoboam's Judah and instead crown Jeroboam, and he becomes their king.

O Christ our Lord, you were whipped bloody with a cat-o'-nine-tails so that we need never be lashed by our sins. You have healed the wounds of our guilt. We fall down before your wounded feet and worship your steadfast love for us. Amen.

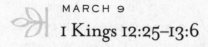

MARCH 9
1 Kings 12:25–13:6

Since all the Israelites worship in Jerusalem, Jeroboam fears that he might lose control of his tribes, now called the kingdom of Israel. So he builds altars where his people can worship.

When Moses was on Mount Sinai, receiving the Ten Commandments on two tablets, his brother Aaron carved a golden calf. Israel worshipped that calf, then got up and danced as if they were drunk. Jeroboam doubles Israel's sin. He molds *two* calves of gold and says to the people, "These are your gods."

Likewise, when Jacob was fleeing from Esau, God appeared to him in a dream: "I am with you wherever you go." When Jacob woke he called the place Bethel, "the house of God." Jeroboam, for his part, turns the house of God into a house of shame. He makes idols and adopts pagan rituals.

The Lord God is not with Jeroboam.

PRAYER
Grant us, Savior, the boldness and the courage to walk among faithless people and by our behavior to be witnesses of your faithfulness. Amen.

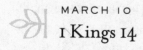

MARCH 10
1 Kings 14

King Jeroboam reigns for twenty-two disastrous years. He fights failing wars. His kingdom is weakened. And his son falls sick with a killing fever.

Jeroboam disguises his wife and sends her to the prophet Ahijah to beg him for healing. But rather than healing the boy, Ahijah utters a dreadful prophecy against Jeroboam. Ahijah is a blind man and cannot see the woman, but God tells him of the ruse.

"Don't flatter yourself, Jeroboam. God blames you for ripping David's kingdom apart. David was righteous, but you have rejected the Lord whom he obeyed—you, worshipping idols! You, calling your people to worship idols too! He will burn your house like dung. And because of your sins and the sins you have forced your people to sin, horror will befall Israel. Your child is dead. The kingdom will mourn for him but not for you."

Jeroboam dies in misery.

PRAYER

Fools say in their hearts, "There is no God." They are corrupt. They commit abominable acts (Psalm 53:1). Once, Lord, (when one I loved had died) I slipped and thought the same, though I scarcely knew it when I thought it. For every little sin and for every great sin, forgive me. Amen.

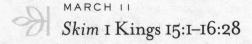

MARCH 11
Skim 1 Kings 15:1–16:28

Now the northern ten tribes are called "the kingdom of Israel," and the southern two tribes, "the kingdom of Judah."

Now follows a list of the wicked deeds and the murders and the deaths of the kings of Israel and of Judah. The "Book of the Annals" is a history of the royal lines of the two kingdoms.

Because Asa, the king of Judah, obeys God, he is given a long life, and the Lord allows a lamp of hope to burn in Jerusalem. But then evil follows evil. Baasha, the king of Israel, dies. His son Elah is assassinated. Zimri commits suicide. Then Omri reigns. He's the commander of Israel's army, and it is his warriors who proclaim him king. Omri becomes the greatest king of the realm, an energetic, foresighted, and diplomatic man. He arranges a marriage between his granddaughter Athaliah to the crown prince Jehoram of Judah, and so brings peace to the two kingdoms. Just as David did, Omri builds his own capital city. His son and his grandsons will rule as a mighty force in Israel.

PRAYER

Let all those who govern us govern wisely: senators, representatives, presidents, school principals, pastors. Let their purposes not be selfishly for their own power or gain. But help them to act on our behalf. Amen.

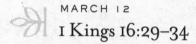

MARCH 12
1 Kings 16:29–34

Ahab is the son of his father. Like Omri, he secures Israel's defense against the Arameans in Damascus. He makes alliances with neighboring states, especially with Judah and Phoenicia. Marriages bind the kingdoms together: Ahab's sister Athaliah marries Jehoram of Judah. Ahab marries the Phoenician princess Jezebel. Peace prevails, and King Ahab begins to build.

He builds a royal palace called the Ivory House because the walls are decorated with miniature ivory carvings. He fortifies cities in strategic places such as Megiddo and Hazor. He constructs water systems of masterful engineering. At Hazor a long water shaft leads by a gentle descent to the level of the groundwater table. At Megiddo the much longer shaft reaches the spring outside the city.

Then King Ahab builds that which outrages the prophets—a temple to Baal and an altar to Baal, the god whom his wife worships.

PRAYER

I have dreamed of other temples, temples devoted to gods of fame (hoping that my writings would make my name remembered), gods of wealth, gods of illicit pleasures. Good Lord, deliver me. Amen.

PART 5

The
PROPHETS

1 Kings 17:1–7

The name Elijah means "Yahweh is my God." The prophet Elijah is like John the Baptist, who will appear more than nine centuries later. I like to imagine that Elijah's intensities have wasted his body to bones; he's a wiry man whose eyes can flash with fire.

Baal is a fiction. He is known as the storm god. The Lord's drought, then, reveals who is the more powerful of the two. Baal is also known as the god of fertility. When Ahab's crops wither, it is as if Baal has been imprisoned. The priests of Baal seek to kill the prophet, so the Lord instructs Elijah to cross the Jordan to a place where *his* food is plentiful. Ravens bring him bread and meat twice a day. But because they're considered unclean birds of prey, this story astonishes Israel. I AM WHAT I AM. God chooses to do what God chooses to do.

PRAYER

We trust in you, Lord. We trust in your promises and your words and instructions and are not afraid. What can mere kings do to us? Amen.

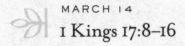

1 Kings 17:8–16

Over and over again God commands Israel to take care of its widows and orphans because a widow without a husband is unprotected, destitute, and impoverished. Generally, the Lord speaks of the widows "among you," among the Israelites. But just as God used unclean birds to feed Elijah, now he chooses a widow who is a foreigner living in the land of *Jezebel's* birth and is, therefore, a worshipper of Baal.

Here the land is as hard hit with famine as is Israel. Of course, she hasn't enough flour or oil to make more than a wafer of bread. Yet Elijah asks her to bring him that last wafer. She can't. She's gathering dry sticks to bake a bite for her son and herself, a last taste before they die. But the prophet assures her that the flour will not be used up nor the oil run out until rain falls again.

The widow wonders whether Elijah's God can be superior to her god. And then, when Elijah's prophecy proves true, she must admit that the Lord is indeed more powerful than any other god she's ever known.

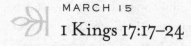

MARCH 15
1 Kings 17:17–24

Well, maybe Elijah's God is not so powerful after all. Perhaps in gratitude for the miracle of a continuous supply of food, the widow offered Elijah a room built on the roof of her house. But her kindness is repaid with a death. Her little boy sweats and yet he shivers. He thrashes in his bed until morning, when he is lying perfectly still.

The widow howls at Elijah, "You killed my son!"

Elijah doesn't respond. Rather, he gathers the boy into his arms, walks out the door, and climbs the stairs attached to the side of the house and lays the widow's son on his own bed.

So significant is this miracle that Jesus will remember it in Luke 4:25–26: "There were many widows in Israel in the time of the famine. Yet Elijah was sent to a widow in Zarephath."

As Jesus will heal the son of a widow in the city of Nain, so Elijah now stretches his body on the boy's body. The boy suddenly sucks a breath of air and comes alive, and his mother believes in the truth of the prophet's words. "I know," she says, "that you're a man of God." She implies that Elijah's God has become her God too.

Lord, grant us the serenity to accept the things we cannot change, the courage to change the things we can, and the wisdom to know the difference. Amen.

—REINHOLD NIEBUHR

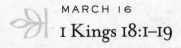

MARCH 16
1 Kings 18:1–19

At the end of three years, the Lord God is ready to send rain.

Obadiah's name means "servant of the Lord," and so he is. Yet he's torn between his service to God and service to his king. He fears the one and is scared of the other. Obadiah holds a high-ranking office in Ahab's government. He knows how the king thinks and acts, so it doesn't surprise him that the lingering drought has caused Ahab to worry more for his royal animals than for his people. His horses need fodder. Primary on his list is to *find* fodder. To that end he and his entourage travel east while Obadiah travels north.

Queen Jezebel is a she-lion, a murderer of the prophets of the Lord. Obadiah has been putting himself in danger by hiding the prophets in caves.

On his way north Obadiah recognizes the man ahead of him—a prophet. He dismounts immediately, then runs to Elijah and bows down. Without a word of greeting, Elijah issues a command: "Go to King Ahab. Tell him I have come into his country." "The king? No," says Obadiah. "He will kill me." The man's fright overcomes his faith. But Elijah steels his nerve with an oath and a promise: "As the almighty God before whom I stand lives, I will myself confront King Ahab." From fright to faith again, from cowardice to courage. Thus, is Obadiah empowered and obeys.

PRAYER

Jesus says to us, "Don't let your hearts be troubled. Peace I leave with you, my peace, not like the peace of this world." Whatever the task you give us,

Lord, however much it frightens us, we will do it because you've promised always to be with us. Amen.

MARCH 17
1 Kings 18:20–40

Baal, the god of Jezebel, has turned the heads and hearts of many an Israelite. Elijah's condemnations can be fire-eyed and fierce, but his methods? They can be funny.

Elijah invites the people to meet him on the top of Mount Carmel for a little entertainment. He lures the prophets of Baal, too, with a challenge. "Prove that your god is true." There is an altar to Baal on top of Carmel. "Tell you what," Elijah says, "lay wood on your altar. Sacrifice to Baal, the storm god, then ask him to burn it with fire." Here's a single, bony man, while these prophets are well fed and five hundred in number. So they prepare the sacrifice and start praying—a whole morning in prayer. But Baal seems to be neglectful. "*Tsk, tsk,*" Elijah says between his teeth. The prophets throw themselves into a frenzied ritual dance, and still no flaming arrow. Not a spark. Elijah makes a sympathetic face. "Poor fellows. Baal must be sleeping." The priests go to extreme measures, gashing their skin till blood soaks their clothes. "Okay," says Elijah. "My turn." He repairs a fallen altar to God. He puts wood on it, and on that, the sacrifice. Furthermore, he digs a ditch around the altar and pours so much water on the sacrifice and the wood and the altar that even the ditch itself is full. Then he prays one brief prayer: "Lord, prove that you are the one true God."

Suddenly, a bolt of lightning strikes down. The sacrifice bursts into flame, and the stones themselves are burned to ashes, and the ditch is as dry as the desert.

PRAYER
When, Lord, you shared the cup of wine with your disciples, you said, "This cup is the new covenant in my blood." During the storm on Calvary, you made yourself our sacrifice. Amen and amen.

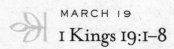

1 Kings 18:41–46

The God who licked the land dry is the same God who now prepares to send rain.

Elijah asks his servant lad to go down from Carmel and to tell the king that Elijah hears the rumbling sound of rain. While the lad is gone, Elijah sits and puts his head between his knees. He might be praying as intensely as Jesus prayed in the garden. But because the prophet can be melancholy, he might be suffering a black despair. When the lad returns, Elijah doesn't lift his head. He says, "Watch the sea's horizon, and tell me what you see." The lad looks out. "Only blue sky," he says. Elijah says, "Do it again." Breakers are leaping and foaming on the waters, but that is all he sees. "Again," says Elijah. "Again, again." The seventh is the charm. "I see a single white cloud no bigger than a fist."

Now Elijah looks up. He says to his servant, "Go now and tell Ahab to harness his horses and to drive his chariot back to his city before the mud sucks at the wheels and even his horses can't pull the chariot forward."

Thick, black clouds darken the earth. A wild wind gets up and blows rain like bullets in people's faces. Baal might be called "the fertility god," but only the one true God makes things grow.

PRAYER

I planted a sweet-corn seed. God gave my garden rain. And I ate the fruit thereof. Amen.

1 Kings 19:1–8

Yes, the prophet is capable of despair.

After Ahab has returned to his palace, he tells Jezebel the whole story of Mount Carmel. She flies into a rage and sends Elijah a saw-toothed message: "Look out for me! You killed my prophets! I am going to kill *you*!"

The prophet flees with his servant to the southernmost city in Judah. He says to the lad, "Wait here." From morning to evening Elijah walks into the wilderness until he comes to a desert bush and sits. "I can't bear this. I can't *do* this anymore. Lord, let me die and be done with it." A heavy desolation can make a person fall into a heavy sleep.

Someone touches Elijah. He wakes. The moon shines on an angel of the Lord. "Get up and eat," says the angel. Elijah sees beside him a little cake baked on hot stones and a jug of water. He hasn't eaten since he fled Israel. He eats, and he drinks, and he falls back to sleep.

How long later? An hour? A minute? The angel touches him again. "Eat. Drink, or the journey will be too long for you." Again the prophet refreshes himself, then travels for forty days to Mount Sinai.

<u>What a wonderful thing to do for someone who is very sad: a touch, a word, a little food, and nothing more.</u>

PRAYER

Even so, Lord Jesus, did you touch the eyes of two blind men and speak to them, and they were healed (Matthew 9:27–31). Even so, please touch my heart. Say, "Little one," and I will feed on your bread. Amen.

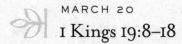

MARCH 20

1 Kings 19:8–18

Elijah climbs Sinai just as Moses climbed that same mount centuries before him. And as the Lord spoke to Moses then, so he speaks to Elijah now, asking a question to which he knows the answer: "Why are you here?" But it was God who brought him here. Perhaps the question is meant to make Elijah repeat his old complaint, and Elijah does, with a whiny exaggeration: "The Israelites have killed the prophets. I am the only one left, and they're out to kill me too!"

God tells Elijah to stand in a cleft of the mount—possibly the same cleft where Moses stood when the Lord passed by.

But things have changed. For Israel, the mighty God appeared in fire and cloud and a storm so powerful that it shook the mountain.

But for Elijah, the Lord is not in the fire or the storm or the earthquake that shook the mountain. No. The Lord God is in a whisper softer than whispers. What does that mean? That he doesn't want to frighten his poor, woebegone prophet? That he comes in mercy rather than in judgment? Elijah stops thinking about his hard life and turns his attention to God alone. "Do this," says God. "Anoint Hazael to reign in Damascus. Anoint Jehu as king of Israel. And anoint Elisha as the prophet who will take your place."

PRAYER

We are often moody, often grumpy about our chores, and often too depressed to get up and do them. But you, Lord, have anointed us in the baptismal waters. You don't shout. You call us by the gentlest of voices, and our ears hear you, and our hearts are glad. Amen.

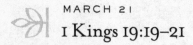

MARCH 21

1 Kings 19:19–21

The rain has softened the soil. Twelve farmers have cleared one long field of its rocks and stones and are prodding their oxen to plow the earth. The twelfth plowman is a young fellow named Elisha.

The prophet Elijah comes up behind him while he's still holding the plow handles steady. Elijah removes his cloak, a mantle woven of goats' hair, and casts it over Elisha's shoulders and says, "The Lord has appointed you to inherit my ministry after I've departed this world."

Elisha understands at once. He does not hesitate, but says, "Let me first go to my parents and kiss them farewell forever." Elijah says, "Go." So Elisha unyokes his ox and leads it home and, in the presence of his family, sacrifices the beast to thank and praise and prove that his trust is in the Lord.

Jesus said to Peter and Andrew, "Follow me." They did not hesitate, nor did they ask a question. They left their nets and followed. A teacher of the law said to Jesus, "Teacher, I will follow you wherever you go." Jesus answered, "Foxes have dens and birds have nests, but the Son of Man has no place to lay his head." Evidently the scribe didn't want to follow a homeless man.

PRAYER

The Lord said, "Whom shall I send, and who will go for me?" Only by faith are we able to answer, "We will go. Send us. Send us." Amen.

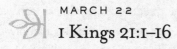

MARCH 22
1 Kings 21:1–16

A land of milk and honey—and of well-producing vineyards. God compares his people to vineyards—*his* vineyards, so the people always offer him the firstfruits of their harvest. Long ago God established a law that a farmer's field must always remain with his descendants. Ahab and Jezebel flout the will of the Lord.

A farmer named Naboth, a worshipper of the Lord, owns a vineyard close to Ahab's palace. Ahab covets it, not for its grapes but to root out the vines—stem and branch—to plant a vegetable garden. He tells Naboth he will pay a good price to buy the vineyard. "I can't," says Naboth. "I'm bound by a law of the Lord."

Ahab, mighty in battle, can be a sulking child. He lies down and refuses to eat. Jezebel shakes her head. "All right," she says, "I'll do what you're too gloomy to do." She commands a fast. Naboth wouldn't come except that two ruffians drag him, then crowd him at the table. They pretend to hear him say something, then cry out in mock horror, "Did you hear that? This fellow *cursed* the king! And God too!"

Queen Jezebel glowers. Her priests hold a quick rump trial. They find Naboth guilty of treason. Soldiers carry him out of the city and stone him to death. Then they shame Naboth's body by leaving it unburied where vulture and wolves savage the man—and King Ahab has his garden.

Lord Jesus Christ, you were humiliated, dragged out of Jerusalem (though we should have been dragged into outer darkness), and put to death (though it should have been us). Rise, rise up, you people, and give thanks unto the Lord, for he is good, and his mercy endures forever. Amen.

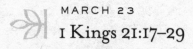

MARCH 23
1 Kings 21:17–29

"Don't covet." Coveting leads to outright greediness. Greediness leads to fraud, and fraud leads to power plays, and power plays to a violation of the laws of the state and the laws of God.

Ahab strolls in his garden with his hands behind his back, pleased by its green growth. Though he took the plot by a violence, it's doubtful he feels remorse.

Suddenly, there stands the prophet Elijah! "You have loved gain more than you love the Lord! You worship your properties and your wealth and your armies and your power! But idolatry does not go unpunished!"

Ahab narrows his eyes. "Well, if it isn't my enemy come back again." Elijah says, "Listen to what the Lord God has to say: 'You killed a man for nothing that you didn't already have. And you left his body on the wayside where the ravens plucked out his eyes. Therefore, *your* body will be thrown to the dogs and the vultures, and your bones will lie unburied.'"

Elijah's prophecy and his absolute conviction shatter Ahab's composure. He trembles. He tears off his clothes and covers his nakedness in rough sackcloth. He fasts and goes about in public desolated and ashamed.

So the Lord says to Elijah, "Ahab has repented. Tell him that wrath will not fall on him but on his sons."

PRAYER

If I covet what belongs to my neighbor, if my sinful greed persuades me that I have a right to his property, I will try to take it guilt-free. Even so do the rich do to the poor; even so do the poor embitter their lives by hating the rich. Even so, even so. But I must not give my allegiance to two masters. One Master only. You, Lord. You are my Master. Amen.

2 Kings 2:1–8

Moses had his rod. Elijah has his mantle. Moses led Israel by a round way to the promised land. Elijah leads his disciple Elisha from Bethel to Jericho and from Jericho to the west side of the Jordan River. At every stop the sons of the prophets warn Elisha of what's to come. Even Elijah tells Elisha to remain behind. But Elisha's love for and his commitment to the God of the prophet will not allow him to stay behind. *Where you go I will go.*

The younger man follows the older man wherever he goes.

When they arrive at the west side of the Jordan, Elijah rolls his mantle—which signifies his godly authority—into something as stiff as a rod. He strikes the water, and the waters part, and both prophets cross on dry ground.

PRAYER

Lord, lead me like a shepherd, and I will follow you, for I am your lamb. Across the waters, Lord, whether they be at peace or else at flood. Through the fires, whether they warm my feet or else rise to consume me. I am Jesus's little lamb. Ever glad at heart I am. Amen.

2 Kings 2:9–12

Elijah and Elisha walk a while in the region where Moses died, then Elijah turns to his disciple and says, "What do you choose before I am parted from you?" Elisha asks for one thing only: "A double portion of your spirit."

"A hard thing for a man to give," says Elijah. "But if you witness my departure, then the Lord God will give it to you."

Suddenly, the two men are divided one from the other by a bright, blazing chariot and horses with flaming manes. A wind whirls around Elijah and catches him up, and he ascends in a blaze and is seen no more.

"My father!" Elisha cries. "My father! My father, the chariots of Israel and the horsemen!" Elisha has been given to see the very hosts of heaven, the angels riding the sky, yet he covers his face and grieves because the prophet has been taken away from him.

PRAYER

Father! The Father of our Lord Jesus Christ, you raised your Son like the daystar until he vanished in a cloud to sit at your right hand. Before he ascended, he breathed on his disciples, saying, "Receive the Holy Spirit." We are your disciples. The Holy Spirit dwells in us, and we will witness his glory in heaven. Amen.

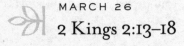

MARCH 26
2 Kings 2:13–18

When Moses died, no one knew where God had buried him, and Joshua took his place. Then Joshua, having received the spirit of Moses, parted the Jordan, and Israel crossed on dry ground (Joshua 3:7–17). Now it's Elisha's turn.

As Elijah whirled into heaven, his mantle billowed down to the earth. Elisha picks it up, and yes, he has received a double portion of his father's spirit. He rolls the mantle straight and stiff and strikes the Jordan, and its waters part.

The prophets who were at Jericho watching as Elijah and Elisha crossed the water to the east, now they see Elisha returning on dry ground. "Something happened," they murmur among themselves. Elisha approaches them wearing Elijah's mantle, and the prophets bow down in wonder. Elisha says, "Stand up." They do, then ask, "What happened? Where's your master? Praying in the wilderness? Prophesying in other cities?" Elisha says nothing. The prophets beg him to say *something*. "We have to search for him, or else what will we do?"

"The Lord," Elisha says, "has already done it for you. He has gathered his prophet to himself and has given you another."

But this company of distressed prophets divides into pairs, and they rush off to search anyway. When they come back empty-handed, Elisha says, "Why didn't you believe what I said to you? From now on I will speak on behalf of the Lord my God."

PRAYER

High and low and hither and thither, people search for the god that cannot give them what they want. But you are the giver of great gifts, Lord Jesus Christ. We don't have to search for you, because you have come to us. Amen.

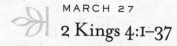

MARCH 27

2 Kings 4:1–37

Elisha inherited a double portion of Elijah's spirit and does what the prophet did before him.

A creditor lends money to a widow-woman drowning in debt. His rates are exorbitant. He comes directly on the due date and demands, "Pay what you owe me!" But she can't. She has nothing left but one cruse of cooking oil. "If don't pay me by tomorrow," he says, "I'll take your children!" When Elisha learns of the widow and the loan shark, he takes pity on her. The little cruse pours forth a flood of oil. She sells the oil and pays the debt in full, then supports herself and her children on the proceeds.

Elisha finds favor with a wealthy woman. She offers him the guestroom on her roof. One day he prophesizes that she will bear a child, and—just as the angels promised Sarah when she laughed—the woman bears a tiny baby boy. He grows old enough to follow his father into the fields. But while working under a searing sun one day, the lad clutches his skull and drops to the ground with a sharp cry. While his mother is stroking his hair at home, the boy is suddenly struck blind by the pain in his head. He thrashes and then lies perfectly still. When Elisha hears the mother's wails, he descends the stairs. He lifts the dead boy in his arms and climbs to his room and prays that the boy be given life again. Yes, Elisha has received Elijah's spirit. He stretches his body over the boy. The boy sneezes and sneezes, sits up, rubs his nose, and asks for a drink of water.

PRAYER

Christ, you raised Jairus's daughter from the dead. You raised the widow's son at Nain. And when you cried, "Lazarus!" the man whom you loved came out of his tomb. Even so will you say to us, "Arise," and we will rise and with the angels sing a choral hallelujah to you. Amen.

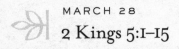

MARCH 28

2 Kings 5:1–15

Which is the greater? The military chief of all the Aramean armies? Or the young Israelite girl who serves that man's wife? Of course. The girl.

Naaman's face and the tissue inside his nose and his lips are marred with reddish lesions. The skin around the lesions has lost all feeling, and none of the Aramean physicians have been able to heal his leprosy. But the servant girl knows a prophet in Israel who is capable of miracles. She tells her mistress about the man named Elisha, and the mistress tells her husband. By now Naaman will try anything. The king of Aram sends a diplomatic letter to Joram, the king of Israel. The king reads: "I require you to heal my captain," then trembles with anxiety. He can't do such a thing!

Naaman arrives with a gaudy entourage and sacks of gold and more silver than one camel can carry. Joram sweats bullets. But the Israelite servant girl named the name of Elisha. Naaman mentions the name, and straightway, Joram sends him to the prophet. With horses and his chariots and a large retinue, Naaman rides to the prophet's house, expecting a magical mumbling of spells over lesions. But Elisha doesn't deign to meet the military chief face to face. He sends out a servant who says, "Bathe seven times in the Jordan River and you'll be clean." "What?" sneers the Aramean. "In that sludge?" He steps back into his chariot and begins to ride away.

But Naaman's more sensible servants urge him to return. "You thought that something easy would cleanse you, a magical word. But the prophet told you to do something difficult. Doesn't that prove his power?" So he submerges himself seven times in the river and is made whole again. He returns to Elisha and says, "Now I know there is no god on the earth except the God of Israel."

PRAYER

You, Lord, have healed our souls in your baptismal waters, and we will trust your word all the days of our lives. Amen.

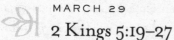

MARCH 29

2 Kings 5:19–27

Naaman leaves Elisha changed and in peace. Gehazi, the prophet's servant, chases after him in greed, wanting to take advantage of the rich and grateful Aramean, unaware that Elisha's spirit follows him.

The first lie: "Elisha sent me to tell you that two men are in need, each of a talent of silver and new clothes." For having been cured of his leprosy, Naaman is happy to oblige, and the gifts are given.

When Gehazi has returned to Elisha, Elisha asks, "Where were you?" Gehazi tells a second lie: "Nowhere." The prophet says, "Did you think I wouldn't know the truth?" Then the consequence of lying—a tit for a tat. Elisha says, "The leprosy I took from Naaman I give to you. And not only you will suffer his leprosy, but so will your descendants."

Ananias and his wife, Sapphira, lied not only to Peter but also to God, and the consequence was both swift and terrible. They fell down dead at Peter's feet (Acts 5:1–11).

Do we think a little white lie is of *no* consequence? Did we fudge on our tax forms? (Commission.) Did we gossip, oh, just a sentence or two? Did we choose not to mention some small sin we did in secret? (Omission.) The Spirit of God knows the truth.

PRAYER

I was angry with my friend:
I told my wrath, my wrath did end.
I was angry with my foe:
I told it not: my wrath did grow.

—WILLIAM BLAKE

This, Lord, is my confession. Heal me of my soul's leprosy. Amen.

MARCH 30
2 Kings 8:7–15

Ben-Hadad, king of Aram, contracts an acute disease. He sends a man named Hazael to Elisha to ask whether the king will live or will he die. Elisha says that the king will live, then he starts to weep. "But you, Hazael," the prophet says, "because of the treachery and the horrors you will commit, you will be punished by a horrible death."

Hazael returns to Ben-Hadad and changes Elisha's truth into a lie, saying, "You will live," then he soaks a blanket in water and covers the king's face, suffocates him, and usurps his throne.

Oh, how people of power suffocate the poor by keeping them impoverished: inferior schools, inferior housing, filthy and crime-ridden neighborhoods, jobs that don't pay enough to support themselves or their families, oppressing other people who don't look like them, refusing to help—or even rejecting—immigrants. "They made their beds. Let them lie in them."

PRAYER

I have the means, O Lord, to lift people out of their miseries. Grant me the goodness to save those who are suffocating from oppression. Amen.

2 Kings 9:30–37

After Ahab and Jezebel killed Naboth for his small plot of land, Elijah prophesied that they would die bloody and ignominious deaths (1 Kings 21:17–24). The Lord waits. The Lord remembers. King Ahab has already died. Now the second part of Elijah's prophecy comes true.

King Jehu is no paragon. He's unscrupulous and cunning and ruthless and brutal—a religious fanatic who kills anyone whose religion is different from his. He slaughtered all of Ahab's offspring. Nevertheless, God made this man to be the instrument of his punishment.

When Jezebel learns that Jehu has entered her city, she chooses to meet him with a glorious defiance. She lines her eyelids with antimony, enlarging her eyes and giving them the striking beauty of Queen Nefertiti. She braids her thick hair and coils the braids around her head. Then, flanked by three palace officials, Jezebel shows herself to her subjects in an upper room and raises her arms: *Behold your queen!* Now Jehu steps forward. Jezebel asks a sarcastic question: "Is it well with you?" No! Judah will turn against Israel. Phoenicia and all Judah's surrounding states will isolate King Jehu. His armies will weaken, and he'll become a vassal to Assyria.

Jehu shouts up to the three officials in the window, "If you're on my side, throw down that heathen whore!" Two of the three seize the queen of Israel and launch her out the window. Her body bursts on the very plot that once belonged to Naboth.

PRAYER

How can I pray after hearing a story of such divine retribution? It's your will, Almighty One. What you ordain is always right. Yet it frightens me. Thou shalt fear and love the Lord. Two emotions struggle in my breast— fear and love. I can only fall before you and mumble my thanksgiving because you have changed your old covenant (your Old Testament) into a new covenant (your New Testament) by the blood of your Son and our Savior, Jesus Christ. Amen.

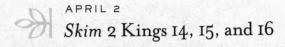

APRIL 1

2 Kings 13:14–21

King Jehoash of Israel seems kindly to Elisha. Though the king disobeys the Lord, he is chosen to receive the prophet's power as once Elisha
received Elijah's power. Elisha has grown old. He lies on his deathbed.
Jehoash comes and weeps over him and cries the words Elisha cried when
Elijah was taken up to heaven: "My father! My father! The chariots of Israel
and its horsemen!" signifying the passage of Elisha's spirit into Jehoash.
Elisha says, "Take your bow and your quiver of arrows. Open the window
and shoot." Elisha lays his hands on the king's hands, another sign of
Jehoash's inheritance. While Jehoash draws the bowstring back to his
ear, Elisha says, "This is the Lord's arrow of victory over the Arameans!"
Then he says, "More arrows, Jehoash. Sting the earth with your arrows."
Jehoash shoots a first and a second and a third and stops. Angrily the
prophet blames him for having shot only three arrows. "You should have
shot five or six. Therefore, you will defeat the Arameans three times only,
though you might have defeated them over and over victoriously."

Elisha turns his eyes to heaven and breathes his last and is buried.
So wonderful was the prophet's spirit that when the dead body of a
Moabite is thrown into the same grave, that body is electrified and lives
and walks again.

PRAYER

*Jesus Christ, three days you lay in your tomb, then rose and raised the
weeping Mary Magdalene from her grief simply by saying her name (John
20:16). This I believe: that on the last day you will call our names too, and
we will rise to eternal life. Amen.*

APRIL 2

Skim 2 Kings 14, 15, and 16

The histories written in the Bible uniformly condemn the kings of Israel
for refusing to honor the God who is God. Judah's kings are praised

for following in the footsteps of their ancestor David—except for King Azariah, who, in his old age, violated the rituals of God and was therefore afflicted with leprosy, King Ahaz, who is said to have sacrificed his son in fire, and others who flagrantly disobeyed the Lord.

PRAYER

We too suffer the sins of our leaders, many of whom elevate themselves to positions of power. They climb up on the backs of lesser people, depriving them of their rights and then neglecting them. "How hard," you said, "it is for a rich man to pass through the eye of a needle?" We, like Saint Peter, say, "What about us? We've left everything to follow you." You answer with an affectionate grace, "Those who have left everything and have placed their faith in me will receive their reward, both in this world and in heaven." You've given us the power of your salvation. Amen.

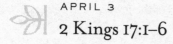

APRIL 3
2 Kings 17:1–6

The succession of the evil kings of Israel ends with its last king, Hoshea. Tiglath-Pileser III, the king of Assyria, Israel's enemy, has overpowered Hoshea's kingdom, forcing him to pay a hefty tribute. Hoshea rifles the temple treasury to make the payments, then tries to make an alliance with Egypt. But when Israel attacks Assyria, Pharaoh's armies fail to appear. Hoshea is imprisoned. Long ago, kings Ahab and Omri surrounded their capital city with a massive, impregnable wall. Its stalwart people are able to hold out against the Assyrians. But Assyria's new king, Shalmaneser V, lays siege to the city. By the third year, the Israelites are so gaunt and so famished that they surrender after all.

PRAYER

Jesus Christ, my sure defense, you have rounded me with spiritual walls that cannot be conquered, not by sin or death or the devil. Who am I that you should protect me? No more than a worm. But your Easter resurrection resurrects me from a worm into a flying butterfly. Amen.

2 Kings 17:24–28

During his defeat of Israel, King Shalmaneser dies, and Sargon II replaces him on the throne. That king deports 27,290 Israelites, scattering them among his various provinces. Next he populates Israel's cities and towns and fields with people from the various parts of his empire. They don't know that the land belongs to God. Because the people worship the idols they've brought with them, lions leap out and savage those they find in the open.

The people cry out to Sargon, who knows from experience that a foreigner must assimilate, must learn the customs of the land he's entered, and must worship its god. Therefore, he sends a priest to teach the people the laws and the commandments of the true God.

That land is called Samaria. By the time Jesus walks from Judah through Samaria to Galilee, the Jews scorn the Samaritans because, though they also worship the God of Moses and David, their teachings are slightly different from the teachings of the Jews.

PRAYER

Lord God, you send rain on the just and the unjust alike. And the Bible assures us that you love the whole world (John 3:16). Yet we vaunt ourselves, feeling superior to those whose ways are different from ours. But you, Jesus? You healed foreigners: the Gadarene madmen filled with legions of devils (Matthew 8:28–34) and the Canaanite woman who begged you to cast out the spirit that bedeviled her daughter. You said, "Woman, you have great faith! Your request is granted" (Matthew 15:21–28). I am a foreigner. I am the Gadarene. I am the Canaanite. Heal me. Amen.

APRIL 5

2 Kings 18:1–16

Out of the darkness and into the light.

God gives Judah a king who walks the paths of righteousness.

King Hezekiah destroys the hill-sanctuaries where the Judeans worship idols. Judah has also made the serpent which Moses cast of bronze into a cultish idol. Hezekiah breaks it into pieces. But, like his ancestor David, even King Hezekiah sins. David killed Uriah. Hezekiah pays tribute to Assyria with the silver and gold in the temple. He even strips the golden overlays from the temple's doors and hinges.

Be patient, King Hezekiah. The Lord will yet do good things for you and for your kingdom.

PRAYER
I come to you, Lord Jesus, weary, worn, and sad. As you did for David and Hezekiah, take my sins away. Make me righteous again, and I will be glad. Amen.

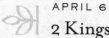

APRIL 6
2 Kings 18:26–19:13

Sennacherib, the king of Assyria, has laid siege to the city of Jerusalem. His warriors are at the wall, some even sitting on the wall. The Judeans fear for their lives. They try to save themselves by bargaining with one of the king's high officials: "We beg you to speak to your people on our behalf, but not in our language. In *your* language."

Nevertheless, the official speaks in the language of Jerusalem because he wants Jerusalem to hear what he has to say. It is to *them* he speaks. "Your king is a liar! He says that he, Hezekiah, can defeat us. He tells you to trust in your God. Ha! Neither he nor his God can save you. *No* god has ever defeated Assyria!"

The Lord who is God promised Israel a land flowing with milk and honey. Now Sennacherib makes the same promise, but deceitfully. "Come with me. Plant your own vineyards. Drink wine. Eat the bread you yourselves have baked and the honey of your hives."

The Judeans tear their clothes because they believe the words of the king of Assyria more than they believe the words of Hezekiah.

I love you, Lord, my strength, my rock, my fortress, my deliverer, and I call upon you to save me from my enemies (Psalm 18:1–3). Reward me according to the righteousness of your Son. Amen.

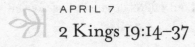

APRIL 7
2 Kings 19:14–37

The cherubim on the ark of the covenant are not chubby little cherubs. They are mighty angels ranked higher than archangels and only one level below the seraphim. Their wings are powerful guardians. It is before these that Hezekiah prays to the Lord, the creator of the universe, to save his kingdom. The prophet Isaiah sends a messenger with an oracle that the zeal of the Lord God is about to work out Judah's salvation. Then the Lord provides a sign for King Hezekiah.

From of old, God planned to use the kings of Assyria as his agents. Now he knows Sennacherib's every move and harnesses that king like an ox. That very night the angel of destruction kills much of the Assyrian army. Sennacherib races back to his stronghold in Nineveh, but no strength can save him, for his sons assassinate him. The words of the Lord are always an act of the Lord.

PRAYER

You, my God, have broken the bows and shattered the spears of those who would poke at our faith and mock our trust in you. "Be still, and know that I am God." Yes! We exalt you (Psalm 46:9–11). We exalt you in all the earth. Amen.

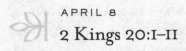

APRIL 8
2 Kings 20:1–11

Hezekiah takes to his bed with a wasting disease. By his own volition, Isaiah comes into the king's chamber and tells him to accept his fate, for the word of God declares that this disease will kill him. "Set your affairs in order." After Isaiah has left him alone, Hezekiah turns his face to the wall, weeping, and prays for deliverance. At that moment Isaiah returns. The Lord can change his mind. He has seen Hezekiah's tears and will heal him after all. He will add fifteen years to his life.

King Hezekiah asks for a sign. Isaiah predicts that the shadow on the sundial will turn backward ten hours. Hezekiah objects. He says that the shadow on the dial can't turn backward, only forward. "What sort of sign can *that* be?" The Lord does indeed make the sun retreat ten hours. In three days the king stands up and goes into the temple.

PRAYER

> I feel better, so much better
> Since I laid my burden down.
>
> I feel like shouting "Hallelujah!"
> Since I laid my burden down. Amen.
>
> —"GLORY, GLORY, HALLELUJAH"

APRIL 9

2 Kings 22:1–23:25

Josiah is the great grandson of Hezekiah, and just as that king walked in the ways of David, so this king walks in the ways of the Lord his God.

Previous kings allowed the house of the Lord to fall into ruin. Josiah decides to redeem the time by repairing the temple. He disburses money to the workers who are restoring it. While the high priest Hilkiah oversees the recovery of the temple's sacred vessels, he discovers the Book of the Law of God and sends it to King Josiah. When the book is read aloud, Josiah tears his robes, grieved by the past sins of Judah.

Though there are many male prophets on which the king could call, he begs a word from the prophetess named Huldah, who predicts that Josiah will die in peace. Straightway he institutes a sweeping reform with an angry hand. Josiah is the storm of the Lord, destroying every last vestige of Judah's idolatrous worship.

PRAYER

We too have worshipped the idols of covetousness and false witness and adultery and payback to those we think have wronged us. But you, Lord Christ—you were wronged even unto death, and what was your payback? Mercy. Forgiveness. Even so have we been forgiven in order that we may forgive our neighbors. And we do. Amen.

ABOUT THE PROPHETS

 The *chronological* sequence of the prophets is different from the *biblical* sequence, which we'll follow in the devotions to come. Below is a chronological/historical succession of the events of the prophets with their approximate dates BC:

Amos, 760

Hosea, 750–724

Isaiah (chapters 1 to 39), 738–701

Micah, 730–700

Zephaniah, 630–620

Jeremiah, 627–583

Nahum, 612

Habakkuk, 609–597

Ezekiel, 593–573

Obadiah, dates uncertain

Isaiah (chapters 40 to 66), 550–538

Daniel, 597–539

Haggai, 520

Zechariah, 520–518

Malachi, dates uncertain

Prophets are intense, passionate, anguished, and urgent. Their words are often outbursts of violent emotions. The sorrows of the people distress them. They stand on a middle ground between God and his children. Their words will slash and after that, console. They may predict the future, but their mission is mostly to speak on behalf of God.

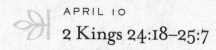

APRIL 10

2 Kings 24:18–25:7

The people of the kingdom of Israel were exiled in the year 722 before the birth of Christ. The people of the kingdom of Judah are soon to be exiled in the year 586.

It's Nebuchadnezzar and not God who places Zedekiah on the throne of Judah.

For a while King Zedekiah sends tributes to Babylon, but then schemes a rebellion. Now it is King Nebuchadnezzar of Babylon who lays siege to Jerusalem. After eighteen months the Babylonian armies breach the city's walls. Zedekiah leaps into the saddle and flees north and east. He hasn't gone far when he's captured near Jericho.

Nebuchadnezzar slaughters Zedekiah's sons before his eyes and, so that this sight will be Zedekiah's last, the king of Babylon sears his eyeballs blind.

The retributions of God are too terrible to contemplate. Yet he can change his mind. His Son cancels the old and brings in the new. "You have heard that it was said, 'An eye for an eye and a tooth for a tooth.' But I say to you, 'Don't challenge the evildoer. If he strikes you on the right cheek, offer the other. If he wants your coat, give it to him. And if he wants you to walk a mile with him, walk two'" (Matthew 5:38–42).

PRAYER
Lord Jesus, you turned your cheek to the spiteful and didn't denounce them even during your crucifixion. Now you walk beside us our whole lifetimes through. Grant us your goodness to turn a cheek, to give our possessions away, and to sit by the sick. Amen.

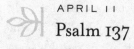

APRIL 11

Psalm 137

The exiles are homesick for the city that has been ruined and heartsick for the temple that has been demolished. They hang their harps on willow trees in Babylon and weep. They live among their captors. They live between the Tigris and the Euphrates Rivers, along a system of foreign canals. Their grief is sharpened by the Babylonians' sarcastic demand: "Sing for us one of those songs you sang on Zion!" How can Judah sing? But they remember. They must remember. If they forget Jerusalem, then music and singing will be lost forever. A withered hand can't pluck a string. A paralyzed tongue can't sing at all.

Judah's grief turns their hopeless rage against the captors who killed their children in the conquest. Let the punishment fit the crime. "O Daughter Babylon, you destroyer! Happy would be that man who takes *your* children and dashes their heads against stones!"

To express such an outlandish rage is not wrong, for to feel nothing is to submit. The psalmist prays with passion and an utter honesty, for God alone can hear without judging. God alone can listen with divine compassion. And God alone can say, "Rise up and live."

PRAYER

Oh, how I want to hurt those who hurt me or the ones I love. Though I may not say it, I think it. But who has ever hurt you worse than those who hated you and crucified you? But you didn't hurt them in return. You prayed to your Father to forgive them—forgiving me too for having assailed you with my sins. Yet you blessed me with your wounded hands. Amen.

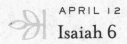

APRIL 12
Isaiah 6

Now we return to the time when Hezekiah was king of Judah.

At dawn a young priest kneels on the threshold of the doors of the temple. His back is turned to the Mount of Olives in the east. When the sun rises over the mount, it shoots its rays past the man and straight into the temple, where it illuminates a cloud of smoke that fills the temple. The hem of the Lord's robe! The seraphim, the burning ones, soar on six wings inside the temple. Two wings cover their faces. Two wings cover their nakedness, and on two wings they fly. The angels cry,

"Holy, holy, holy is the Lord God!" Holiness belongs to God alone, for it means that the Creator is above everything he has created. The angels cry, "The whole earth is full of his glory!" Glory is God's weightiness, his authority over the whole universe, over the stars as well as over every blade of grass. So majestic are the angels' voices that they cause the doorposts and its hinges to tremble.

The young man, overwhelmed with the sound and the glory of the Lord, fears for his life. His lips have uttered sinful words. But one of the seraphs sears his lips with a burning coal, saying, "Your guilt is gone."

The angels are silenced by the mighty voice of God. "Who will go with me? Who will be my prophet in the land?" The young man murmurs, "I will go."

PRAYER

I am that young man. I am Isaiah. I tremble before your presence, O my Lord. Yet you have touched my ears and my tongue and have given me speech (Mark 7:34–35). I will go for you. I will teach the nations. Amen.

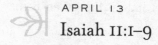
APRIL 13
Isaiah 11:1–9

Isaiah prophesies, "They will not hurt or destroy on all my holy mountain." And again he prophesies, "They will beat their swords into plowshares and their spears into pruning hooks. Neither shall they learn war any more [Isaiah 2:4–5], for there shall come a kingdom of peace."

Isaiah may be referring to King Hezekiah, but future peoples will understand that his "Messiah," his "anointed one," is Christ Jesus.

And that peace? That cosmic peace? Predators will cease eating their prey. Wolves will live with lambs, and leopards with little goats. There will be such peace that a nursing child will put her hand on the hole of poisonous snakes with no fear of being bitten. Eden will have come again.

Those who want peace must work for justice, for corruption always leads to destruction.

Jesus, grant us the peace that the world cannot give. Amen.

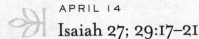

Isaiah 27; 29:17–21

Leviathan, that dragon of the sea, is identified in the book of Revelation 12:9 as the "ancient serpent called the devil, or Satan, who leads the whole word astray," whom, on that great and holy day, God will put to death, and on that same day God will redeem Israel.

Was Israel's exile seen as a punishment, pure and simple? Well, now God says that it was a goodness after all, for the people's suffering purged them of their sins, and God will be Israel's benevolence. "Make peace with me. Make peace with me. Cling to me. There is a stump in Israel that will put forth a shoot, and the shoot will bear a flower." God will crush the stones of the idolatrous altars as if they were chalk. He will cause pagan fortresses to be deserted and windblown and forsaken. And on the day when the trumpet's blast proclaims a new harvest, God will gather his people in like grains of wheat and will bring them home to worship in Jerusalem.

PRAYER

Lord, you work salvation in the earth. You crushed Leviathan's head under your heel. You fed meat to the creatures of the wilderness. You made the summer. You made the winter. There is none like you. Who should we cling to if not to you? Amen.

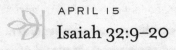

Isaiah 32:9–20

The prophets consistently rebuke the people of the Lord for abandoning him. Here Isaiah condemns women who represent the whole of Israel.

Rather than working, they gather on the rooftops of connected houses and idle the time away, gossiping. Isaiah warns them, "Shudder at what God will do. The vineyards will dry up, and the grapes will become as hard as pebbles. Strip yourselves," Isaiah says. "Cover your genitals with sackcloth. Beat your bare breasts. Mourn for the desolation of your land." Harsh and caustic words! But God can turn his doomful judgments into mercy.

Isaiah now predicts that the Lord will restore the fortunes of Israel. The forests of Assyria will wither and become a wilderness. Babylon will be utterly destroyed, but the vineyards of Israel will be showered with rain, will grow green leaves and fat clusters of purple fruit. The children of the Lord will live beside the still and peaceful waters. Farmers will sow their seeds. Their fields will be well irrigated, and their harvest will produce a hundredfold.

PRAYER

We drink water from the wells of your salvation, Lord. We wash our children in the waters of baptism. We gather at the river, the beautiful, beautiful river of God and say, Amen.

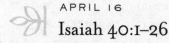

APRIL 16

Isaiah 40:1–26

While Judah lives in exile, Isaiah prophesies the revelation of God's glory, for he will lead his people home from Babylon. "Comfort ye! Comfort ye, my people!" Judah's sins have been blotted out. The desert will be washed with water and grow like a garden. The sands that burn the soles of a traveler's feet will be cooled by ponds of water (Isaiah 35:6–7). A voice will cry out in the wilderness—promises to fill in the valleys, to flatten the mountains, and to make a straight, smooth path for Judah's return. "The voice of the Lord has spoken it." He knows the names of every sheep in his flock, and his lambs he will carry in his arms, just as mothers cuddle their children (John 10:1–5; Luke 15:4–6).

The Lord, the everlasting Creator says, "Cry out!" Isaiah says, "What shall I say?" "This," says the Lord, "that all people are like the grass that withers and dies but that I will breathe life into them again." Death and resurrection. "I will empower the weary. They will mount up on wings like the wings of eagles."

PRAYER

> There is a balm in Gilead
> To make the wounded whole.
> There is a balm in Gilead
> To heal the sin-sick soul. Amen.

—"THERE IS A BALM IN GILEAD"

APRIL 17
Isaiah 42:1–9; 43:1–13

Upon his "servant" (his "anointed one"), God puts his spirit. Centuries later he will send his Spirit in the form of a dove on his Son (Matthew 12:15–21; Mark 1:9–11).

God's servant doesn't shout in the streets. He doesn't hurt the wounded nor extinguish the small flame that warms the heart and life of the sick. He is the light that opens the eyes of the blind. He sets the prisoners free. New things are springing forth. Don't you see them?

Even so will Jesus give sight to the blind. He will make the lame to walk, the lepers clean, the deaf to hear, the dead to be raised, while the poor and the oppressed will receive good news and jump for joy (Luke 7:18–23). God will save his people from ordeals by water and by fire because "you are precious in my sight, and I love you."

PRAYER

My God, I know your love and have received your love. You are my rock in a shaky land, and you are my salvation. Amen.

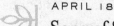

Song of Solomon (or Song of Songs) 1

(First read the book at one sitting.)

"Song of Solomon" can also be translated "Song *to* Solomon." It was written about four hundred BC.

The maiden yearns for kisses of her beloved. "Or leave a kiss within your cup, and I'll not ask for wine." She's black and beautiful—African black, or sun-scorched black—as black as Bedouin tents woven of goats' hair. Her half brothers forced her to work their vineyards, while hers went weedy and unpruned.

The maiden loves a youth, and he loves her: "You are beautiful, beautiful, my love." Bangles hang over her cheeks from jewels worn on her forehead. She wears a love-charm between her breasts, a pouch of spikenard.

PRAYER

How beautiful on the mountains are the feet of the messenger who brings good news. How beautiful are you, my Lord, and how beautiful is your good news! We are your brides, dressed in white. You are our bridegroom, dressed in glory. Amen.

Song of Solomon 2:4–17

Early rabbis said that the maiden symbolized Israel and the youth symbolized the Lord. Christians have long said that the maiden represents the believer and the young man represents Jesus (see Revelation 21:2). In either case, the song is boldly sexual and is about the consummation of love.

"The banqueting house" can be a "house of wine," where something like window drapes hang from the ceiling. Raisin cakes can be an aphrodisiac. The maiden's yearning is so strong that her face is warm and her knees are weak. "Hurry!" the youth urges the maiden. "The turtle-doves are singing. Spring is here." The lovers go out and walk through the vineyards. "We should catch the foxes," says the youth, "before they dig among the roots and ruin the grapes." But his beloved has other thoughts on her mind: "Hurry! Hurry! Leap like an antelope, twenty feet at a bound."

PRAYER

Jesus loves me, and I love Jesus, and the banner over us is Love. Amen.

APRIL 20
Song of Solomon 3; 5:2–8

The maiden dreams two dreams, one of longing and relief, the other of fear and loss.

In the first dream she can't find her lover. She runs to the city. A watchman at the gates cries, "Halt! Who goes there?" She answers with an earnest question: "Watchman, have you seen him? Did you stop him too?" Well, women aren't threats. The watchman lets this woman pass. And when she finds her lover, she falls on his neck and weeps.

In her second dream the maiden has undressed for the night when she hears a knock on her door. "My love, my darling, open up," he calls. "It's drizzling. I'm wet through and through." The maiden gets up and puts on her clothes and goes to the door. But when she opens it, her lover isn't there. The poor maiden panics and rushes out into the night. At the city gates, two drunken guardsmen laugh and grab her and strip her bare. The maiden wakes from her nightmare, her sheets soaked with sweat, her bones quaking with fear.

PRAYER

We too have been troubled by nightmares, some minor, some so terrible we thrash in our beds, and some we can't forget. Lord Jesus, like a mother wake us, and like a mother hold us to yourself, and soothe our troubled spirits.

Song of Solomon 5:10–16

The starry-eyed maiden sings a song about the charms of her young man.

His complexion is as red-ruddy as was King David's. He is taller than King Saul. If he stood among ten thousand men, she would pick him out at a glance. His face is her treasure. His black hair falls in waves down his back. ("My beloved is mine and I am his.") His eyes have the tenderness of doves, of turtledoves whose love for their mates is steadfast. His kisses are as soft as the petals of a lily. And, oh, his stature! Arms molded of gold. Legs like columns carved of alabaster. He stands as lofty as the trees of Lebanon. His forehead shines like polished gold. And he sings in a seductive baritone. "This is my beloved. This is my friend."

PRAYER

My Savior, you are more beautiful than that maiden's lover. And loftier, for your stature reaches from the earth into high heaven. You are the lily whom your Father clothes. You are mine and I am yours. Amen.

Song of Solomon 4:16; 5:1

Although this passage falls in the middle of the songs, it indicates the lovemaking that finally fulfills the couple's desires.

The north wind and the south wind blow the maiden's scent abroad, alluring her young man to her garden. The garden is walled. Its soil is fertile, and its fruit is delicious.

And what is the maiden's garden? Why, it is herself, her body.

And he comes. The spices belong to him. The honeycomb belongs to him. All is his, and all is hers. *Consummatum est.* It is finished.

PRAYER

My soul says, "Yes."
My soul says, "Yes."

Yes to your will,
> (Yes, yes.)

Yes to your way.
> (Yes, yes.)

I praise you, my Lord.
> (Yes, yes.)

I thank you, my Lord.
> (Yes, yes.)

Come by us, O Lord.
> (Yes, yes. Yes, yes, and amen.)

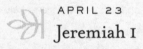

APRIL 23
Jeremiah I

(Turn to page 100: Jeremiah prophesied about a century *after* Isaiah. I'm not following the prophets' chronological order. I'm following the biblical order.)

Jeremiah was born in Anathoth, three miles northeast of Jerusalem, 627 years before the birth of Jesus. God says to him, "I knew you before I formed you in your mother's womb." In Psalm 139:13–15 the psalmist says much the same thing: "You knit me together [*knit one, purl two*] in my mother's womb." The Lord chooses his servants even before they're born.

Jeremiah is twelve when the Lord calls him to prophesy "to the nations." As Moses did before him, the lad hesitates: "I can't. I'm too young to speak." The flaming seraph touched Isaiah's lips with a burning coal. Now the Lord himself touches Jeremiah's mouth and proves by a sign that he has endowed Jeremiah with the authority of a prophet. He asks the boy, "What do you see?" "I see an almond branch and a pot of boiling water." These are signs of God's commission: "Uproot gardens. Trample on wheat fields. Break the altars and the temples dedicated to Baal." But God isn't only a punishing judge. He is also a merciful Father: "<u>Destroy, but build up too. Encourage the farmers to plow their fields</u>. Tell them to sow new <u>seed, and they</u> will gather into their <u>barns</u> abundant harvests. But you, Jeremiah, must also gird your loins like a warrior prepared to fight."

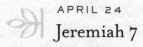

APRIL 24
Jeremiah 7

This may be Jeremiah's first full sermon. The Jews are in God's temple to worship. Jeremiah stands at the temple's gates, <u>accusing them because their worship is hollow and meaningless</u>. <u>They worship not God but the temple itself</u>, assuring themselves that their safety lies in "the temple of God, the temple, the temple of the Lord." "But you," Jeremiah harangues them, "ride roughshod over the strangers in your land. No compassion for widows and orphans! You break God's commandments, stealing, murdering, committing adultery. Worse than that, you have shed innocent blood! This house is called by the Lord's name. But you have made it a den of robbers!" (See Jesus's accusation in Luke 19:45–46: "Made it 'a den of robbers.'")

"Because you have rejected the Lord," cries Jeremiah, "mourn. Cut your hair. Put on sackcloth. Grieve. Confess that you have burned your children in the 'Valley of Ben Hinnom.'" Jesus will call that valley "Gehenna," where there will be wailing and gnashing of teeth.

God's vexation burns so hot that he warns the people, saying, "Your corpses will not be buried but left on the roadsides, where vultures and jackals will feed on them."

commandments. You know them, every one. I pray for, and I believe in, your faithfulness, your compassion, and your full forgiveness. Amen.

Jeremiah 8:18–9:3

Jeremiah's passionate denunciations are interspersed with his passionate anguish for the people, "my poor people." When they hurt, he hurts with them. When they mourn, he mourns for them.

"Is there no balm [the sap of silver fir trees] in Gilead [the forests east of the Jordan River)]?" God and his prophet are so sick at heart that they don't have tears enough to weep for the fate to befall the people.

Psalm 1 distinguishes the wrong path from the right. If only Judah would listen to the prophet and choose righteousness, she would be well watered and produce an abundance of fruit. But because the people have chosen the path of sinners, they will be blasted away like chaff in a strong wind.

"This," says the Lord, speaking through Jeremiah, "shall be the future of my people. Because they've made weapons of their tongues, their enemies will triumph over them with iron weapons."

PRAYER
"Blessed are you who are poor, for yours is the kingdom of God…. Blessed are you who weep now, for you will laugh" (Luke 6:20–21). Again and again, Lord Jesus, you change our lives from distress to assurance. Again and again you lift us out of the pit and cause us to smile. Amen.

Jeremiah 26:1–15; 7:1–3

When Jeremiah has finished his sermon against the Judeans who worship in the temple (the temple, the temple—sound without meaning), the priests seize him. They place him in the city gates, where the elders hold court. "This," the priests declare, "this, this false prophet deserves to die!" Jeremiah protests that the words he speaks are the words of God. As for dying, he shows no fear. "Kill me, if that's your plan," he says. "But if you do, my blood will be on you and on Jerusalem."

Yet often and often God forgoes his wrath and chooses mercy. Jeremiah's sermon doesn't end before he says, "Amend your ways, and the Lord will live with you in the land he gave to your forebears, to Abraham and Isaac and Jacob forever and ever."

PRAYER

I trust in your mercy, O Lord my God. My heart rejoices in your salvation. I sing to you because you have dealt bountifully with me. Amen.

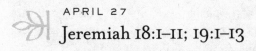

APRIL 27
Jeremiah 18:1–11; 19:1–13

Jeremiah not only preaches to the people, he also symbolizes the judgments of the Lord by what he does.

The prophet watches a potter working at his wheel. When the pot becomes blemished and misshapen, he punches it down and starts again. Then he glazes the new vessel and fires it in his kiln. "Listen," says Jeremiah to Judah. "Listen to the word of God: 'House of Israel, like clay in the potter's hand, you are in *my* hand. Blemish yourselves and I will destroy you. But if you change your ways, I will change my mind and build you beautiful again.'"

Next God instructs Jeremiah to go again to the potter's house and buy a slender, well-worked flask. The prophet purchases the flask. Then the Lord instructs him to take some of the city's elders and some of its priests to the Valley of Slaughter, a sort of garbage dump. By a sign, then, Jeremiah prophesizes a horror to come. He throws the flask down into the valley, shattering it so completely that it can't be mended. "Even so," says Jeremiah to the elders and the priests, "will God break you and your city into so many pieces that they cannot be joined together again."

Nevertheless, the Lord also says, "I will break the bow and shatter the spear." And, "Be still, and know that I am God" (Psalm 46:9–11).

PRAYER

You are the potter. I am clay, blemished by my iniquities. But you reworked me on Calvary and baked me with your love and glazed me with your blood, and I will never be shattered again. My mind and my heart are at peace because you are my God. Amen.

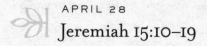

APRIL 28
Jeremiah 15:10–19

Jeremiah is passionate in his prophetic denunciations and passionate in his suffering for the sake of the people's suffering. He is also passionate in his complaints against God for the trials visited upon him. Yes, he ate the words of the Lord willingly. But now he hates his life.

Jeremiah has obeyed God in everything, however difficult the task. He has never married, has never danced with merrymakers. He is despised, even within his family. "I am innocent!" Jeremiah shakes his fist at God. "You have made me burn with indignation! I suffer the insults and the curses of Jerusalem! My wounds will not heal! I depended on you, God, but you've left me high and dry. I'm like the traveler who crosses the desert past the place of no return, a thirsty man looking forward to a drink from a stream of water. But when I get there, that stream is baked and dry!"

If ever you're angry at God, speak your anger. Shout it if you have to. This Father is unfazed by your complaint or Jeremiah's. He says, "If you turn back, I will take you back."

PRAYER

I contracted an inoperable lung cancer and was told to get my affairs in order. Should I shake my fist at God? I didn't, but I could have. And if I had, God would not have taken it amiss but would have only said, "Turn back. I will strengthen your faith." It was from you, my Lord, that I received my faith and my peace in the first place. Amen.

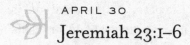
Jeremiah 20:1–12

Jeremiah stands in the court of the temple and utters the words of the Lord: "I am about to destroy Jerusalem and all its surrounding towns!"

When the priest named Pashhur hears Jeremiah's prophecy, he seizes him and beats him and locks him in the stocks like a criminal. Passersby hiss at him. Then as soon as the prophet is released, he spits fire at the priest. "They call you Pashhur? *I* call you Terror on Every Side. The Lord God will terrorize *you*! He will do to you what he did to Israel—drive you and yours into exile!"

As quick as Jeremiah is to condemn others, he is just as quick to blame God all over again. "My life has become a misery." *If you will . . .* Right. Jeremiah's anger cools, and he says, "But the Lord is with me like a terrorizing warrior."

PRAYER

Not always and not often, O Lord, but sometimes my life is embittered by scornful, self-satisfied people. They ridicule me because I'm different. They mock me because I won't join their rough fun or their drinking parties or their joyrides or the tricks they play on others. But you are with me, my shield and my protector. Amen.

Jeremiah 23:1–6

The word *pastor* derives from the word *shepherd*. What Jeremiah says to the religious leaders in his day he also says to the religious leaders in our day:

"You are pastors without principles, motivated by self-aggrandizement and not by love for your God. *You* have scattered his flock! *You* have driven them away. You have *not* tended to their wounds, nor do you save them from the mauling teeth of wolves.

"'I,' says the Lord, '*I* will gather my flock again, but you I will sweep away and will give my sheep humble pastors who will lead them by example and by faithful preaching. And,' says the Lord, 'I will raise a branch from David's line, a king who will deal justly with my people.'"

PRAYER

My grandfather was a pastor with soft, brown, and gentle eyes. My father was a pastor who preached in German for German congregations, a scholar-pastor whose wisdom blessed his people. Lord Jesus, our Good Shepherd (our Good Pastor), thank you for giving us pastors who both preach in and who live your image. Amen.

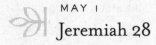

MAY 1
Jeremiah 28

The truth of a prophet's prophecy and a prophet's false interpretation of the times—"Peace, peace" where there is no peace—are reckoned by the outcome of their prophecies—what happens and what does not happen.

Hananiah preaches a peace that will not come. Jeremiah preaches a disaster that will surely come.

Hananiah says, "The Lord spoke to me, saying, 'In two years I will bring back the treasures which King Nebuchadnezzar stole from my house. And I will bring my people out of exile.'"

Jeremiah says, "Amen to that! The peace you preach would be good for us all. But I am bound to preach a different fate for Judah." Jeremiah wears a yoke around his neck to symbolize how heavy is Babylon's continuing oppression. Hananiah breaks Jeremiah's yoke. "This," he says, "is how God promises to break the yoke of the Babylonians' oppression!"

Jeremiah walks away. But later the Lord tells him to return to that charlatan and to say, "These are the words of the true God. 'You have broken a wooden yoke. But I have given Nebuchadnezzar an iron yoke which you can't break! Neither you nor the people of Judah. For your lies, Hananiah, I will sicken you until you go down to your death.'"

There are pastors whose preaching reaches for fame, TV pastors who beg for money, pastors who use their authority to abuse others. But thanks be to God for pastors willing to preach your truth, however hard the consequences. Amen.

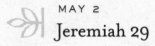

MAY 2
Jeremiah 29

Because he prophesied Babylon's iron yoke, Jeremiah now thinks about the Judeans still living under King Nebuchadnezzar's yoke. He sends his countryfolk a letter, urging them to make peace with their circumstances.

"Settle down in Babylon because your captivity will last seventy years," which is the length of a very old person's lifetime. "Build houses. Marry. Have children. Live as you would live here in Jerusalem in times of peace. Be patient. Your present suffering is working out the expiation of your sins. There is hope for you. God will bring you home again."

Comforting words indeed. But Jeremiah's next words come as a shock: "Pray for those who persecute you. In *their* welfare is *your* welfare."

Three false prophets live among the people in Babylon: Ahab (not the Ahab that once ruled Israel), Zedekiah (not the Zedekiah who will prophesy in the future), and a man named Shemaiah. Jeremiah writes: "Don't trust their lies or the dreams they dream."

Shemaiah writes to rebuke Jeremiah: "Seventy years? Seventy *years*? Outrageous! God can set Judah free in the twinkling of an eye!"

Jeremiah fires back: "The Lord will punish you. You will not see all the good that he plans for his people."

Jesus, you have said to us, "Peace I give you. Not the peace the world gives, but my peace." This world may pretend that peace is the winning of wars or good health or happy times. But your peace calms our inward spirits. Your peace is the hope that allows us to pass through this world with no fear for the future, because our future is in your hands. Amen.

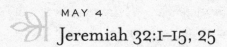

Jeremiah 36:1–26

Baruch, an educated scribe, is Jeremiah's secretary and an eyewitness to many of the events in the prophet's life. Jeremiah's memory is flawless. He dictates his sermons word for word to his secretary, who records them on a long scroll.

"Take this," says Jeremiah, "and read it to the people in the temple and then to King Jehoiakim's palace officials." When Baruch reads it to the officials, they react with alarm and take it to the king. Jehoiakim is in his winter chamber, warming himself before the fire kindled in his brazier. While one of his men reads the prophet's sermons aloud, the king grows angry and angrier. "That arrogant toad!" Jehoiakim cuts the scroll and piece by piece burns it in the brazier until every last scrap has turned to char. "Arrest Jeremiah!" the king commands. "Arrest his secretary!" Baruch escapes, and the Lord God hides him and Jeremiah with him.

Jeremiah repeats the entire scroll to Baruch again, word for word.

PRAYER

Let the words of my mouth and the thoughts in my heart be acceptable to you, O Lord, my Rock and my Redeemer (Psalm 19:14). Amen.

Jeremiah 32:1–15, 25

Hanamel rides to Jerusalem to visit his cousin. "Jeremiah," he says, "there's a field for sale in Anathoth. You know we have to keep it in the family [see Leviticus 25:23]. But I'm in debt. Surely you can purchase it." Baruch takes six and a half pieces of silver from his pouch. Jeremiah tells him to draw up the proper documents, then tells Hanamel to go back and buy the field. Then he himself will go north to inspect the property.

Anyone else would think Jeremiah's act is absurd. Babylon is about to overrun Judah and take *all* its lands. Jeremiah's purchase will be mute—except that Judah's hills and valleys and good earth belong to God. *His* hand guides the affair.

Baruch writes two copies of the deed, one to prove Jeremiah's ownership and one to seal in a jar as a symbol of his conviction that God will surely bring his people out of exile and home again.

"For it's you, O Lord God, who told me to buy the field."

PRAYER

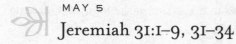
Everything I own is in your hands, O Lord, and my trust is in you. You own the mansions of heaven. I look forward with joy to dwelling there with you. Amen.

MAY 5
Jeremiah 31:1–9, 31–34

In the past God told Isaiah to say to Israel, "Comfort, comfort my people!" Here in the present, Jeremiah consoles God's people: "He loves you. He loves you with an everlasting love, with the love of a father for his children."

Comfort: God has abandoned all the old covenants which the people broke (covenants with Abraham, with Jacob, with Israel at Mount Sinai, with David) and is instituting a new one which will prompt joy and the shaking of tambourines and dancing—though this too the people will break hereafter. Had the Lord written his early covenant on two tablets of stone? Well, now he writes his new covenant on his people's hearts. "Wait," he says to them, "and I will bring you home from the farthest regions of the earth. Wait, wait for me."

PRAYER

Our Father, who art in heaven, your name is holy, and we do wait. We wait for the coming of your kingdom. Amen.

Jeremiah 37:11–38:13

When Jeremiah sets out to claim his property, a watchman at the city's gate seizes him and snarls, "You traitor! You want to fight on the side of Babylon!" The watchman binds the prophet's wrists and takes him to the palace officials. "A deserter!" Jeremiah denies the charge. Enraged by the prophet's constant condemnations, they beat him and imprison him, then confront Zedekiah (the present king of Judah), saying, "This man must be put to death!" Instead of death, the king makes sure that Jeremiah receives a loaf of fresh bread every day.

A cistern is made to catch and to save rainwater against the dry season. It's shaped like a bottle, its opening only big enough to swallow down a human body, its walls plastered smooth and unclimbable, its floor wide and muddy. The officials drop Jeremiah into a cistern, letting him down by ropes. He sinks to his ankles in the mud, and there he remains for several days.

Judah is in peril, and Zedekiah is weak in the knees. He sends a delegation to Jeremiah, begging the prophet to pray for him. Yet and still, Jeremiah insists that the king should submit to Babylon.

When Zedekiah's servant Ebed-Melek hears of Jeremiah's confinement, he goes to the king and says, "Wicked men are starving the prophet to death." Zedekiah has always respected Jeremiah. "Find three men," he says, "and draw the prophet up to freedom." Ebed-Melek drops ropes into the cistern, together with two towels. "Put these under your armpits," he says to Jeremiah, "to cushion the ropes when I draw them taut."

PRAYER

I stand in the mud of my transgressions, isolated, helpless. Savior, save me by the ropes of your great mercy. Amen.

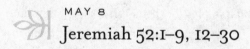

Jeremiah 38:14–28

King Zedekiah says to Jeremiah, "Have you heard some word from the Lord?" Jeremiah answers, "My prophecy concerning the destruction of Jerusalem is coming true. A word from the Lord? Yes. He spoke to me."

"Of freedom?" "No. Of judgment. Jerusalem will fall to the forces of King Nebuchadnezzar." Indeed. The Babylonians have laid siege to Jerusalem. Zedekiah can no longer doubt the prophecy.

PRAYER

O Lord, protect our nation. Enemies outside its borders seek to destroy it. Certain citizens inside its borders fear that they will be displaced by people of other cultures and religions, fear that they will lose their rights and their power to other "inferior" races. They hate our nation's institutions, its traditional ethic of acceptance, its traditions of equality, unity, indivisibility, even the nation's laws that they think are stealing their "freedom." These citizens march, protesting (sometimes loudly and angrily) a government that, they think, wants to take away their liberty.

How often I've prayed, "Give thanks to the Lord, for he is good, and his mercy lasts forever." Be good. Be merciful. Save us from sinners and from our own sins. Amen.

Jeremiah 52:1–9, 12–30

"O break, my heart," says Jeremiah. "My bones are out of joint. I stumble like a drunkard because of God's holy words."

Jeremiah sits on the Mount of Olives, weeping for Jerusalem. The hordes of Babylon have breached Jerusalem's walls. The prophet grieves as he watches its destruction.

Solomon's Temple is in flames. A stinging black smoke darkens the sun. The beams of the houses stand on end, burning like candles. The Babylonians stuff Jerusalem's treasures into sacks, throw them into wagons, and cart them away. The captain of the Babylonian armies orders his soldiers to break into pieces the two bronze columns that stand on either side of the temple doors. Its lampstands, the altar of burnt incense, the high altar of sacrifice—everything good and holy is looted. The temple vomits clouds of black fire. A lazy wind blows the smoke toward the east.

O break, my heart!

Hot stones explode, and the house of God collapses.

Finally, Jeremiah comes down the mount and walks the smoldering streets of Jerusalem.

"Is it nothing to you who pass by? Behold and see that there is no sorrow like my sorrow" (Lamentations 1:12).

In the end, Nebuchadnezzar has driven into exile 4,600 Judeans. Jeremiah's prophecy has been fulfilled.

PRAYER

Our dead shall live. They will wake up and sing. The earth will burst with life, giving birth to those who have been buried. For our resurrection we praise your name and thank you, O Lord, our heavenly Father. Amen.

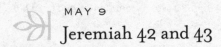

MAY 9

Jeremiah 42 and 43

The handful of people who were left in Jerusalem when the rest were driven into exile beg Jeremiah to pray for them. What should they do? Surely it would be best to flee to Egypt. But the prophet tells them to stay right where they are and that God will build them up. "But if you go, you will be struck by the sword. You will suffer drought and famine and pestilence. The Egyptians will curse you. They will sneer at your broken-down and humiliated condition, and you will die in that foreign land."

Nevertheless, the remnant of Judeans accuses the prophet of telling lies. In the face of his warnings, they travel to Egypt anyway, taking Jeremiah and Baruch with them.

After their emigration, the Lord tells Jeremiah to bury some stones close to Pharaoh's palace. As he digs, and as the remnant watches,

Jeremiah delivers the last prophecy that we know of: "The Babylonian king, Nebuchadnezzar, will build his throne on these stones and will ravage Egypt. But you have chosen it."

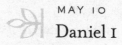

MAY 10

Daniel 1

Nebuchadnezzar recognizes the value of four men among his exiles: Daniel, Hananiah, Mishael, and Azariah. Therefore, he elevates them to serve in his court and gives them Babylonian names. Belteshazzar means, roughly, "protect the king's life," and Abednego, "servant of Nebo." Shadrach means "shining," and Meshach may mean, "Who is like (the moon god) Aku?" or else it's a derivation of the religious name "Mithra."

The Babylonians' meat is offered to idols before they eat it. But Daniel chooses not to break the law of God. Because he eats only grain and fruit and vegetables, the palace master fears that he will become gaunt and sickly, a bad comparison with the other young men. "This king will have my head."

Daniel says, "Take it easy. Give me and my companions ten days without meat, and see what happens." After the allotted ten days, the four Judeans are smooth and strong and glossy. King Nebuchadnezzar approves. Moreover, Daniel has the charisma to interpret dreams and a wisdom that outshines that of every Babylonian enchanter.

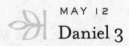

Daniel 2

These days King Nebuchadnezzar sleeps restlessly. In that zone between sleeping and waking, he dreams a dream he can't understand. Nor can any of his sorcerers interpret it. He threatens them with execution—and not only them but also every court official, including Daniel.

It is dangerous to come to a monarch uninvited. But Daniel braves the danger. He can do what the Babylonian magicians can't. By the strength of God, he interprets dreams. And Daniel knows Nebuchadnezzar's dream even before the king describes it.

"You are standing before an enormous and frightening statue. Your dream predicts four ages and a fifth glorious one. The statue's golden head represents your golden reign. Its silver chest and arms represent the kingdom that will follow yours. Its bronze abdomen and thighs represent a third kingdom to follow the second. And the feet of iron mixed with clay? That signifies a fourth divided against itself.

"But I tell you that after the destruction of these four ages, the Lord my God will raise up a kingdom of his own which will last forever and ever."

Because Daniel's God is the Lord of all mysteries, and because Daniel speaks wisdom plainly, boldly, and with authority, the king bows down and says, "Now I know that your God is God above all other gods."

PRAYER
King of Kings and Lord of Lords, I pray that I might come into your kingdom that Daniel prophesied, the kingdom that lasts forever and ever. Amen.

Daniel 3

Did Nebuchadnezzar dream of an enormous statue, and did he recognize Daniel's God as the God above all gods? Well, that attitude doesn't last long. The king constructs another towering statue, this one *completely* golden, and commands his subjects to bow down and worship it, since it represents himself. (Think of the Tower of Babel.) "Those who will not bow down and worship, I will throw them into the fire of fires!"

Nebuchadnezzar's command spreads throughout the kingdom. It isn't long before certain of his officials come, loudly condemning "those scurrilous Hebrews." "They refuse to worship your statue, O King of might and right decisions!" In a fury Nebuchadnezzar shouts, "What I said, *do* it!" Soldiers rope the three men. They stoke the fire in the furnace! They make it blaze so hot that after they've pitched God's men into it, they fall back, dead.

Shadrach, Meshach, and Abednego stand—no, walk—on the white-hot coals and seem to chat with one another. Yet God is with them as he was with Israel (Exodus 14:19). The ropes alone have burned away.

Nebuchadnezzar comes and peers into the flames, expecting to see the three Jews' bodies reduced to ashes. But not even a hair on their heads has been singed. More astounding, there is a fourth man walking with them! An angel? More than an angel. God promised, "When you walk through the fire, you will not be burned; the flames will not set you ablaze" (Isaiah 43:2).

How often does Nebuchadnezzar need proof that the Jews' God is God indeed?

PRAYER

> Ah, what availed King Herod's wrath?
> He could not stop the Savior's path.
> Alone, while others murdered lay,
> By Christ, in safety, borne away. Amen.

—"SWEET FLOWERETS OF THE MARTYR BAND"

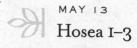

MAY 13
Hosea 1–3

(Turn to p. 100 for the actual chronology of the prophets.)

The English language cannot fully appreciate the breadth of the Hebrew word for *word* because God's "words" are at the same time his deeds. By his word, he commands Hosea to *do* something symbolic: to marry a promiscuous woman, just as God married Israel. The prophet obeys and marries a woman named Gomer. She bears three children, each emblematic of God's attitude toward Israel. Their first boy is named Jezreel—the valley in which the Lord will trample the Assyrians. The little girl, God names "Not Pitied," as a mother would not deny her child comfort or compassion. And the next baby boy is named "Not My People," for God said to Israel, "You are not my people, and I am not your God."

Now God tells Hosea to divorce his wife, "Even as I have divorced my people."

Gomer goes off and paints her face to entice other men to support her, a quid pro quo, a favor for a favor.

But God's grace prevails. "She has suffered enough. She is penitent. Call her back. Marry her again. Before, you married Gomer because I commanded it. Now I tell you to love her."

PRAYER

Lord, restore our fortunes (Psalm 85). Forgive us, O God of our salvation. Speak to us. Speak peace. Then your righteousness and our peace will kiss together. Amen.

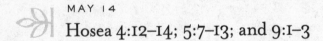

MAY 14

Hosea 4:12–14; 5:7–13; and 9:1–3

"O Israel! How long will you be pieces of wood? How long will you go whoring after promiscuous women, and how long will you let your very daughters play the whore? I will not punish them, because *you* are the aggressors, and *you* have turned away from me. Look for me and tremble because I will not be found."

She said no, but the man did not take no for an answer. He let his desires overpower him. And her. He drank to excess. In the morning he couldn't even remember what he did to the woman in a dark room. Old men and young men demean women by their crude jokes, their whispered innuendos, their promises to reward a woman with a promotion or a role in their movie or endless devotion—"if only you spend the night with me."

Even so, and even in these terms, does the prophet Hosea condemn Israel. "On them, says the Lord, I will pour out my wrath like water."

PRAYER

Though I have never done such things as these, I have, from time to time, thought about them, and you, O Lord—you know my inward thoughts. But you said to me, "Though your sins are like scarlet, they shall be white as snow. Though red like crimson, they shall be washed as white as wool" (Isaiah 1:18). It is by your love that I am able to obey you. And by your love I am forgiven. Amen.

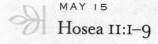

MAY 15
Hosea 11:1–9

This chapter often causes me to weep. Truly. How good is our God. How like a parent.

"When Israel was my baby, I loved him." God is the Father/mother who led Israel out of Egypt and called him by name. But, like so many of our teenage sons and daughters, Israel turned a deaf ear to his Father/mother's wishes.

"But it was I," says the Lord, "who loved them like my own son and daughter. I took my little baby in my arms. I kissed his cheek. I taught him how to walk. I led him by the cords of my love. But he has turned away from me. I will send him into Assyria! Ah, my son, my son, I cannot do to you what I did to Admah and Zeboyim, how I destroyed their cities with sulfur and salt even as I destroyed Sodom and Gomorrah [see Deuteronomy 29:23]. My heart grows warm with compassion. I can't help it. No, I will not destroy. I am God! I am not created. I created you, and I cradle you, and I carry you on my shoulders like a lamb."

What a beautiful new note. What consoling music. It is like the lullaby a mother sings to her sleepy child.

MAY 16
Amos 1:1–2; 2:6–8; 9:14–15

(See p. 100. Amos prophesied before Hosea)

The city of Tekoa lies ten miles south of Jerusalem. Here Amos
raises sheep, some to be sacrificed in the temple, and pricks green syc-
amore figs so that they will be edible in their season.

Yet in spite of his rural occupations, Amos is an uncompromising
prophet, one who condemns the wealthy on behalf of the poor.

He levels his eyes at Amaziah, the high priest of Bethel, and utters
prophecies to be heard throughout the land of Judah:

"This is what the Lord says to Israel: 'Because of your transgressions, I will not withhold my punishment. Because an innocent man
can't pay his debts, you sell him into slavery and add the money to
your treasure chests. You neglect—no, you *trample* on the heads of the
poor. Profligates! You blaspheme my holy name! When you ride your
chariots through the streets, heedlessly you knock sick people to the
ground. You share the same slave girl. You party in my temple. You
fall down drunk before my altar. I will turn your parties into death
marches.'"

But we must never think that the God of the Old Testament is an
angry man whose beard is torn by the wind, one whose tongue is thunder and whose eyes are flashes of lightning. Never—because his mercy
endures. Here is hope: "I will restore Israel. His harvests—grain, vineyards, gardens, fruit, wine—will be abundant."

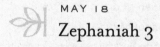

Psalm 121

A pilgrim is ascending the road to Jerusalem, the road to the maker of the universe, singing his praises: "My help comes from the LORD" (v. 2). The pilgrim's foot won't slip and twist his ankle. He won't stumble on a stone (see Psalm 17:5). His Lord is his security (Psalm 125:1–2). The mountains will not tremble under his foot. God remains awake and watchful over the pilgrim's way.

Amos prophesied that the Lord would blacken the sun at noon. Now the psalmist declares that the Lord is the protector who shades the sun for sweating travelers. "Hide me in the shadow of your wings" (Psalm 17:8). The Lord covers the moon with his hand so that it will not cause lunacy by night.

Those who are mounting the road to the Holy City confess that they are strangers and pilgrims on the earth (Hebrews 11:13–14). God will guard his people when they come and go, when they depart and when they come home again. Blessed be the name of the Lord.

PRAYER

Nothing, Jesus, can come between me and you, between my helplessness and your love. Not death or life. Not angels or rulers. Not things present or things to come. Neither powers nor the dizzying heights nor the great chasms. Amen.

Zephaniah 3

Zephaniah (his name means "the Lord protects") was the descendant of dark-skinned Africans. He prophesies to Judah and the nations shortly before the days of the prophet Jeremiah. He prophesies when the Judeans have gathered in Jerusalem to celebrate the Festival of Tabernacles, a "harvest home" celebration. Assyria has fallen on hard times. Babylon has come to power.

This chapter opens with a doomful judgment. Jerusalem's leaders, elders, prophets and priests decry their Lord. They are like the roaring lions that consume people, like wolves that prowl and slaughter by night. By morning they skulk back to their dens, leaving nothing behind except skulls and bones. Even so does God convict his people in the morning. "Wait for it, wait for that day," says the Lord, "when I will banish the haughty from my holy mountain. Nevertheless [always and always that 'nevertheless'] I will call a remnant of my humble people to myself."

Zephaniah can't help himself. "Sing! Shout! Don't be afraid! The Lord who dwelt in his temple before it was destroyed, dwells among you now! [See Psalm 47:1–4.] He rejoices! He will save the halt, the lame, the blind, and the poor! He will change Jerusalem's shame into praise!"

PRAYER
How great and how faithful you are, my God. Every morning your mercies are new. Amen.

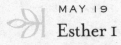

MAY 19
Esther 1

We wouldn't be wrong to start Esther's story with "once upon a time."

King Xerxes rules Persia, an empire that covers most of the known world.

Xerxes marries the high-minded woman named Vashti, then celebrates the marriage with a lavish banquet. His servants cover the wide lawn outside his citadel. A crowd of noblemen sit on benches to eat. At the same time, Vashti spreads another banquet in another place for the noblewomen. Food fattens the men. Wine flows like rivers. Usually a king's subjects wait to drink until he's lifted his own cup. But on this occasion, they guzzle the alcohol straightaway, then drink and keep on drinking. It's a gay and noisy feast. Xerxes can hold his liquor, but today he drinks to excess, drinks till he can't distinguish his golden bowl from his silver cup. "By God!" he cries to his eunuch Memukan, "bring me my queen!" Xerxes wants to show off his new beautiful bride. But Vashti's headstrong and refuses her husband's command. Sloppy with drink, the emperor breaks into a rage. He has his wife stripped of her royalty and immediately promulgates a new law: "Every man shall dominate his wife!" A Persian emperor's law can never be revoked.

The once-upon-a-time storyteller laughs at Xerxes's bluster and bullying, just as we laugh at the chuckle-headed pomposity of the leaders of our present age.

PRAYER

When the Lord restores the fortunes of Zion, we will laugh, and our tongues will shout with joy (Psalm 126:1–2), and you, Lord God, will laugh with us. Amen.

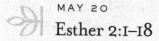

MAY 20
Esther 2:1–18

Mordecai is a Jew. He's a man of intelligence and good sense and has therefore been made an official in the court of the king. Mordecai's complexion is dark because he descends from generations of Africans. His niece is likewise dark-skinned. Because Esther (her name means "star") is an orphan, her uncle adopts her as his own daughter. Esther, thirteen or fourteen years old, is a shy, quiet girl who has the discernment of an adult.

After Xerxes has sent the proud Vashti away, he casts about for a new wife. She must be humble, she must be beautiful, and she must be a virgin. Xerxes commands that the virgin girls who live in his city of Susa be brought to his royal palace and given an apartment where they will be prepared to meet the king. They are instructed in court etiquette. Their bodies are massaged with the oils of myrrh. If one of them has an abrasion, it's healed by a poultice of olive oil. The pretty girls are taught how to appease the king, to apply perfumes such as aloe and nard, and how to enlarge their eyes by lining the lids with dark antimony. One by one the girls are taken to the king that he might find the girl who meets his specifications.

When Esther stands in the king's presence, her eyes cast down, she pleases Xerxes more than the rest. "This one," he says. "She's fit to marry me."

Beautiful souls have been invited to the table of the King of Kings. We come to you, O Lord, ready to serve you in everything. Your bread (Christ's body) and your wine (his blood) satisfy our longing. Your kingdom is splendid and everlasting, and we bless you (Psalm 145:10–13). Amen.

MAY 21
Esther 2:19–23

Mordecai overhears two of the emperor's eunuchs plotting to kill Xerxes. Mordecai wants to increase Esther's standing in the eyes of the king. "Listen," he says, "I could reveal the plot of the eunuchs to the king, and he wouldn't doubt me, and nothing would change. But if you carried the message, things *would* change. He would respect you all the more, and it's likely that he would come to love you."

Though she's shy, Esther is also a confident woman. She presents herself before the king. "This better be important," he says.

Esther says, "Judge the matter for yourself, then do to me what you will."

"Say on."

She explains the plot. "To assassinate you, my lord."

"How can you know this?"

"Your servant Mordecai heard the eunuchs whispering outside the gate."

Not yet trusting the word of a girl, the king investigates and learns that her word is indeed true. He does two things: he hangs the conspirators (hanging is another way of saying "impaled on a stake").

And the second thing? He admires his queen all the more.

PRAYER

Your "stake," my Lord, was the spikes on the cross. You suffered the stripes of my sins. You died the death I should have died. But the cold grave could not hold you, nor death's cold iron band. Amen.

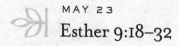

Esther 3–7

This is the central event of Esther's story. Five years have passed since she became queen of Persia.

During that time the emperor honored an Agagite named Haman by giving him the position of satrap, the highest office in the realm. Haman hates Jews. When Mordecai refuses to bow down to him because he obeys the laws of the Jews, Haman takes it as a vile impertinence. He goes to the king of Persia and persuades him to kill Mordecai by a hangman's rope. "And all the Jews in the empire." The king agrees. Heralds spread the news.

But Queen Esther plans a plot of her own. She prepares a banquet to which she invites many guests and Haman and the king as well. While the people are eating, she leans close to her husband and asks a favor. "Ask anything," says the king, "even up to half of Persia." Ether says, "Haman wants to kill my people. My king, save them." *My people!* Who knew that Esther is a Jew? The king glares so fiercely at Haman that he begs for his life. But his life is not saved. He is hung on the gallows he had built for Mordecai.

PRAYER
Justice is yours, O Lord God. You treat the sin as the sinner deserves. Yet you save everyone who repents.

Esther 9:18–32

What started with "once upon a time" ends with "happily ever after."

Haman has fallen. The king of Persia has raised Mordecai to the highest office in the realm, in which his authority is second only to the emperor.

The root of the word *Purim* is "Pur," which indicates the casting of lots, just as we roll dice today. The Jews' festival of Purim was celebrated at the beginning of March, shortly before the barely harvest. Esther's story has all along been moving to this point: how Purim came to be. Mordecai need only ask his niece, and Queen Esther makes sure that it is done for him. She, who once was soft-spoken, now speaks with a sovereign voice.

Oh, what a holiday is Purim! Feasting. Laughter. The exchange of presents, such as food and clothing, and charity to the poor.

PRAYER

How good, Lord, are your banquets! And how blessed are your guests: prostitutes, tax collectors, the crippled, the scorned, the old, the young— all who have found favor with you. Amen.

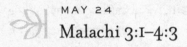

MAY 24
Malachi 3:1–4:3

Malachi's book ends with promises of health and freedom and brightness and jubilation. God will send his messenger to proclaim it.

But first, as always among the prophets, the Lord blames his people for neglecting sojourners, widows and orphans, blames them for being stingy with their hired workers. Moreover, they have neglected to tithe (Deuteronomy 14:22–29). The Lord won't destroy them. But he will refine them, will purify them in his crucible, will change their dross into silver. Suffering leads to perfection.

And who will be his messenger? Elijah. And who is Elijah? The New Testament identifies him as John the Baptist (Matthew 11:11–15). Malachi's prophecies look forward not to tomorrow, not to years, but to that great day of the Lord when he will reappear at the end of time.

Leap up! Frolic in the sunshine like young calves set free! The sun will rise with healing in its wings, and the wings of angels will fly us home.

PRAYER

Great day! Great day when the Lord will rebuild Zion in heaven and fly us home. Amen.

BOOK 2

THE
NEW
TESTAMENT

PART I

The

WORD

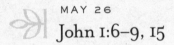

John 1:1–5

In the beginning God uttered the word *light* and there was light. He uttered "day" and "night," "waters" and "dry land," and by his word God spoke the universe into being. God also created time: there was evening, and there was morning—the first day (Genesis 1:5).

John the Evangelist remembers that Word. It was (*he* was) with God from the beginning; nothing that was created was created without him. The Word was with God. He was God from the beginning. That Word was Jesus Christ. He penetrated the universal darkness clothed in human flesh. In him was life, and all who believe in him are children of God the Father, and we can ourselves utter the words, "I want Jesus to walk with me," with confidence that he does.

PRAYER

In your light we see light (Psalm 36:9). Lighten our darkness, O Word of God, and defend us from the perils of the night. Amen.

MAY 26

John 1:6–9, 15

John switches from the deep past to the historical present. A living human enters the story. He is John the Baptist, the messenger about whom Malachi prophesied, who will prepare the people for the appearance of the Messiah: "This is the one I told you about. His rank is higher than mine because he comes before me." Like Elijah, John lives in the wilderness. He eats locusts and wild honey. He wears a rough garment of camel's hair and baptizes the Jews in water, those who come confessing their sins.

My father was the minister who baptized me. My mother was the Baptist who made me aware of my transgressions. But it was Jesus who baptized my soul. He was in the water.

Don't forsake me, Holy Spirit. Be the wind that blows over me. Be the very breath that I breathe, or my soul will perish. Amen.

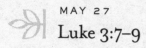
MAY 27
Luke 3:7–9

John the Baptist is like the man of God (1 Kings 13:1–3). They both speak harsh words—the man of God to Jeroboam, the Baptist to the crowds who come without repenting, who think John's water will be some sort of magic to cancel their sins.

But John's condemnation scorches them. They are snakes trying to outrun a field fire! "God has sharpened his ax to chop you down like a sick tree that bears no fruit and to consume you with the Holy Spirit and a *heavenly* blaze!" (see also Matthew 7:15–20 and Luke 13:6–9).

On the other hand (with God there is always an "other hand"), John implies that if the people will bear good fruit, God will take them back again.

There are those among us who have come to the waters of repentance without repenting. Their works will prove them fruitless. But we are commissioned to preach good news, to heal the sinful sick, to cleanse those whose iniquities are like leprosy (Matthew 10:5–8), and to lift the lost out of the pit of despair.

PRAYER
Lord, strengthen our faith and our zeal. Grant us the love and power of the Holy Spirit to persuade people to forsake sin and to return to you. Amen.

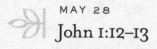
MAY 28
John 1:12–13

Those who believe in Jesus are God's people. But more than that, they are God's *children*. They weren't born of blood (think of a man's sperm, which was thought at that time to carry life into a woman's womb), nor of a decision made by two people, nor of a man's sexual desire (Galatians 5:16), but of God himself!

Jesus was the Father's Son, his only Son, and we were born as Jesus's brothers and sisters. In our ways and our days—there's no one else who can guide us and empower us to accomplish his mission.

In spite of a people's foolish rejection, the Word's words end on a note of hope and promise. By Christ's own ending, all will be well with us.

PRAYER

Heavenly Father, the Father of all your children, you have given us earthly fathers and mothers to love us and to train us up in the way we ought to go. But you are our eternal Father, and your love lasts forever. Amen.

MAY 29

John 1:14–18 and Philippians 2:1–6

John the Baptist preached that Jesus was and is and always will be greater than any other on earth. In him we've seen the very glory of the Father. Yet he clothed himself in human flesh and came and dwelt among us, he, the Father's grace and truth. He clothed himself in human flesh and descended to live right here among us in humility.

The apostle Paul urges us to put on Christ's clothes, to live as he lived, to humble ourselves, to put away selfishness, to empty ourselves to serve the world as if we were slaves, and to be obedient, even unto death.

The cross that Jesus speaks of is not some trouble we might suffer in our lives. It is, like his cross, the cross of death.

Yet all those, yesterday and today, who believe in him are given the sight, that is *in*sight, to see his glory, which reflects the glory of his Father, and can comfort themselves because the Father loves them.

PRAYER

Jesus loves me, this I know,
For the Bible tells me so. Amen.

Psalm 148

The psalmist calls on the whole universe to praise the Lord. His song is first to the heavens (vv. 1–6), then to the earth (vv. 7–10), then to human-kind (vv. 11–13), and ends with the communities of all God's people (vv. 13–14). The song starts and ends with the same cry, "Hallelujah!" (praise the Lord). Sing "hallelujah" forever and forevermore.

The psalmist follows the sequence of creation (Genesis 1–2:4) and remembers the covenants God established with his people: Noah (Genesis 9:9) and with every living creature (Genesis 9:10, 12, 15–16). The psalmist takes the plain words of Genesis and refashions them into a poem of striking beauty.

Likewise, Saint Francis of Assisi rewrote this 148th psalm into a hymn he called "The Canticle of the Sun." He calls the sun, the wind, and fire "my brothers," the moon, the earth, and all waters "my sisters."

Humanity joins nature to sing hallelujah to God and also to keep nature, keeping it and tilling it (Genesis 2:15). This is our injunction too. Yet human beings persist in devastating nature. Count the ways: polluting the oceans and rivers; impairing earth's atmosphere by our emissions; wiping out the lives of crawling creatures, four-footed animals, and the winged birds; wounding our frail island-planet. And leaving no good place for the health of the masses of people.

PRAYER

O God, you are mighty. You alone are able to change our minds and our deeds. Then exert your love. Save our world and us too. Amen.

PART 2

BEGINNINGS

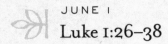

Luke 1:5–25

Malachi prophesied the reappearance of the prophet Elijah: "He will turn the hearts of parents to their children, and the hearts of the children to their parents" (Malachi 4:6). Compare these words to Gabriel's description of the new Elijah, the Christ, in Luke 1:17.

While the old priest Zechariah is burning incense in the temple, Gabriel announces the good news that Zechariah and Elizabeth will bear a child.

Lo! A new age is dawning, the age of the Messiah!

Zechariah doesn't laugh as Sarah laughed when she was told that she'd bear a son in her withered old age. Yet he finds it hard to believe in the angel's words. "No," he says. "I'm long past pleasure, and my wife's womb has been dry for decades."

"Old, you say?" the angel responds. "Well, *I* say that I am Gabriel, the messenger of God. Your faithlessness is foolishness. Because of your unbelief, you will be mute until the babe is born indeed."

PRAYER

There are mysteries, Lord, that I find hard to believe. Three Gods in One? How can that be? A virgin gives birth to a boy? Impossible. But I want with all my heart to believe the things I can't understand. Help my unbelief. Amen.

Luke 1:26–38

It's midnight. Mary is sleeping on her straw-filled mattress, tired because she spent the day weaving at her loom, an obedient sixteen-year-old maiden.

Suddenly, a radiant, glorious light fills the room, and she snaps awake.

"Hush, Mary. God loves you and has chosen you to bear a son—not the son of some man, but of God."

How can this be? An angel here in her room? Yes, the archangel Gabriel.

Gabriel dims his radiance. "Listen to a wonder, Mary," he says. "Your tiny baby boy will be holy. And just as his ancestor King David ruled Israel, your child will rule all the kingdoms on earth and in heaven."

Mary may be a soft-spoken girl, yet she has a backbone and is bold enough to say, "No, sir. It can't be. I've never slept with a man." Gabriel says, "Didn't I tell you the babe would not be born of a man? He will be called the Son of the Almighty. And here's a sign: your old, old kinswoman Elizabeth is already six months pregnant. With God nothing is impossible" (see Mark 10:27).

Immediately, the bold, obedient Mary believes the angel's promise and says, "I will be—no, I am—a maiden ready to serve my God."

PRAYER

Stir up your power, O Lord, and come. Plant in us the seed of faithfulness, whatever may come. Water it in your own waters, not with your tears, but with the water that springs up to eternal life. Amen.

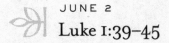

JUNE 2
Luke 1:39–45

After Gabriel has left, after the room is once again dark with the night, Mary can't sleep. Her heart pounds with anticipation. She packs a bag with raisins and dried fish and a flask of water and a change of clothes. At dawn she hurries from Nazareth and makes the long journey into the hill country of Judea, then goes straight to the house of Zechariah and Elizabeth.

"Cousin," she cries, "I have such a thing to tell you!" Elizabeth says, "I already know. My baby kicked, my baby *jumped* in my womb!" She laughs and cries out, "The Holy Spirit tells me to tell you that no woman, no one is more blessed than you. And most blessed is the fruit ripening in your womb! Yes, and me too, because the Lord has allowed me to see his mother!"

Be glad! Rejoice! Shout to the Lord, because his steadfast faithfulness surrounds us (Psalm 32:11). Amen.

JUNE 3
Luke 1:46–56

And Mary sang, "He remembered me.
He remembered his maiden of low degree.
With tender care and gentility,
     He remembered me.

I breathe and my breathing laughs in the Lord;
I live and my living enlarges his name;
For I have heard his mighty word,
Obeyed his bright, genetic word,
     And I that Word contain."

And Mary sang, "He remembers you.
He will lead you, exalt you, and love you too.
Children of old, be children new.
     He remembers you.

And where are the full? God gives them no food.
And where are the hungry? God fills them with good.
The powerful by God shall fall,
The proud be taught to drop and crawl,
     The poor rise up renewed."

And Mary sang, "He remembers me;
He's made me the place of the Savior-seed.
Oh, let it be, Lord, that I like you
     Will remember too,
     Will remember you too."

So sing we all with your ordinary, commonplace, obedient people. Amen.

JUNE 4
Matthew 1:18–19

In the olden days, adulterers were stoned to death (Deuteronomy 22:23–24)—the women because they didn't cry for help, the men because they violated their neighbor's wife. In Mary's days the punishment is less severe. A man can divorce with a simple writ. A woman's body may not suffer a punishment of pain, but her reputation does because she's been profoundly humiliated, and worse than that, she has become a destitute outcast.

Joseph and Mary aren't married yet, but an engagement is as good as marriage. Joseph has already met with Mary's father. They've already made a formal contract. Joseph has already paid Mary's father the bride-price. It's customary for a couple to wait one year before making their vows and spending their first night together. But before the year is up, Joseph sees the pooch in Mary's belly, and he is grieved to recognize her pregnancy. He loves his Mary, yet there's no help for it but that he will draw up that writ of divorce and put her away from himself.

Joseph is a righteous man. He'll make their separation a private affair. But there's no assurance that the whole village of Nazareth won't find out about it. This causes Joseph no end of agony on behalf of his once betrothed.

PRAYER
Can even a good law make a good thing bad? Perhaps it's someone's false righteousness. Perhaps it's an arrogant self-righteousness that's bad from the start. Do I think I have the right to blame my neighbors and to punish them—say, by turning my back and refusing to ever speak to them again? O my Lord, cleanse thou me of my secret faults. Amen.

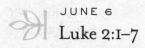

Matthew 1:20–25

Joseph's small compound forms a square, with two sides of his house forming an *L*. The third side is a stable for his donkey and several sheep, and the fourth is a low wall with an entrance, forming a court-yard wherein is a clay stove-fire and is where the carpenter does his work. Before anyone steps over the threshold into the house itself, they remove their sandals. Right now, while Joseph sleeps on his roof in the cool of the night, he dreams a dream.

The archangel Gabriel appears beside him and says, "Joseph, don't divorce Mary. She has *not* shamed herself. She has *not* lain with another man. Believe this, that the child she will bear is God's by means of his Holy Spirit. Mary accepted this impossible promise. You should do no less than her. Oh, and name the baby 'Jesus' [Yeshua], for he will save his people from their sins."

Joseph wakes. His faith too has awakened. Joyfully he bestrides his mule and rides to Mary's house and says, "Marry me."

Oh, and what a wedding it is! Mary's friends, Mary's maidens, process from her house, while Joseph's friends, Joseph's groomsmen, process from his house, and they meet in the middle with boisterous shouts of celebration.

PRAYER

Immanuel, God with us. Jesus, the Holy One of God who lives among us, you promised never to leave us as motherless and fatherless orphans (John 14:18). So come with us. Abide with us. Amen.

Luke 2:1–7

The carpenter lifts his heavily pregnant wife onto his donkey. Joseph and Mary travel slowly. It's some seventy miles from Nazareth to Bethlehem. They stop to sleep as they go. When they enter Bethlehem,

Mary's first contraction takes her breath away. Joseph is a lout where woman-things are concerned. Mary needs a midwife. He dashes through the city's streets, knocking on doors, asking for a place where his wife can lie down. No, no, no midwife and no inn that isn't already full. There's no help for it, then, but that he must find a stable to protect Mary from the weather. He does, and he lays his Mary down on stable straw. The contractions come faster and more painful. "Mary, I don't know what to do."

She turns onto her stomach and kneels in order to raise her bottom. "Sit behind me," she says. "When he crowns, press your hand to his head." Poor Joseph. Sweat rolls down his forehead. Mary suffers a series of god-awful contractions. "Joseph," she says between grunts, "ease him out slowly, or I'll be torn." There he comes—a patch of slick hair. One more almighty contraction, and the baby slurps onto Joseph's two hands. He has *done* it! Jesus has entered the universe. Mary rolls onto her back. Joseph gives her the infant, and she puts him to her breast. She tells Joseph to make strips of clean cloth. The mother binds the tiny boy, singing a soft "Coo coo, coo coo, my sweeting. Coo coo, my baby Jesus and my Lord. Joseph," she murmurs, "I'm tired. Lay the child on the straw in the feed trough."

PRAYER
Mary has given birth to a king. Jesus, my King of Kings, I am the babe in your arms. Embrace me. Feed me your bread and your wine and your love. Amen.

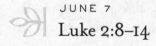

JUNE 7
Luke 2:8–14

In those days people called shepherds a shiftless, dishonest lot who graze their flocks in richer men's fields. But God, as Mary sang, brings the powerful down from their thrones and lifts up those of low degree. It is to the impoverished, ordinary shepherds that he breaks through the midnight, and the angel gives *them* the good news.

The shepherds cringe and cover their eyes. But the angel says, "Hush, hush. Tonight a child, the Son of the Most High, was born in Bethlehem. Go to the stall east of Bethlehem. The boy lies in a feed trough, wrapped in swaddling clothes. See how dearly his mother is kissing him. The mother's name is Mary."

Now the stars, the hosts, the armies, the chorus of the Lord, raise a marvelous song: "Glory to God in highest heaven! And peace, peace to his people on earth!"

PRAYER

Holy are you—most holy in the universe! Though the darkness hides you, and though our eyes are blind to your brightness, your love enlightens our hearts. What more can we ask of you than that? Amen.

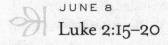

JUNE 8
Luke 2:15–20

It is said that Caesar Augustus has brought peace to his empire—the *Pax Romana*. Moreover, the Romans call Caesar "the son of god." Well, they may say so, but all his power and all his glory are mere smoke compared with the son of a carpenter. Caesar's rule will die when he dies. But the rule of Christ will last forever and forever.

The glory that is Rome? The pride of its empire? Forget that. God chooses a pack of despised shepherds to witness and to worship the infant in the manger. For the sheer joy of it, they rush from the stable and into the city, crying, "You've *got* to believe us! We have seen the glory of God!"

As for the Virgin Mary, she meditates on this marvelous event that has come to pass. Mary, faithful and the mother of our faith, our bold young woman, is an early theologian.

PRAYER

Your birth and our Christmas, Lord—turn our minds from the busyness of getting and selling to your giving and our receiving the joy of your coming and of your coming again. Amen.

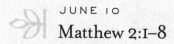

Luke 2:22–38

If a woman gives birth to a son, he will be circumcised on the eighth day, but she remains unclean for thirty-three days, during which time she's prohibited from entering the temple, and after which she can be purified by a sacrifice (Leviticus 12).

Joseph's carpentry earns enough to support his family, but only just enough. He hasn't the wherewith to sacrifice an animal larger than two pigeons. Now he and his wife and her suckling child go up to the temple, and Mary is purified.

While they are there, a very old man named Simeon separates himself from the crowds. He approaches Mary and gazes at the infant in her arms. Jesus gazes back at him. Simeon's rheumy eyes fill with tears. "The Holy Spirit promised that I wouldn't die until I saw the consolation of Israel," he says. And to Mary he says, "Can I hold your baby?" She places him in Simeon's arms. He lifts his eyes to heaven. "Here he is," the old man says. "Lord, I have seen your salvation." He returns the child to his mother and predicts that the child will cause many to fall and many to rise. Simeon predicts one more thing, a sad thing: "Woman, in time a sword will pierce your soul." What does that mean? Maybe it means that the mother of our Lord will stand at Jesus's cross, sharing his pain.

Now there hobbles to the couple a widow-woman who is almost one hundred years old. She places her crooked fingers on the Christ-child's head and blesses him, the Son of Man and the Son of God.

PRAYER

Our Advent wait is over. Christ Jesus, we celebrate your Christmas birth. You are the sunrise of our mornings and the wings that cover us all our nights long. Amen.

Matthew 2:1–8

How many days does it take for the eastern astrologers to ride from Persia to Jerusalem?

When they arrive in Jerusalem, they ask its citizens where they can find the king. The citizens answer, "In his palace." "We have come to worship the child." What? A *child*? "King Herod is a grown adult." Well, then, the king will surely know where the little king lives. They gain an audience with Herod and say to him, "In our country we saw the rising of a remarkable star and interpreted it to mean that the king of the Jews has been born. So we followed that star till it stopped over Jerusalem." Herod growls, "*I* am the king! What? Are you telling me there's a pretender to my throne?" The astrologers know nothing about pretenders. "We want to know where the child lives."

The cunning King Herod plans a plan. He puts on a pious face and says, "Of course, of course, I want to honor him too." Privately he commands his scribe to find out where this "king" lives. The scribe searches the Scripture until he comes upon the prophet Micah and reads the passage to the king: "But you, O Bethlehem of Ephrathah—though you are least among the tribes of Judah, from you shall come forth one who will rule the kingdom of Israel."

Herod then says to the astrologers, "In Bethlehem, a five-mile walk to the south." Herod smiles and says, "Listen. When you have found him, come back and tell me where he is so that I can also worship him."

PRAYER
You, Lord, are a remarkable star. It is you who are the light that lightens our way, even from here to eternity. Amen.

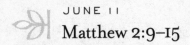

JUNE 11
Matthew 2:9–15

The traveling star stops directly over the house where the two-year-old Jesus is playing with a toy hammer and a nail and a piece of wood. It doesn't matter that the astrologers are gentiles. God receives gentiles as well as his own people. These men's profession usually requires solemnity. But at the sight of the boy, they rejoice. They kneel, and Mary doesn't deny them that. She takes their coming as divine. Jesus puts down his little hammer, and the wise men open gifts fit for a king—gold and frankincense and myrrh. Joseph the carpenter gapes at such wealth. Mary nods, and Jesus wonders how to play with such strange things.

That night the astrologers dream a dream. An angel appears and says, "Go home by a different route. King Herod plans to kill the child king." Faith accepts the warning, and faith skirts Jerusalem.

Joseph too dreams a dream. The angel tells him to get up and to escape with his family to Egypt and to stay there. "Herod will send his soldiers to Bethlehem to murder your son."

PRAYER

We walk in danger wherever we go in this hostile world. Lord Jesus, be our sure defense. Amen.

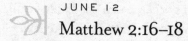

JUNE 12
Matthew 2:16–18

King Herod has lost patience. Unreliable foreigners! Devious easterners! Just as the angel predicted, the king commands his troops to ride to Bethlehem and to slaughter every boy two years old and younger. Soon their blood runs in the city's streets. The mothers gather their dead sons in their arms. The boys' blood stains their robes. Oh, how the women howl aloud their grief.

Five hundred years before, Jeremiah prophesied the despair of another mother. He said, "A voice is heard in Ramah [north of Jerusalem], lamentation and bitter weeping. Rachel is weeping for her children. She refuses to be comforted because her children are no more" (Jeremiah 31:15).

In our time it isn't much different. Children have been gassed in Hitler's ovens. Many children the world around are born in squalor. They starve. They cry for food, and their mothers don't eat so that their children can be fed. Children grow up without an education. Many can't find work. There is no safety net for those who are impoverished. And their parents must work two jobs in order to survive.

Jesus, I pray that you will give me a right mind and the willingness to work for justice for the poor and for those whom society has forgotten. Amen.

JUNE 13
Matthew 2:19–23

Ever since God sent Gabriel to the Virgin Mary, the Lord has continued to appear in people's dreams. Tonight the angel enters Joseph's dream. "King Herod is dead," says the angel. "It's safe to take your family home." Joseph packs his bags and goes. Herod was cruel, but his son, King Archelaus, rules as bitterly as his father.

Joseph skirts Judea, and the Lord leads him into Galilee and to Nazareth, among gentiles. Jesus grows up in the favor of the people while his father trains him in the skills of carpentry. They build furniture. They build houses in the large city to the north. Joseph is content. But it won't be long before Jesus leaves his father and his mother to apply himself to his Father's work in the world.

PRAYER

That other work, my Lord, is something like carpentry, because it is the building of faith in your people. And your wood was the two beams of the cross, and you have already built houses in the heavenly places—mansions to be our homes. It is with a great gratitude that we say, Amen.

PART 3

MINISTRY *and* MIRACLES

John 1:29–30

When John the Baptist points to Jesus and explains to his disciples who that man is, they probably expect to hear a name and maybe to learn of his occupation. But John startles them by calling him a lamb—"The Lamb of God who takes away the sin of the world."

What sort of Lamb? In the Bible we find four sorts of Lambs, each of which defines our Lord. (1) Jesus is the ram that Abraham found in a thicket, the ram he sacrificed instead of his son Isaac. (2) He is the Passover Lamb, who sacrificed himself for us. (3) He is the sacrificial Lamb who was led to the slaughter (Isaiah 53:7). (4) He is the Lamb in the book of Revelation, who looks as if he has been slaughtered (Revelation 5:6) and who is exalted by thousands and thousands of voices. "Worthy is the Lamb to receive power and wealth and wisdom and might and honor and glory and blessing" (Revelation 5:12). And he, Jesus, will be the temple in the new Jerusalem, and its light (Revelation 21:22–23).

Our Lord Jesus spans the Bible from its first book (the Word) to its last, when he will reign with God the Father, in a world without end.

PRAYER

O Jesus—God made flesh—you are unchanging. You are the way and truth and life. Please be the light that lightens our pilgrim paths. We follow you. We adore you. We sing your praises now and always. Amen.

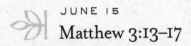

Matthew 3:13–17

John baptized unto repentance. Jesus has no need to repent. Yet he comes to John by the Jordan and asks to be baptized. John says, "No, Lord. You are righteous. I need to be baptized by *you*."

Jesus answers, "As a man here on earth, I must fulfill *all* righteousness." So Jesus is baptized, backward, under Jordan's waters. Then he fairly explodes out of the water, and the blue sky is torn apart like a sheet of papyrus. No one sees what Jesus sees: the Holy Spirit swooping down in the form of a dove. Think of the dove that flew back to Noah's ark with an olive leaf of life in her beak (Genesis 8:11). And Jesus hears the thundering voice of the Father: "You are my Son, my beloved one!"

Thus does the Spirit of the Son of God infuse the waters of our baptisms with grace and life.

PRAYER

Dear Jesus, God's Son and our servant, you are the mediator. You are the golden cord; you are the holy prayer that reaches down from heaven and binds our hearts to the Father. And we cherish you. Amen.

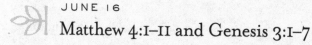

JUNE 16

Matthew 4:1–11 and Genesis 3:1–7

Satan starts his temptations by trying to make his target doubt the words of God: God said, "You are my Son." Satan says, "*If* you are the Son of God, change these stones to bread." In the same manner, he tries to make Eve doubt God's warning: "*Did* God say . . . ?" Jesus answers not with his own words but by quoting the words of Scripture, a passage which also speaks about words: "No one lives by bread alone, but by the words of God." Eve answers Satan correctly: "If we eat of the middle tree in the garden, God says we will die." Well, she *almost* answers correctly, except that she adds a child's whine: "We can't even touch it." "*If* you are God's Son," Satan says to Jesus, "jump down from the highest tower of the temple." Then, snidely, he quotes Scripture too: "See if his angels catch you." Again Jesus answers with words from the Bible: "Don't put God to the test." To Eve, Satan says, "Go ahead and touch it, eat it." Then he tells her the greatest lie in the universe, "You won't die." Eve looks at the fruit hanging on the Tree of Knowledge of Good and Evil and wonders if it would be tasty. Satan takes Jesus up to the world-mountain and offers him everything. (He is, after all, the prince of the world below.) "You only have to worship me." Jesus answers with a sharp tongue, "Get away from me!" Then, once more, he assails the Evil

One with the words of Scripture: "Worship God only! Serve him only!" Satan says to Eve, "God fears that you will become like him. There can't be two sheriffs in town." With that, Satan's temptation succeeds. Eve plucks the fruit and eats it and is cursed. From that point on, her life moves year by year toward death.

Jesus also moves toward death, but *his* death brings life.

PRAYER

If you, my Christ, are by my side, I can a host defy. Amen.

JUNE 17
John 1:35–42

In many church denominations, just before celebrating communion, the congregation sings, "Lamb of God, who takes away the sins of the world, have mercy on us." John the Baptizer declares as much, and two of his disciples follow Jesus. The prophet Isaiah (53:6–7) referred to the Suffering Servant this way: we are sheep who disowned the Shepherd. He was the lamb led to the slaughter in our place.

On the second day, as Jesus is walking, he suddenly rounds on the two disciples, saying, "What (who) are you looking for?" Their answer is the cry of people even today, yearning to fill the hollow spaces inside themselves: "Is there a God? *Where* is God?" They need something greater than themselves.

Jesus's response both to them and to us is one that will be repeated again and again in John's gospel: "Come and see." Seeing where Jesus dwells and who he is and what he does is the beginning of faith. "See me and know that I am the Son of God."

"Whom are you looking for?" The question asked here at the start of John's gospel is the same question, word for word, which Jesus asks Mary Magdalene after his resurrection. The two questions bracket the whole of Christ's ministry on earth. As he descended from heaven, even so he ascends. Blessed be the name of the Lord.

Those two disciples are Andrew and his brother Simon. Jesus knows the man's gruff personality and names him Rock-Man, Peter.

PRAYER

I love you, O Lord, for you are my rock, my fortress, and my deliverer. Amen.

Matthew 4:18–22

It often happens that the four gospel writers see the same things but from different perspectives. Matthew's account of the calling of Jesus's first disciples is somewhat different from that of the other three gospel writers.

Jesus is in Capernaum, a city stinking of fish—fish filleted, fish salted, fish pickled in brine, fish sun-dried. Capernaum sells its fish abroad.

Andrew and Simon Peter are fishermen who know the right times and the best places to net shoals of fish. It's possible that their father owns their boat. If so, he and they are members of the middle class, with money enough to be taught the higher things in life.

Peter and Andrew are onshore, washing their nets, when Jesus approaches them.

Although they've never met him before, his are words of authority. "Follow me." Thus, he changes them forever. "Are you fishers of fish? I will make you fishers of souls." Immediately, they leave their nets and follow him.

Next Jesus finds James and John, the sons of Zebedee, and says to them, "Be my disciples and follow me." They don't go home. They don't kiss their parents goodbye. They pick up and go without another word.

PRAYER

I pray with Saint Augustine: "Christ, I could not seek you if you hadn't already found me." Nor could I today preach your gospel if you hadn't first put the words into my mouth. Amen.

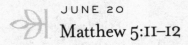

Matthew 5:1–9

Christ's "Blessed," spoken on the mount, refers not only to his present time but also to the end times, when his blessing will be established forever.

"Poor"—the poverty-stricken.

"In spirit"—those whose internal hearts are not proud, those who humbly know that they don't depend on themselves but on God.

"Mourn"—people who grieve because the world is broken.

"Comforted"—in the coming kingdom.

"Meek"—not fainthearted, but meek as Moses was meek (Numbers 12:3) when he outfaced Pharaoh.

"Righteousness" does not mean to hunger for a right piety, but to be filled with the righteousness of the Savior.

"Merciful" isn't an attitude. It is those who do *acts* of mercy.

"Pure in heart"—those with an undivided devotion to God alone. (See Psalm 86:11.)

"Peacemakers"—people who reconcile those who are in conflict (as is the Truth and Reconciliation Commission in South Africa).

PRAYER

I am blessed, Lord, only because you blessed me first. Amen.

JUNE 20

Matthew 5:11–12

It is here that Jesus stops speaking in the third person, "they," to speak in the second person, "you," meaning his disciples, meaning us.

Why should we "rejoice and be glad"? Not because we will escape persecution, but because we *will* be persecuted. Those devoted to Jesus will always be pilgrims and aliens in this spiteful world. Their words will draw the hoots of the scornful. When they talk to others about the necessity of righteousness, many people of the world will hear an intolerable law and reject it. When they talk about love, people will laugh at their silly understanding of love.

Nevertheless, they belong to the company of the prophets who were entrusted with the mission of the Lord. *That* is their blessing. *That* makes them bold.

PRAYER

Jesus, let me never be ashamed of you, for in you and your gospel are the power of God and his righteousness. Amen.

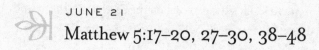

JUNE 21
Matthew 5:17–20, 27–30, 38–48

Jesus preaches to the multitude sitting before him on the mount. "I have not come," he says, "to change the laws of Moses but to fulfill them" (by his death and his resurrection). It is right here that the old covenant (the Old Testament) becomes the new covenant (the New Testament).

No longer an eye for an eye or a tooth for a tooth. Rather, if someone slaps my right cheek, I'm to offer him my left. What then? Is Jesus saying that I can't revenge myself? Yes, I can never take revenge.

Jesus doesn't abolish the commandment not to commit adultery. He adds to it. A man or a woman is adulterous even if they only think about it, even if they merely look at someone, meditating, "What if?"

In the olden times you could love your neighbors and hate your enemies. Now the *whole* law is love. This is the perfection that Jesus wants. But we *can't* be perfect unless ours is the perfect faith that springs from our Savior.

PRAYER

Who can stand, Lord, when you appear in power and might? Purify me. Refine my dross into silver, and I shall stand before you rich with your own riches. Amen.

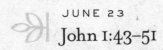
Matthew 6:9–13

When you pray, pray like this:

Call God "Father," for we are Jesus's sisters and brothers. His Father is our Father. He's in heaven and, by his Son, is also present on earth.

A name is more than a name. It indicates the whole person. "Hallowed"—honor God as the only Holy One.

"Your kingdom come," the kingdom of God's Son, already here and also at the end of time.

"Your will be done in heaven," where the saints and the angels and all the company of heaven live in perfect obedience to the Father. And "here on earth," where Jesus fell facedown on the earth in Gethsemane and prayed, "Abba, Father, not my will but yours be done" (Matthew 26:39).

"We need food to sustain us day to day. As you forgive the debts we owe to you, empower us by your grace to forgive the debts we owe to one another.

Evil surrounds us all day long. Save us, protect us, deliver us."

And conclude your prayer with a shout of conviction, believing that all our petitions are heard by our heavenly Father and will be answered, every one: "Yours is the kingdom! Yours is the power! Yours is the glory forever and forever!"

And declare your faith in the Lord's prayer with a glad "Amen."

PRAYER

What better prayer can we pray than this, the prayer that Jesus has taught us? Amen.

John 1:43–51

Come and see. Believe and go.

Andrew and Peter and James and John heard Jesus's "come" and went to call others. Jesus finds Philip and says, "Follow me." Then Philip goes to Nathanael and says, "I've found the One the prophets predicted!" "Right," says Nathanael. "I suppose he dropped from heaven." "No. He comes from Nazareth." "It's an old saying: 'Can anything good come out of that backwater village?'" Philip says, "Come and see."

Jesus is often glad to meet a doubter. They speak their minds.

So here comes Nathanael, prepared to put Philip in his place. Nathanael says to Philip, "This guy's a prophet?" Philip answers, "His name is Jesus." Then Jesus speaks to Nathanael: "Even before Philip found you, I saw you sitting under a fig tree." "Teacher," Nathanael answers, "you are the Son of God." "Do you believe this," Jesus says, "because I saw what eyes can't see? You—all of you—will see greater things than this. The heavens will open, and angels will be ascending and descending, heaven to earth and earth to heaven." (Think of Jacob's ladder.)

In those days the Roman emperor was called "a son of god—of the gods." But his gods were illusions, and his empire would fall before its enemies. Jesus Christ is God's Son truly. He will defeat the Prince of Darkness, and his kingdom will stand indestructible, even forever.

PRAYER

Because you are the Son of God and the Son of Man, you, Lord, are my lifeline between your Father in heaven and me here on earth (1 Timothy 2:5). That makes you my mediator, the one who descends to hear my petitions and ascends, taking them to your Father and mine. Thank you. Amen.

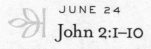
JUNE 24
John 2:1–10

It takes two days for Jesus and his disciples to ride their donkeys from Capernaum to Cana. Or if they walk, three days. They're off to join a wedding party. Whether Jesus was invited or not doesn't matter. He goes to show forth his glory.

At wedding feasts the guests wash their hands in stone jars filled to the brim with water. At this feast it's *six* jars, each containing twenty to thirty gallons of water.

The wedding celebration lasts a week—drinking, dancing, singing, eating, telling riddles, laughing at jokes. It's no surprise, then, that the wine is gone before the celebration is done. Jesus's mother has a backbone, bold and self-assured. She says to her son, "Do something." Jesus says, "Woman"—that word isn't a slur or a brush-off but the usual way a woman is addressed—"what does this have to do with me?" Neither is that a rebuke. Jesus has begun to separate himself from ordinary human relationships in order to work the works of his heavenly Father and to make a new family of his followers.

No matter what her son told her, Mary goes to the servants and says, "Do whatever he tells you to do." Then it seems that Jesus does nothing remarkable—no gesture, no magical word. He simply tells a servant to dip a cup in a jar and to carry it to the master of ceremonies. "Tell him to take a sip." The master of ceremonies sips, then runs to the bridegroom. "Why were you hiding this wine? And why did you save it till now? You know that a drunk doesn't know that he's drinking the dregs."

The wine with which Jesus gladdened the wedding guests in Cana should also be known as the gift of a giving Lord God, for he said, "I am sending you grain and *wine* and oil, and you will be satisfied" (Joel 2:19).

PRAYER

Oceans of wine! What a beautiful image! And you are the groom, and the bread and the wine we eat and drink in our pews or at the communion rail, and we are drunk on your love, and your wedding feast will last forever. Amen.

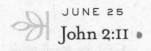

JUNE 25

John 2:11

While driving east on US 30 from Merrillville to Valparaiso, Indiana, I pass a green sign that reads "Valparaiso, 10 miles." Any fool knows that the sign is not the city itself. It *points* to the city ten miles ahead. But in the gospel of John, Jesus's signs (in John there are seven) don't *point* to him. They *reveal* him, because he *is* his signs.

In the other three gospels, signs are essentially miracles that display Christ's power and his authority. But in John, Jesus says, "I am the bread of life. I am the light of the world. I am the good shepherd. I am the resurrection and the life."

In the Old Testament, God names himself "I AM." Every time Jesus says of himself, "I AM," it is a hidden reference to his own godhead.

And one thing more: seeing is believing. When the disciples see water changed into wine, they come to believe in him—that he *is* the sign they see.

PRAYER

Jesus, when I hunger, feed me with the bread of your righteousness. When I walk in nights of sorrow or despair, be my light. When I am lost and as lonely as a wandering sheep, be my good shepherd. Be, O Lord, my great I AM, and I will live my life in you. Amen.

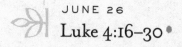

JUNE 26
Luke 4:16–30

Worship in the synagogues often consisted of seven parts. (1) The reading of the creed (Deuteronomy 6:4–5), (2) a recitation of the Ten Commandments, (3) a recitation of the eighteen benedictions, (4) readings from the Torah and the prophets, and (5) a psalm. (6) Then the scroll was passed to the one invited to interpret a passage of his own choosing, after which (7) a blessing closed the service.

Jesus has come to his people in Nazareth. He is given the scroll and unrolls it to Isaiah 61:1–4. "The Spirit of the Lord is on me, because he has anointed me to proclaim good news to the poor." Jesus rolls the scroll up and hands it back to the leader. He scans the people before him, then says, "Today this scripture has been fulfilled." Wow! Nazareth gets to be the first to hear this wonderful thing! They say to one another, "Who knew that a carpenter's son could be so eloquent?"

Jesus listens, then tells them what they think is an entertaining riddle: "I suppose you're going to say, 'Doctor, heal yourself.'" But it isn't a riddle. It's a serious statement—and a judgment. "Well, I say to you that a prophet is never accepted in his own hometown."

"No, but we—Wait a minute! He is blaming *us*! We won't stand for it!"

Jesus continues: "The prophet Elijah was hated in Israel, so he went to a pagan widow and healed her son."

Enraged, the people in the synagogue cry, "That tears it!" They drive him out to the edge of a cliff above the Jezreel Valley, ready to push him down to his death. But Jesus's hour has not yet come. He passes through them and is gone.

PRAYER

Too often I've been angry at too many people. I have justified my anger by saying, "They did it to me!" Jesus, I beg you to direct my anger at the one true enemy—Satan, who seeks to make my soul his own. Keep my soul as your own. Amen.

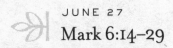

JUNE 27

Mark 6:14–29

Herod Antipas divorces his wife and marries his brother's wife, a woman named Herodias. Antipas has breached a code of Moses (Deuteronomy 24:1–4), and John the Baptist cannot keep silent. He stands below Herodias's palace window and cries out to her, "Adulteress! Adulteress!" The queen so hates this razor-tongued preacher that she commands her husband to lock the man in jail. He does, but he also admires the Baptizer. Therefore, he often visits John in jail.

Then comes the king's birthday. Lords and ladies shower him with gifts. Swains whirl their girls around. Jugglers juggle. Drummers drum. Athletes do backflips. And everyone drinks themselves silly. Even Herod pickles his brains, and Herodias sees an opportunity to revenge herself on the Baptist. She goes to Herod and smiles and says, "It would please me, my Lord, if you would grant me a favor." The fuddle-brained king spreads his arms in a grand gesture and cries, "Whatever!" "Swear to give my daughter what she asks for." "Done and *done*!" cries King Herod.

So Herodias dresses her daughter in a lovely linen gown, and the girl dances.

Herod is charmed, overcome with delight. "Whatever you want," he cries, "it's yours!" The child tells Herod what her mother told her to say: "John's head on a platter." Herod is suddenly sober. "No," he groans. "Anything but that." Herodias says, "The king who made a vow must honor his vow."

Herod slumps. Herodias commands a guardsman go to the prison and draw his sword.

PRAYER

> For all the saints who from their labors rest,
> Who thee by faith before the world confessed,
> Thy name, O Jesus, be forever blest.
> Alleluia! Amen.

—"FOR ALL THE SAINTS"

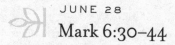

JUNE 28
Mark 6:30–44

Whenever Jesus's ministry drains him—teaching, healing, casting out demons, traveling here and there by foot—he steals away to some private place to pray.

Now the tumultuous crowds have become too much to bear. Jesus invites his disciples to go with him to some quiet haven. They board a boat and sail away from Capernaum, along the shores of the Sea of Galilee. But there is no haven. Jesus lifts his eyes and sees the same crowds running after him along the shoreline. Five *thousand* people. Jesus sighs with compassion, for they are like sheep without a shepherd.

He says to the disciples, "Drop anchor." They do, then Jesus stands up in the still boat and teaches the people from noon and into the late afternoon. By this time everyone is hungry. Philip says, "Send them home to find food for themselves." But Jesus says, "Beach the boat. I will feed them." Philip says, "But there's nothing here but five small barley loaves and two dried fish." "Nevertheless," Jesus says, "tell them all to spread out and sit on the ground." Five thousand?

When they have all arranged themselves on the green grass, the Lord takes the loaves and the fish in his hands and blesses it and breaks it (see Mark 14:22–25). He then has his disciples distribute the loaves and the fish to the crowd.

Everyone eats, and the disciples are astonished. There are twelve baskets of leftovers. But why should they be astonished? This is Jesus, after all.

PRAYER

Miracles on miracles! That you love me in spite of my failures, that you satisfy my hungers with the bread of righteousness, that you will turn my dying into a sleep, and that you will wake me in the morning to an ever-lasting life—O Lord, that is, and you are, the greatest miracle of all. Amen.

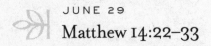

JUNE 29
Matthew 14:22–33

After the breaking of the bread and after the night has fallen, Jesus wants to go to a private place alone. He tells the disciples to board the boat and to continue their voyage while he stays behind.

The disciples sail through the night. But in the grey before the dawn, storm winds whip the sea into huge billows. The disciples bail furiously, fearing for their lives, while the boat slews up and down.

All at once they see a dim, white figure walking toward them across the water. A ghost! "God, *help* us!" But as the figure comes closer, they see that it is a living man. He calls to them, "Why are you afraid?"

John says, "It's Jesus." But Peter needs proof. "If you're truly *you*," he says, "let me walk on the water too." And Jesus says, "Come."

So Peter swings his legs over the side and takes several watery steps.

But then his feet begin to sink. "Jesus!" he cries. "Catch me!" Jesus lifts him by his arms. "Why did you doubt me? Simon! Where is your faith?" The storm passes. The lake lies smooth. And dawn smiles in the sky.

PRAYER

Eternal Father, strong to save,
Whose arm has bound the restless wave,
Who bade the mighty ocean deep
Its own appointed limits keep,
Oh, hear us when we cry to thee
For those imperiled on the sea. Amen.

—"ETERNAL FATHER, STRONG TO SAVE"

JUNE 30
Mark 5:1–20

Not only the Israelites but people in general carved tombs into the sides of limestone hills.

East of the Sea of Galilee, in the land of the Gerasenes, a naked madman skitters among the tombs, lacerating his skin with sharp-edged stones. The Gerasenes have tried to bind him with chains, but devils have the strength of a thousand, and the wild man snaps his chains and breaks free. He will not be clothed. Nor will he stop shrieking.

The disciples beach their boat. Jesus steps ashore, and that demoniac races to him and bows, his glittering eyes deep in their sockets. Demons know what sane people don't. An evil spirit shouts through the poor man's mouth, "What do you want with me, Jesus, you Son of the Most High God?" Jesus commands, "Come out of him!" To know a demon's name is to dominate him. Jesus says, "What is your name?" A cacophony of voices wails, "Legion, for we are many." A Roman legion consists of six thousand infantry and two hundred cavalry. Not one demon, then. A multitude. Jesus commanded them, and they are commanded.

The legion whines. "Don't throw us into the abyss. Send us into that herd of swine!" Now, there are swineherds watching their herds grunting on the hillside. Jesus says to the demons, "Go." Suddenly the pigs squeal, rush and tumble down the hill, and leap into the sea, where they drown, their bodies rolling over and over like barrels on the water.

The swineherds are frightened. They race back to the city. When all the citizens come out, they stop dead. The madman is in his right mind, dressed, and sitting peacefully. "Get away from us!" the Gerasenes yell. Jesus goes back to the boat. The healed man follows and begs to go with his healer. But Jesus says, "It's better for you to stay here and proclaim what God has done for you."

Thus has Jesus appointed his first missionary to the gentiles.

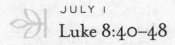

JULY 1
Luke 8:40–48

After the disciples have beached their boat at Capernaum and Jesus has disembarked, he is surrounded by the crowd he fed several days ago. The people clamor, "Feed us like you fed us before."

A man named Jairus, a leader in the synagogue, presses forward through the crowd and falls at Jesus's feet. "My daughter, my only child," he pleads, "is sick unto death. Please come to my house." Jairus gets up and starts to make a way for the Master.

Just then Jesus feels a little power pass out of him. He looks around and says, "Who touched me?" Peter says, "There's no telling in this mob." But Jesus knows the hearts of the people. It was a woman who's suffered a flow of blood for twelve years. Doctors haven't been able to heal her. The woman fears that Jesus is angry. She falls at Jesus's feet and mumbles, "But as soon as I touched the hem of your robe, my bleeding stopped."

Maybe Jesus wants Peter to compare his faithlessness on the Sea of Galilee to the faith of this unknown woman. "Daughter," he says, "your faith in me has healed you. Go in peace."

"Peace I leave with you, my peace, and not as the world gives."

PRAYER

Jesus, I believe. Help my unbelief. Amen.

JULY 2
Luke 8:49–56

While Jesus is still in the crowd, one of Jarius's servants comes to Jairus and says, "I'm sorry, sir, so sorry to tell you that your daughter has died."

Jairus is about to tear his clothes when Jesus touches him and says, "Don't grieve. The girl will be saved." The servant retorts, "I know what I saw. She's *dead*."

Jesus tells Jairus to lead him to his house. Once there, Jesus takes charge. He tells Peter and James and John to come with him. Then they, with the girl's parents, enter her room. The child lies—her face pale, her lips blue—on her bed. Ah, a child no more than twelve years old.

Jesus takes her hand and says in Aramaic, "*Talitha, kumi.*" Immediately, the girl sits up and looks around. Still holding her hand, the Great Physician helps her to stand, then sees to mundane matters. He says to her mother, "She's hungry. Heat a bowl of broth."

When my wife and I adopted our own baby daughter, we named her Talitha because she was given a new life in our home.

PRAYER

Lord God, we implore you always to take the children onto your lap. "Let the little children come to me. Do not stop them. The kingdom of heaven belongs to them" (Matthew 19:13–15). We believe, Jesus, that you keep your promises and that you answer our prayers. Amen.

Matthew 13:1–43

Jesus interprets only three of his parables: the sower and the seeds, the wheat and the weeds, and the net cast into the sea. Otherwise, he wants his hearers to live inside the parables, to *experience* them, and perhaps to realize that they are themselves characters in the stories. Each of these three speaks of the kingdom of heaven, as do the following five parables in the gospel of Matthew.

"The kingdom of heaven" refers both to the present times (of the disciples *and* of us) and to the end of time, meaning that the kingdom exists both now and not yet.

Why parables? So that those who see only the parables' surface, but not their depths, will resist understanding (Isaiah 6:10) and those who see with the eyes of faith will understand their deeper meanings.

Christ is the sower. The seed is his gospel. And the ground on which the seed falls can be dangerous. The seed that falls on a hard path can't know the true meaning of the Word. Satan perches like a bird and pecks that seed into himself. The seed sown on stones covered by a thin layer of soil hears Christ's Word with a missionary joy. The seed sends up a small green stem, but persecutions wither it as under a scorching sun. And the seed that falls among weeds is choked, even as a believer turns and rejects faith to enjoy the glittering things of the world. Dangerous!

But the seed that falls on rich soil is one who hears the Word and understands it. Their faith grows up in such great measure that their harvest yields a hundred times more than any other seeds that are sown.

PRAYER

Lord, you have planted in us the sure hope of the coming of your kingdom, where our joy will increase a hundred times more than we deserve. Amen.

Matthew 16:1–4

The Sadducees and the Pharisees are not on the same team. They disagree with a passion. Nevertheless, they've joined forces here in order to test Jesus. Matthew's word "test" is "tempt" because he sees this confrontation between Jesus and his enemies as a struggle between universal evil and the universal goodness of God.

"Show us a sign from heaven." This is the temptation. They expect to humiliate Jesus. He'll have no sign to show them. But Jesus accuses them of blindness to any spiritual sign. They can read the signs in the sky. Matthew's word for "sky" is the very same word for "heaven." Red sky in morning, sailors, take warning. Red sky at night, sailors' delight. Right. This generation can read the weather, but for their hardness of heart, they can neither read nor see the signs of God's time.

Far from being tempted, Jesus lambasts his tempters. (Remember the "Get away from me!" that Jesus threw in the face of the Devil?) Jesus accuses them of the adultery they commit with Old Mister Law against God, who would marry them, the God right now standing before them in the person of Jesus.

"Then he left them and went away." Matthew's word for "left" is "abandoned." Those who know nothing of signs have no idea of the thing that Jesus just did to them.

"Woe to you, Scribes, Pharisees, hypocrites! Cups! Dishes! You wash yourselves on the outside, but inside are the worms and the maggots of your greed!" (Matthew 23:25–26). Tell me: should we think of Jesus as meek and mild?

PRAYER

O God, you strong warrior defeating the fortresses of the wicked, you are my rock. You are my fortress. Never let me be taken captive, not by the Devil, not by my own sins. Amen.

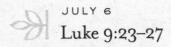
Matthew 12:9–14

Who can farm, or who can do carpentry or fire a forge or weave a shawl or sharpen a knife on a whetstone or prune vines with just one hand? One Sabbath, while Jesus is in the synagogue, he sees a man with a withered hand. He can't support himself, let alone his family. (Think of the farmer whose hand gets caught in a combine.) To accuse Jesus as a scofflaw, the Pharisees ask him a leading question: "Surely you know the law? That no one should heal on the Sabbath?"

Jesus knows that they know what *is* permitted on the Sabbath: to save the life of a sheep in distress (see John 10:14). Now he compares a mere animal to the need of a *human* in distress. He says to the man, "Stretch out your withered hand." The man does so, and he is immediately made whole. He can save his family. He can go to work.

The Pharisees' effort to denounce Jesus has been thwarted by a simple healing. But the Lord's goodness is to them a rank humiliation. From that moment they begin to find some way to destroy him.

PRAYER

O thou great Physician, heal me. When my love begins to wither and I can't work in the vineyards of your kingdom, heal me. When my faith begins to wither under the bright sun of the world's delights, heal me. When I droop in the gloom of sadness or despair, heal me. Strengthen my hands, O my God, once again to labor in your vineyards. Amen.

Luke 9:23–27

Two sorts of gospels, one false and leading to the loss of one's self, the other true and leading to salvation.

Some time ago, when Western missionaries first began to convert certain tribes in Africa, their home churches would send them necessary goods by airplanes. It wasn't long before people began to call it a "cargo religion." Jesus blames those who do the same in his day. "What does it profit you if you gain the whole world?" There are preachers who preach and people who believe that when Jesus said, "You shall have life abundantly" (John 10:10), he was talking about wealth and prosperity. I know a man whose book sold so wildly that he earned a million bucks. (This is a fact.) He announced to a full auditorium, me included, "I prayed for a million, and praise God, he *gave* me a million." This is the false gospel, for Jesus's "abundant life" is not for this life but for the heavenly life to come.

The true gospel asks faithful Christians to take up their crosses and follow Jesus. (See Matthew 16:24–26.) Our crosses are not some worldly burden. "My mother-in-law's Alzheimer's is the cross I have to bear." My teenager, my cancer, the weather, the crime, and so on and so forth. No, the cross Jesus has in mind is *his* cross. "Take up *that* cross and follow me." "Follow you where?" "To Calvary."

Disciple, if you will suffer as Jesus suffered, you will live to see the glory of the Father and the Son and the Holy Spirit.

PRAYER

I must not complain of tribulations and trials, or even of the death that waits for me, because you, Lord, wait to welcome me home. Amen.

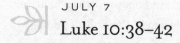

JULY 7
Luke 10:38–42

Jesus's disciples include women, such as Mary Magdalene and Joanna (Luke 8:2–3) and Martha's sister Mary, who sits where men sit, at the feet of a teacher. The student of a rabbi is called that rabbi's disciple.

Martha chooses to serve as every good hostess should. The social order expects as much of women. We cook for our guests. We offer them juice or soft drinks or wine. But Mary has chosen the better part, devotion to the Lord's word above any other thing. The better part because this is a manifestation of her love for God. Faith comes by hearing. And faith increases by learning.

The good Samaritan demonstrates the second great commandment, love for one's neighbor. Mary demonstrates the first great commandment, love for one's God.

Even so do Christians choose to serve their church buildings (vacuuming the carpets, repairing the roof), to serve most piously, rather than serving the Lord their God with all their hearts. There is a fine line between the two, which is why so many people *think* they're serving God.

PRAYER

I commit my ways, my Lord, to you alone (Psalm 37:5). I trust in you. Guide me. Guide me even to the promised land. Amen.

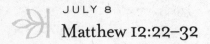

JULY 8
Matthew 12:22–32

Two kingdoms as long as this world endures: the kingdom of Satan, prince of this world, and the kingdom of God. The two kingdoms struggle together in a deadly combat, and even now we stand between them.

Perhaps the crowd listening to Jesus will choose God's kingdom and become the disciples of Christ. Perhaps not.

Once more Jesus heals. This time it's a man with a demon that has rendered him speechless and blind. And once more the Pharisees attack Jesus, slandering him in the hearing of the crowd, perhaps to make them *their* disciples. (Note that their greatest evil is to block others from entering the kingdom of God.) They charge Jesus, saying, "You collude with Satan! You cast out demons by the power of a demon!"

Jesus crushes their logic. "A house divided against itself cannot stand. If Satan casts out Satan, then Satan is divided. He battles against *himself* and will not win the cosmic war."

Jesus says, "I go my way yesterday, today, and tomorrow, empowered by the Spirit of my Father. But you blaspheme the Spirit! You will not be forgiven, neither in this present age nor on the last day, when God will judge you without mercy."

We must realize that *this* is the "unforgivable sin," the rejection of the Holy Spirit. It is not suicide or dying without having confessed one's sin and receiving forgiveness or the terror people feel when they fear that the gates of heaven will be locked against them.

PRAYER

Jesus, receive me. Cast out my sins. At my dying day I will still be clinging to you. And this I believe, that you will open the gates of heaven and take me in. Amen.

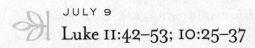

JULY 9

Luke 11:42–53; 10:25–37

The healing Jesus can also be an angry Jesus. On the mount (Matthew 5), Jesus said to those whom he was teaching, "Blessed are you whose hearts are pure." But now he reverses his pronouncement: "Woe, woe to you, you presuming Pharisees, tithing worthless herbs but hauling others into a rump court!"

In these days Jews revile Samaritans. A man asks Jesus, "Who is my neighbor?" Jesus answers with a parable.

"As a merchant was traveling from Jerusalem to Jericho, robbers waylaid him. They stripped him of his clothes, beat him, stole his money pouch, and left him lying half dead.

"So here came a priest and a temple-Levite, both lifting their noses and passing on by. But then came a Samaritan who took pity on the unconscious merchant. He dismounted. He cleaned the bleeding man's wounds with wine and bandaged them with strips of cloth infused with oil. Then he lifted the fellow onto his mule and took him to an innkeeper and said, 'Take care of him.' The Samaritan paid the innkeeper now and promised more when he returned.

"Tell me," Jesus asked the man who had questioned him, "two Jews and a Samaritan—who was the true neighbor?"

Jesus's parable had a good effect, for the man answered, "The one who had pity."

No one knows the trouble I've seen except you, O Lord. Have pity on me. Cleanse me with your wine. With the oil of your mercy, bandage the wounds of my sinning, and lift me high and higher onto the green fields of heaven. Amen.

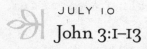

JULY 10

John 3:1–13

Nicodemus has a good reputation: a Pharisee well versed in the law and a leader of the Jews. He comes to Jesus by night (in John "night" often implies a blindness to the true significance of the Lord). Moreover, Nicodemus has heard about Jesus's signs but thinks they're nothing more than miracles. "Rabbi," he says, because he knows Jesus to be an influential teacher.

Jesus speaks to Nicodemus in ambiguities: "If anyone wants to *see* [remember, it's night] the kingdom of God, they must be born again." It's important to know that the Greek word for *again* also means "from above." We can't read one without the other. "Born again" means knowing who Jesus is and putting faith in him. "Born from above" means to have become a child of God. (See John 1:13.)

Nicodemus is baffled. He thinks Jesus is talking about an impossible and foolish reality. Who can squeeze back into a mother's womb? But Jesus is talking about spiritual matters: "Born of water and Spirit." Water—a mother's amniotic fluid? And the Spirit, a radical *re*birth. "How can this be?" says Nicodemus, not really expecting an answer. But Jesus shakes his head and says, "A teacher of Israel, and *still* you haven't plumbed the depths of a right understanding?" Hereafter, Nicodemus shuts up and listens to what Jesus has to say. "I tell you about earthly things, and you don't believe. Then how can you believe these heavenly things I'm telling you now?"

PRAYER

I want to walk in your light, O Lord. I want to believe your signs and the mysteries of the faith. There are so many things that my reason can't make sense of: a virgin birth; a God and a man in the same body; the Trinity, that three Gods are one God. But what my mind can't understand, my heart can believe. Amen.

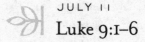

JULY 11
Luke 9:1–6

Jesus commissions his twelve disciples to go out among the people to witness to the gospel. Perhaps they will be able to turn the hearts of many to God, the great and gracious Lord, not only by their preaching but also by the miracles they've been empowered to perform. And Jesus says, "Take nothing for your journey."

We too ought to take a lesson from his instructions.

While I was pastoring my inner-city congregation, I was paid scarcely enough to support my family. This is not a complaint. The church hadn't the money to pay me a full wage. I planted a vegetable garden and raised chickens, while my wife sewed hand-me-downs and cooked the simplest meals. Now, I tell you that to tell you this: to live as poor as our neighbors taught me a very important lesson. How could I truly know the circumstances of the poor if I were not poor myself? How could I preach to them the gospel without favoring people of privilege, people comfortable in their pews? I stayed with my congregation for eighteen years.

As for demons, I salved the anxieties of those who had been abused (girls raped by a relative). I helped to heal the downcast and prayed with the ailing—and all this not because I was good, but because my Shepherd is good.

PRAYER
Lord, when John the Baptist wanted to know whether you were the one to come, you responded by speaking of your deeds: healing the blind and healing the lame, cleansing lepers, and preaching good news to the poor (Luke 7:18–23). By you and in you, sustain me in doing what you do and have done. Amen.

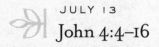

Mark 2:1–12

The house is jam-packed. While Jesus is teaching those who are hungry to learn, as well as a few scribes who have studied every jot and tittle of the law, he's interrupted by a chunk of baked clay that drops from the roof and lands at his feet. Jesus looks up. A man looks down through the gap he's opening in the roof and says, "Apologies, Master." Three more men help the first man to widen the hole, then they let a fifth man down by ropes. This one lies on a pallet, mute and rigid with paralysis. As always, Jesus reads the human heart and knows the faith of the paralytic's friends. He says to the paralyzed fellow, "Son, your sins are forgiven." That vexes the scribes. They mumble among themselves that only God forgives sins and that Jesus has just blasphemed.

Jesus says, "I know your minds. Let me put a question to you. Which is easier? To say to this man, 'Your sins are forgiven' or to say, 'Stand, pick up your pallet, and walk'?" A scribe answers, "Anyone can *say* forgiveness, but it doesn't mean that someone is truly forgiven. It's harder to prove your power, especially when it proves that you are powerless."

To show that his forgiveness is of God, Jesus tells the man to stand, to roll up his pallet, and to carry it home. Immediately the paralytic does exactly that and leaves the house. The scribes may grind their teeth, but the crowd is amazed and gives glory to God.

PRAYER

Glorify God, all you people. Praise the Lord! Sing praises to him. Praise him as long as you live (Psalm 146:1–2), and with me say, Amen.

John 4:4–16

Jesus and his disciples have been traveling through Samaria. By the time they reach a town called Sychar, Jesus has a mighty thirst. He sits on the rim of a well and sends his disciples to town to buy food. While he waits, a woman comes with a water jug. Usually the townswomen walk to the well in the cool of the morning, chatting and laughing. That this woman comes alone in the heat of the day indicates she's been ostracized. Jesus asks her for a drink of water. The woman is perplexed. "You're a Jew," she says, "and I'm a Samaritan. Why are you talking to me?" Jesus doesn't answer her question. Rather, he responds with a baffling word: "If you knew the gifts God gives and who I am, you'd be asking me for a drink, and I would give you living water." A "living" water is water that moves, streams, flows. The woman says, "You don't have a bucket, and our ancestor Jacob dug this well very deep [at least a hundred feet]. Are you greater than Jacob?"

Jesus says, "Drink any water but mine, and you'll be thirsty again. My water bubbles up to eternal life." "Oh, sir, give me that water." Jesus changes the subject and says, "Call your husband."

The rest of the Samaritan woman's story will come in the devotion for July 15.

PRAYER
"With joy you will draw water from the wells of salvation" (Isaiah 12:3). Jesus, I drink from the chalice of living water that flowed from your side, and I drink the cup of salvation. Amen.

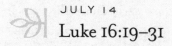

JULY 14
Luke 16:19–31

A rich man's purple robe signified that he was a high-ranking official or that he was a member of the royal family. People like these used bread to wipe the grease from their hands, then tossed the pieces under the table.

Jesus tells a parable:

Lazarus ("God helps") lay at a rich man's gate, hungry and suffering running pustules, but was given nothing. Both men died, and their fortunes were reversed. Lazarus was with Abraham, who took him to his breast, while the rich man suffered the flames of hell. He called to Abraham, "Let Lazarus bring me a drop of water on his fingertip to relieve my thirst." Abraham said, "No one can cross the great gulf between us. You enjoyed the delights of the world. Lazarus's delight is in heaven."

"Then send him to warn my brothers." Does this rich man think Lazarus is his servant? He said, "If someone rises from the dead, that will persuade them to repent."

Abraham said to the rich man, "If they haven't believed Moses and the prophets, they won't believe at all."

It may be a subtle distinction between trusting in the visible world and trusting in the invisible God. Christians can't serve two masters, the supreme Lord and the wealth of the world, for they would love the one and hate the other (Luke 16:13).

PRAYER

I called on you. Out of my misery I cried unto you for help. You heard my voice and healed me and comforted me. Bless you, God of my soul. Amen.

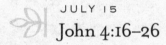

JULY 15
John 4:16–26

"Call your husband." "I have no husband." "Right," says Jesus, "You've had five, and the man you're with is not a husband at all."

Both in the past and still today, people have blamed the woman as a sinner, but Jesus doesn't blame her. "Five husbands" doesn't mean she's a man-killer. Some of the men may have died, and some may have divorced her, and the one she lives with now supports the woman who would otherwise lack any place in her society.

Because Jesus knows what he shouldn't have known, the woman says, "You are a prophet." Prophets often predicted the coming of "the day of the Lord." Jesus now speaks of his hour (as he did to his mother at Cana). The hour (*his* hour) is coming, and is already here, when the faithful will worship God the Father in spirit and in truth—not on Mount Gerizim in Samaria or at the temple in Jerusalem. A spiritual and genuine worship will not be bound to a particular place or time. Nor should our true worship be bound to a particular church or doctrine or season (Christmas, Easter).

Step-by-step the Samaritan woman has been moving ever closer to belief. And this exchange puts paid to it: "Are you the Messiah?" Jesus answers yes in his own way: "I AM," which is the name of the Deity.

We would do well to compare the woman's steps to faith with the steps many people take to Christianity.

PRAYER

> Jesus, where'er thy people meet,
> There they behold your mercy-seat;
> Where'er they seek thee, thou art found,
> And every place is holy ground. Amen.

—WILLIAM COWPER, 1731-1800

JULY 16

Matthew 11:28–30

Jesus calls to himself those whose labors have exhausted them, those borne down by heavy yokes as if they were weary plow-oxen. "I will give you rest."

The "yokes" that Jesus has in mind are the crushing effects of the laws imposed on his people by the Pharisees as well as the heart-hardened ways the Pharisees deal with anyone they think has offended the law. Don't we in the same manner judge those who do not conform to the laws of our various churches?

"And I will give you rest." God rested on the seventh day. The Jews have from times immemorial honored the Creator by resting on the Sabbath. *This* is the same rest to which our Lord calls us. His yoke is "light" because it is the yoke of love.

Often in the Old Testament, a yoke symbolized servitude, and an iron yoke a heavy punishment (Deuteronomy 28:48). Yet it could also be a sign of God's mercy (Isaiah 10:27). Jesus's lighter yoke, then, reveals the mercy of his Father. Our Lord is not a taskmaster. Among his commandments is this: "Love one another as I have loved you."

PRAYER

> In my troubles, Lord, walk with me.
> When my life becomes a burden
> I want Jesus to walk with me. Amen.
>
> —"I WANT JESUS TO WALK WITH ME"

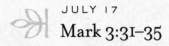

JULY 17
Mark 3:31–35

Joseph has faded into the background. He's done his work. He's raised his stepson. And he is a modest man. Never in the four gospels will we hear of him again.

But Jesus's mother continues throughout the gospels. Mary, this woman of determination, tracks her son's ministry.

It comes as no surprise, then, that she and her other children are standing outside the house where Jesus is teaching.

The word *outside* indicates that Jesus is separating himself from his blood family.

Here comes a fellow shouldering his way through the crowd with a message from Jesus's mother: "Teacher, your family's asking for you."

Jesus takes a moment to scan the crowd before him. Finally, he spreads his arms and says—perhaps loud enough for his mother to hear—"Who is my mother? Who are my sisters and brothers?" Jesus is creating a new family of believers, his own family, which will be completed at the cross when he gives his mother to John and John to his mother (John 19:26–27) and which will last all down the ages. "Here is my mother. Here are my sisters and my brothers, those who do my Father's will."

And this is the will of the Lord: to obey his commandments. And he will bless you abundantly (Deuteronomy 30:8–11).

When I was baptized, my name became "Child of God." Son of God, you are my brother, and I am a member of your glorious family. Here I live. Here I obey. And hereafter, I will abide in your house. Amen.

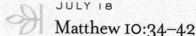

JULY 18
Matthew 10:34–42

Jesus's "sword" isn't a fiery division of people and families. He's speaking about the end of time. As for the divisions, they occur among the Christians of Saint Matthew's church when persecutions separate members of the same families, some choosing faith, and others, fearing lions and fire, despair.

Those who love their human families more than they love Jesus are not worthy to be a part of his spiritual family. Those who do not take up the cross of suffering as Jesus suffered on his cross are not worthy. But those who do take up the cross and follow him will be willing to lose their lives for his sake. These are they who will find their lives again and will be members of his new and true family.

This is what I think, that they will also be given back their human families—but rejoicing in the union because they know that this is the free gift of God.

PRAYER
Here I am, Lord, ready to die the death of social rejection as well as the death of people's (even my relatives') snarking at my "outdated" religion. Here I am, a follower of you to the cross and to the resurrection. Amen.

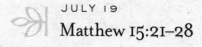

JULY 19
Matthew 15:21–28

There was that demoniac among the tombs who became a missionary. There was that Samaritan woman at the well—also a missionary. Now there is this woman born among gentiles who cries out, "Have mercy on me, Lord, Son of David! My daughter is wracked with an evil spirit."

Son of David? Can that be a cry of faith? If so, it is nothing more than faith in Jesus's miracles.

The disciples are irritated by the woman's interruption. "For heaven's sake," says Peter, "send her away!" It seems, then, that Jesus agrees with his complaint, because he answers the woman with sarcastic words: "God sent me to serve Israel." The woman prostrates herself in a posture of worship and again begs his mercy even as Christians do today, singing, "Lord, have mercy. Christ have mercy. Lord have mercy."

Jesus continues his sarcastic words—but we are beginning to realize that he is turning them against his disciples. "You think [*they* think] that the food given to children should be thrown to the dogs?" Interesting: Jews don't keep dogs as pets. They eat garbage. Now the gentile woman parries with a quick wit and boldness: "Even the dogs get the crumbs that fall from Israelite tables."

Now Jesus says outright what he knows, that her sight is becoming insight and that she's learning the deeper meaning of Jesus's person. He says, "Your faith is inspiring." Jesus glances at Peter, then says to the woman, "Go home. Your daughter has been healed."

PRAYER

Amen, O Lord. Amen!
Have mercy, Lord! Amen!
Sing it over again, amen!

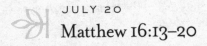

JULY 20
Matthew 16:13–20

Jesus and his disciples travel east to Caesarea Philippi. Nearby is an ancient grotto and a spring where Canaanites used to worship Baal. Jesus speaks about a wholly different worship, asking, "Who do people say the Son of Man is?" "Well," they answer, "some say John the Baptist come back to life. Or Elijah because he was taken up into heaven without dying." Now Jesus makes his question personal: "Who do *you* say I am?"

Simon the Rock speaks for all the disciples: "You are the Messiah, the Son of the living God." Jesus says to Peter, "Flesh and blood didn't reveal this to you, but my Father in heaven did." Yet in speaking the words, Simon has made them his own, an expression of his faith.

Jesus addresses the man who will become the foremost teacher after his ascension. "You are Rock," he says, "and you are the cornerstone on which I will build my church." We, the community of faith, are the building Christ builds" (Ephesians 2:20–23).

The gates of hades (hell) may be understood as the door from which pours forth the power of Satan to attack and to batter the church. It is both popular and silly to think that Peter's keys open heaven to the good and close it to the bad. As the keeper of the keys, Peter has been given the authority to govern the house's (the church's) affairs and to teach (Isaiah 22:20–21).

PRAYER

Almighty God, let your Holy Spirit be the spirit that breathes within your church. Loosen our tongues so that we can freely preach the salvation of your Son. Amen.

JULY 21
Matthew 16:21–23

The church *will* endure, for Christ will be battered on its behalf, battered and scourged and put to death and on the third day rise to life.

It's important to understand that the elders and chief priests and scribes are the *leaders* of the Jews, not the Jewish people themselves—a false application that has justified antisemitism all down the ages and even today.

Simon Peter must not have heard that "on the third day rise to life." The cornerstone of Christ's church now becomes another sort of stone—a stumbling block. He says to Jesus, "Death? I won't have it!"

I can think of three reasons for Peter's rebuke: (1) He loves his Lord. (2)

He doesn't understand that "Messiah" should *require* a death. (3) He's scared. If Jesus will be handed over to his enemies, then Peter might also be killed.

Whatever Peter's reason, Jesus answers with a razor-sharp tongue: "You are more concerned about earthly things than about the will of God." So pointed is his reproach that Jesus compares him to Satan (Matthew 4:10). "Get away from me!"

PRAYER

It is your love that, in spite of my gross iniquities, has never said, "Get away from me" but "Let the little children come unto me." I'm a child who sucked his thumb and drank the milk of your salvation (1 Corinthians 3:1–2) and now have been given the solid food of faith, always feeding on your cup of wine and your bread of life. Amen.

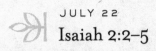

JULY 22
Isaiah 2:2–5

As Jesus is about to take Peter, James, and John up the Mount of Transfiguration, so now we prepare ourselves by looking at God's holy mountain.

Zion is a hill (a mount) in Jerusalem to which Isaiah prophesies that the nations will come, and God will gather his people together. They will come with their sons and their suckling daughters. Their hearts will thrill, and they will rejoice (Isaiah 60:4–5).

All those who climb the holy mountain, believing in its glory, will call to others, "Come up! Be taught the ways of the Lord and to walk his paths." He is a just God, announcing peace—iron swords beaten into the shares to plow the abundant fields, and swords beaten into hooks that cut off the stems of rich bunches of grapes. Wars will cease, but more than *that* peace, God's peace (his shalom) will be healing and will bring a universal holiness.

We say, "Come to the living Lord Jesus Christ. See his transfiguration and be changed forever."

I came to you, Jesus, and you did not put me to shame. Amen.

JULY 23
Luke 9:28–36

Jesus often goes to private places to pray. This time he takes with him Peter, James, and John into the mountains and separates himself from the three disciples.

Suddenly, while they're watching him, a brilliant light smites their eyes. Jesus's human face breaks into a divine radiance; his robe is a bright flash of white. Both Moses (representing the law) and Elijah (representing the prophets) represent the fulfillment of the Old Testament. They are talking with Jesus about his departure, his exodus.

At Mount Sinai, God spoke to the Israelites out of a cloud. On this mountain too, God speaks out of a cloud, saying the same as he said at Jesus's baptism: "This is my beloved Son. Listen to him!"

Good old Peter, always compulsive. After Moses and Elijah have taken their leave, Peter wants to memorialize this glorious moment, to freeze it forever as a commemoration, and says, "Let's build three dwellings right here!" But the cloud casts the three disciples into darkness, terrifying them, and the more so when it surrounds them altogether. After the cloud has dissolved into plain daylight, there stands Jesus in his common appearance, and alone.

Perhaps God's reprimand, "Listen!" changes Peter's mind. Better than to fix the moment is to stand in an awe-full silence, and in silence to retire from the mountain, speaking nothing of what they've seen.

PRAYER

I will tell of the decree of the Lord God, who said, "You are my Son. Today I have begotten you." I will publish it abroad, for Jesus is my brother, and I too am a child of the heavenly Father. Amen.

John 8:31–36

Too often people use the words of Jesus glibly. For them "truth" is less than *the* Truth. A politician might mean, "My campaign promises are true. My opponent lies." A philosopher might mean, "Study. Plumb the depths of human thought." Or a professor, "Literature will lead you to the truth." But faith is ready to learn what Jesus's words truly mean.

"If you hold to . . ." can mean, "If you abide in, dwell in," as though in a Jesus-house. ". . . hold to my teaching . . ." definitely does *not* mean "keep my commandments" but rather, "dwell in me," because Jesus's word is everything he teaches and everything he does (John 1:14).

"Then you will know the truth." This truth is not a *what*. It is a *who*. In John 14:6 Jesus calls himself the way and the *truth* and the life. Pilate will ask him, "What is truth?" Jesus keeps silent, but he might have answered, "Me." *He* is our truth. (See Galatians 5:1.)

"And the truth will [I will] set you free." Jesus's words in verse 36 emphasize the whole of his meaning.

PRAYER

Jesus, my pilgrim-Way; Jesus, my living Truth; Jesus, my Life, my abiding place forever and ever—I did not choose you, but you chose me. Amen.

Luke 15:11–24

Jesus tells a parable.

The younger of two sons demands his inheritance right now. But he wants from his father what he shouldn't receive until his father's death. The son, therefore, is treating his father as if he were dead already. The son has begun to break from his family's relationship.

The father is greathearted. He doesn't scold. He consents, and the boy travels off to live among gentiles. There men pretend friendship—parties and drinking and spending until the boy has nothing left, not even friends. His hunger drives him to find work with a land-rich pig farmer—all the worse because Jews do not eat pork. The son who divorced his father is forced to eat the swine's fodder, carob pods.

It is in the pig-mire that the boy wakes up to the misery of his condition. He admits that he caused it himself—that he sinned against his father and his Father God. No, the son has no claims on his father's fatherhood. But he will go to his father and confess his sins and hope to be accepted as a slave. So he turns toward home.

But the father has always been waiting, worried for the sake of his son. When he sees him coming down the road—slow and filthy and miserable—it almost breaks his heart. The father leaps up and runs out to the boy, who starts to confess, "I've sinned. I'm not worthy—" But the man interrupts, crying to his servants, "A robe! My best robe! A ring! Clean sandals for my boy's weary feet! And kill the fatted calf!" Marvelous. Meat is too precious to be eaten as a daily diet. It's saved for celebrations. Then the father, his Father, says the truth: "He was lost. Now he's found. He was dead [to me and to all the world]. But now he is alive! Let's have a party!"

PRAYER

> Just as I am thou wilt receive,
> Wilt welcome, pardon, cleanse, relieve,
> Because thy promise I believe,
> O Lamb of God, I come. I come. Amen.
>
> —"JUST AS I AM"

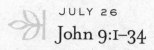

JULY 26

John 9:1–34

Here's a remarkable story, not only because a blind man receives his sight but also because step-by-step he comes to believe and step-by-step makes fun of his accusers.

"As long as I am in the world," Jesus says, "I am the light of the world." In him light and sight are the same.

Jesus comes upon a man whom he knows has been "blind from birth." Jesus spits on the ground and makes a mud, then applies it to the blind man's eyes and says, "Wash in the pool of Siloam." Step 1: The blind man obeys and comes back seeing. Now he's in for some questioning. With every question his faith grows stronger and stronger.

Step 2: His neighbors are confused. "Isn't this that beggar boy?" The sighted man says, "It's me!" They ask, "Who did this to you?" "Jesus." "Where is he?" "I don't know." Step 3: The Pharisees interrogate him, and he repeats what he told the neighbors. "Who do you say Jesus is?" "A prophet." Step 4: The Pharisees haul his parents before them and ask, "How did he come to see?" (To see in order to *see*.) The Pharisees frighten his mother and father. They duck the question: "Ask *him*." Step 5: Again the Pharisees confront the man: "Give glory to God!" which is as much as to say, "Do you swear to tell the truth, the whole truth?" Here comes the man's humor: "Oh, so you want to become disciples like me?" Step 6: Another joke: "I am astonished! Men well-educated in all the laws, yet you can't recognize a divine sign when you see one?" And now his seventh step to faith: "God doesn't listen to sinners. But he listens to me because I've begun to worship him."

The Pharisees are furious. "He calls *us* sinners!" They drive him out of the synagogue. He's been sundered from his family; now he's sundered from his religion, and that without a care in the world.

PRAYER
Blind to Christ I was, but now I go singing a happy song, "Jesus is my sight, and soon my paradise!" Amen.

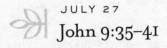

JULY 27
John 9:35–41

Jesus is the Light of the World, who pierces the darkness but lets those who love the darkness rather than the Light to abide in their sins.

The blind man who has literally never seen Jesus is now given the chance to see fully and faithfully, for Jesus comes to him.

Did the Jewish leaders cast him out? Jesus said, "I will never drive out anyone who comes to me" (John 6:37).

When he finds the sighted (and insightful) man, he asks the Christ-question: "Do you believe in the Son of Man?"—he who brings to earth the glory of God, he who is the champion of the poor and the oppressed. The man answers Jesus's question with a question: "Who is he?" And Jesus as much as answers, "I AM." Immediately, the man's faith is made complete. "I believe!" he cries and falls down before the object of his faith and worships him.

Then Jesus speaks what we've already heard in the story: "I've come that those who don't see, will see [me]. And that those who think they see, won't see at all."

Certain Pharisees say, "You don't mean us, do you? *We* see."

Then Jesus puts their pitiful pride to the judgment: "If you were blind [but saw me as the Son of God], there'd be no sin in you. But because you say, 'We see' [but don't see me], you will drink your tears and eat the bread of your iniquities."

PRAYER

> This little light of mine,
> I'm gonna let it shine.
> Oh, this little light of mine,
> I'm gonna let it shine,
> Let it shine, let it shine, let it shine. Amen.

—"THIS LITTLE LIGHT OF MINE"

JULY 28
Matthew 19:13–15; Mark 10:13–16; and Luke 18:15–17

Because the disciples are protecting Jesus from distractions, they tell parents of babies and little children to go away. But Jesus does whatever he wants to do. "Let them come to me." Then he sets them on his lap and blesses them.

Those parents are themselves in need of his blessing. Thirty percent of their infants die in childbirth. Another 30 percent of the children from two to six years old will die because of disease or famine or wars. Another percentage won't survive to the age of sixteen. The parents before Jesus have heard of his healing touch. "But I have calmed and quieted my soul, like a weaned child with its mother. My soul is like the weaned child that is within me" (Psalm 131:2).

Parents today pray for the souls of their children, that they may be kept in the faith and not go wandering after the enticing gods of the world. To sit on the lap of God is to be embraced by a spiritual health.

"It is to such as these that the kingdom of heaven belongs." The trust of a baby who nestles in its mother's lap—that is the same child-like trust we ought to have, faith in our father/Father and our mother/Mother. Such faith will lead us, too, into the kingdom.

PRAYER

> I am Jesus' little lamb.
> Ever glad at heart I am,
> For my shepherd gently guides me,
> Knows my need and well supplies me,
> Loves me every day the same,
> Even calls me by his name. Amen.
>
> —"I AM JESUS' LITTLE LAMB"

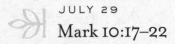

JULY 29

Mark 10:17–22

This is a sad story, for the rich young man who comes to Jesus is truly seeking to inherit eternal life.

"Good teacher," he says. But Jesus takes that *good* and says that his own goodness comes from God alone.

Jesus answers by referring the man to the commandments in which God has already revealed a life well lived.

Jesus believes in the man's piety. The young man says, "I've kept these commandments as long as I've lived." Jesus listens. He looks on him and loves him, and says, "Do one more thing. Sell all your possessions. Give the money to the poor, then come and follow me."

The rich young man becomes a sad young man. He goes away grieving.

No doubt Jesus is sad to see the departure of the young man. "Some of the sower's seeds," he said previously, "fell among thorns. These are those who hear the word, but the cares of this world and the lure of wealth choke the word" (Mark 4:18–19).

Look to the right, my friends. Look to the left, and what do you see? City lights? Skyscrapers? Fashionable clothes? Elevators to well-paying jobs? Do things like these—*can* things like these—draw you away from Jesus? And do you know enough to be saddened by this? Oh, look to Jesus, who is all the wealth you need to know.

PRAYER

My Lord, I have scaled the ladder of self-importance and found only disappointment. Now I'm on the ground, pleading the grace to be taken up into the land of forgiveness. Amen.

JULY 30
Mark 10:35–45

The disciples do not always get along. They've been quarreling (surely Peter has been quarreling) about who's the best and greatest of them all. James and John ask to sit next to Jesus when he comes into his kingdom.

Jesus answers that only God can grant such favors, then draws them right back to reality: will they be able to drink the cup that he will drink? The cup of God's wrath? (See Isaiah 51:17.)

"Yep!" The brothers are so proud their buttons pop. "We can do that!" And Jesus says, "Yes, and you will"—just as John the Baptist has already been martyred.

Now the rest of the disciples glower at James and John. Jesus says to them all, "You talk about greatness? Then think of the lords of the gentiles, some of whom are great, yes, but great tyrants! As for you, if you want to be great, first be a servant. If you want to be a master, first be a slave." Jesus regards his disciples for a moment. Can they accept what he's going to say? Neither greatness nor glory will be his. Only self-sacrifice. "For," he says to them, "even the Son of Man did not come to be served, but to serve, and to give his life as a ransom for many."

PRAYER

My Lord, you have paid my ransom with the golden-red coins of your blood. You have purchased me and bought me and have made me the treasure in your purse. Gratitude is too small a word. Amen.

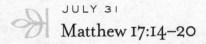

JULY 31
Matthew 17:14–20

The man who separates himself from the crowd and kneels before Jesus is a believer, for he calls him "Lord." In Matthew, "Lord" is on the lips of only those who believe. Thus, the man stands in stark contrast to the disciples' failing faith.

"My son," he says to Jesus, "is an epileptic." The actual word is *moonstruck*, because lunacy was thought to be caused by the moon. "He falls into fire or water. Your disciples have been no help."

Jesus's response includes even his disciples because of their weak faith: "You perverse generation! How you frustrate me! Bring me the boy."

It wasn't epilepsy after all, but a demon who threw him into fire and water. Perhaps with a word, perhaps with a gesture—we don't know—Jesus casts the demon out of the boy, and he is immediately cured. Once again this is a cosmic encounter between the kingdom of Satan and the kingdom of God, and God triumphs.

Jesus turns to his disciples. "Faith like a mustard seed is not small. It's as large as the mustard bush and is great enough to move mountains!" By the presence and the power of God do impossible things become possible.

If we today can't cure, if we cannot pray a friend to health, we ought never to blame God for the failure, nor need we be ashamed of ourselves. Our faith is likely not the problem, but God, the great I AM, always does what he will do. *He* chooses. Faith believes that and worships him.

PRAYER

I believe evil exists in the world, that it infects humanity, tempting people to sin a thousand different kinds of sins, and me too: anger. "Anyone who is angry with a brother or sister will be subject to judgment" (Matthew 5:22). My God, it is impossible for me to forgive myself. But it is possible for you, and I am forgiven. Amen.

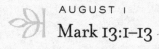
AUGUST 1
Mark 13:1–13

There lived a Jew, a historian named Josephus, who described the Jerusalem temple as having to be approached on twelve steps. Its facade and three sides were covered with massive plates of gold. At sunrise the temple flashed like fire, so brightly that a pilgrim had to turn his eyes away.

While Jesus sits with his disciples on the Mount of Olives, across from the temple, they marvel at what they see. But Jesus says, "It won't be long before the temple is destroyed, its stones thrown down, its gold melted." The disciples ask, "When? What'll be the signs?" Jesus answers, "Watch out! Many will say they preach with the authority of my name. There will be terrifying wars, nations raging against nations, earthquakes, famines, plagues. But don't be worried; these things have to be. As for you, you'll be beaten, and they will make you stand in court before the governors. Witness of me. Preach the gospel. Don't worry about what you will say. The Holy Spirit will give you what to say. Families will hate one another. You too will be hated on account of me. But those who endure will be saved."

The flocks of the Good Shepherd need not fear, whatever befalls them. They *shall* endure because the Shepherd himself suffered their beatings, was hauled into the court of Pontius Pilate, and was killed on their behalf. They shall endure unto the end.

Good and gracious Savior, I know of Christians and missionaries who have been tortured or put to death. Protect them. And if they must die, grant them the faith to meet their martyrdoms still praising your name. Amen.

AUGUST 2
Matthew 25:31–46

When Christ shall return in dazzling glory, attended by his angels, and when he takes his judgment seat, he will gather all the peoples on earth to separate the righteous from the unrighteous, just as sheep are separated from goats. Then both sides will be astonished by what he says.

To the sheep: "Come into my kingdom. I was hungry and you fed me, thirsty and you gave me a cup of cool water, a wilderness wanderer and you took me into your houses and exchanged my tatters for clean clothes." That promise astounds the righteous sheep. "When did we see you, Lord? When did we do these things?" And the Lord King will say, "Ah, but you did when you did it to the least of my children."

Then to the goats: "Go into the hellfire prepared for Satan and his evil spirits. You did absolutely *nothing* for me." Then the goats will be astounded. "We never saw you anywhere. How *could* we serve you?" And the King of Glory will answer, "Oh, yes, you saw me. Everything you did not do for the least of my children, you did not do for me."

Thus will the unrighteous live an everlasting death, while the righteous will live an everlasting life.

Long ago my grandpa superintended a Christian cemetery in St. Louis, Missouri. When we'd walk among the tombstones at night, and when the wind would rattle the tree leaves, Grandpa Storck would tell me this joke: "God and the Devil are counting out the dead."

PRAYER
The homeless child needs a home. The round-bellied baby needs to eat. Those who beg on the streets hope for a warm meal and a job. Cold men

need coats. My old failing grandma needs to be fed by a spoon and washed after using the toilet. I know where you are, my king, my Jesus. Now I am the spiritual beggar in need of your help. Amen.

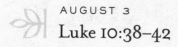

Luke 10:38–42

"Martha, Martha."

Good hosts serve good dinners to their guests, light candles, maybe play soft music. Martha is roasting vegetables, stewing meat, and pouring a carafe of wine because Jesus has come for a visit.

Her sister, Mary, on the other hand, might be called irresponsible because she's neglecting her social duties. She's sitting at Jesus's feet, listening to what he has to say.

Now the Lord judges between the two sisters. Martha's busyness obeys the expectations of public propriety. But if society knew of her sister's "indolence," it would deem Martha's house to be shameful. Society would be wrong.

Remember how Jesus interpreted the parable of the seeds and the sower: "As for the seed that fell among thorns, they are ones choked by the cares and the riches of this world. Their fruit cannot mature" (Luke 8:14). Martha's care for worldly institutions is like the seed among thorns. Far from shame, Mary chooses the "Chosen One," whom she loves with all her heart and all her soul, her strength and her mind, and the words and the love of her Lord will never be taken away from her.

Let Christians likewise serve the Lord with gladness and come into his presence with singing (Psalm 100:2).

PRAYER

Christ, you commissioned women to model the gospel before anyone who chooses to listen. Even so have you commissioned your people. Think on us. Rest your hand on our hearts. Grant us the wisdom and the patience and the persistence and the fortitude to witness to your gospel among those who do not yet believe in you. Amen.

PART 4

JESUS TURNS
His Face to
JERUSALEM

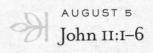

Mark 10:32–34

More than a few times, these devotions have referred to Christian suffering. Remember how Peter responded to Jesus's first prediction that the Son of Man would suffer death. Remember Peter's fear: "This will *not* happen to you!"

Jesus and his Twelve are on their way to Jerusalem when, for the third time, Jesus speaks of his passion, adding terrible details: he will be handed over to the Jewish authorities, who will bind him and demand that Pontius Pilate try him, scourge him with a cat-o'-nine-tails, and sentence him to die an agonizing death.

He will indeed die for us, but here the important meaning is that we ought to pattern our lives on his.

Nevertheless, Christ holds out a hope that the disciples won't understand till after his death: that after three days he will rise again.

We live long after Christ's death and his resurrection. Then why don't we all put our trust in him? Why do we, like Simon Peter, fear death when death is but a sleep?

PRAYER

No, Lord, I no longer fear death, for you will meet me at the door and welcome me home. Amen.

AUGUST 5
John 11:1–6

The village of Bethany is less than two miles east of Jerusalem, the Mount of Olives rising in between. Mary, the sister of Lazarus, will soon anoint Jesus's feet with perfume and dry them with her hair, and Martha sends word to Jesus that their brother Lazarus is sick unto death. At this time Jesus abides outside Judea. He doesn't answer the women's appeal and waits right where he is. The disciples think they understand: Jesus is loath to go on account of the Jewish leaders' plot to kill him. Moreover, he need *not* go because, as he says, "Lazarus isn't going to die." But his *next* words are confusing: "This thing is for God's glory, so that the Son of God may be glorified by means of it."

Glory is good. But what does Lazarus have to do with it?

When we look back on this incident, we know that Lazarus, whom Jesus loves, will die a brief death and will be raised again. At the same time, Jesus is referring to *his* death too. His death and his resurrection—*that's* what Jesus means by the glorification of the Son.

Come, let us take our fill of love until the morning. Let us delight ourselves with love (Proverbs 7:18). Such ought to be a Christian's song to him who *will* come again in the royal glory of a king.

PRAYER

To you, O Lord, is the power and the glory forever. Amen.

AUGUST 6
John 11:7–16

Finally, Jesus says, "It's time we went to Jerusalem." "No!" say the disciples. "They will *murder* you!"

The poor disciples—how long before their eyes are opened to the truth?

It can't be an accident that Jesus begins to talk about sight and the light. He *is* the light (John 8:12). "Those who walk in daylight will not stumble against the stones of danger." Then he says, "Our friend Lazarus is asleep. I'm going to wake him up."

Again the disciples say, "No." But this time they are not thinking about murder. They are speaking out of relief: no going. "Lazarus is on the mend. He'll wake when he's cured."

But by "sleep" Jesus means death, and by the waking from sleep, he means a resurrection. But we know that Jesus is referring to his own death and to his rising again.

Earlier Peter rebuked Jesus's decision to die. Thomas accepts the decision and, for love of his Lord, will follow him to Jerusalem, even unto death.

Today our faith comes by seeing, and by seeing our Lord Jesus truly (he is the Son of God), comes our ability to believe steadfastly in him.

PRAYER
I walk, my Jesus, in your light. You make me able to see the stones of danger. In your light I see light. Amen.

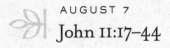

AUGUST 7
John 11:17–44

I can imagine that when Martha sees Jesus coming to her, she beats on his chest with her small fists. "Why did you wait till my brother died?" Jesus knows, and we know the "why," but he doesn't answer her. She relents. "But you've raised people from the dead before" (Luke 7:11–12). Earlier Peter confessed that Jesus was "the Messiah, the Son of the Living God." Here Martha confesses the same: "You are the Messiah." But her confession thinks only about the resurrection on the last day.

Jesus brings the future into the present. "I am [I AM] the resurrection and the life."

Next Mary comes to him and falls at his feet, sobbing. "If only you had come in time."

Jesus too begins to weep. The crowd thinks that his are the tears of sorrow. Actually, these are tears of anger at Satan, who strikes people with diseases. "Where," he asks, "is Lazarus's tomb?" He's shown the way, then tells two men to roll back the flat stone. Martha protests: "He's decomposing. He stinks." Jesus says, "Haven't I told you that you will see the glory of God?"

Jesus faces the black, yawning tomb and cries, "Lazarus, come out!" and the man that was dead comes out alive, still wrapped in his winding cloth. The women unwind the man who has been set free from death, now to live a normal life.

PRAYER
Lord, you freed me from Satan's desire to entomb me. I believe you are my resurrection and my everlasting life. Amen.

AUGUST 8
Matthew 21:1–11

The Passover is celebrated in March or April. Jesus tells two disciples to go into a village nearby and then to bring back a donkey and the colt of a donkey. They do. The air is electric. Some great thing is about to happen. Though people ride donkeys bareback, the disciples remove their cloaks and lay them on Jesus's donkey. Having read the whole New Testament, we know that Jesus is a king, but now he chooses to ride into Jerusalem like a peasant, humble and scarcely worthy of notice.

Yet a host of the Jews who have followed him from Martha's house treat him as if he *were* a king. As Jews pour out of Jerusalem, both crowds cast their cloaks on the road in front of him. They celebrate by waving branches (Leviticus 23:40–41) and shouting, "Hosanna in the highest heaven!" ("Hosanna!" is like crying, "Hooray!") and "Glory to God in the highest heaven!" (See Luke 2:14, where the hosts of heaven sang the same thing.)

The city trembles at such a tremendous arrival. "Who *is* this?"— ever the profoundest question about Jesus's person. The answer is right and very important, but those who answer think only of surface realities: "A prophet born in Nazareth."

PRAYER
Ride on, King Jesus, no man can hinder me. I sit the saddle behind you, Lord; Satan cannot touch me. Amen.

AUGUST 9
Matthew 21:12–17 and Luke 19:45–48

In the temple, in the court of the gentiles, men and women exchange foreign coins (because they are emblazoned with idols) for coins that were acceptable to use in the temple for the selling and the buying of sacrificial animals. It is a necessary exchange because many a worshipper travels too far to bring their own beasts. But the money changers could abuse their business.

Jesus enters and is incensed by what he sees. He grabs the edges of their counting tables, spills the money all over the floor, and upends the tables themselves, then storms at the money changers, saying, "The Lord God said, 'My house is a house of prayer.' But you have made it 'a den of thieves'!" (Isaiah 56:7).

Frenzied, now, the leaders of the people grind their teeth. Even children sing, "Hosanna to the Son of David!" *Children!* With the lie on their lips! Oh, the leaders *will* slaughter him!

Before Jesus leaves the temple, his compassion grows strong. He heals Jews who are blind or lame or diseased. Once more the Son of God and Satan battle each other for the possession of the entire universe!

PRAYER

> Mine eyes have seen the glory
> Of the coming Lord.
> He is trampling out the vintage
> Where the grapes of wrath are stored.
> He has loosed the fateful lightning
> Of his terrible swift sword—
> His truth is marching on. Amen.
>
> —"BATTLE HYMN OF THE REPUBLIC"

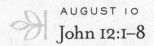

AUGUST 10

John 12:1–8

Jesus returns to Mary and Martha's house. The dinner Martha prepares for him is a meal of farewell (though only Jesus knows this). Neither can Mary know the significance of her extravagant act.

Jesus is stretched out from the low table, his left shoulder on a cushion, his legs extended behind him.

Mary kneels and anoints her Lord's feet with a whole pint of spikenard, a very expensive perfume because it has been brought all the way from the East. That she wipes his feet with her hair is a most intimate gesture between a man and a woman.

Mary is a model of faith; Judas of faithlessness. When the house fills with the fragrance, Judas objects: "She could, you know, have sold it and given the money to the poor." He's probably not thinking about the poor but about the money-purse which he keeps for the rest of the disciples.

Jesus gives the deeper meaning to Mary's anointment. His hour has come. Mary's act bespeaks of his burial, when women will come to his tomb to anoint his body. He turns to Judas, scolding, "You will always find poor in the land. Maybe you'll serve them. Whether you do or you don't, you will not always have *me*."

Consider the reason why.

PRAYER

I have you, Lord, because you first found me. I love you, Lord, because you first loved me. I can't anoint you as Mary did. But you have anointed my head with oil, and I will feast at your table from this time forth and forevermore. Amen.

AUGUST 11
Matthew 23:37–39

Jesus has left Bethany for Jerusalem and is soon to depart the world altogether.

I imagine that he's sitting with his disciples on the Mount of Olives, gazing across the Kidron Valley and grieving for the City of David.

A lamentation: "Jerusalem, Jerusalem, you have killed the prophets [Lamentations 2:20] and stoned those who were sent to you. [See both Ezekiel 16:40 and Matthew 21:37–40.] Now what will you do?"

He isn't scolding Jerusalem. Jesus is like the mother who is sad for her delinquent child. And like a mother hen, he has tried to gather his scattered flock and keep it under the wings of his love, "but you wouldn't have it. Look around you. Your house, your temple, has been forsaken."

Jesus has a deep regard for the people of Jerusalem. He hopes they will have turned to him by the time he comes again in glory and that they are able to say, "Blessed is he who comes in the name of the Lord" (Psalm 118:26).

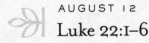

AUGUST 12
Luke 22:1–6

The Feast of the Passover remembers the past. It keeps alive the memory of Israel's exodus out of Egypt.

Luke says that Judas does not assert his own will to betray Jesus but that Satan has entered into him. Judas did not, however, resist. This is an important distinction. He doesn't *have* to be lost. Satan leads Judas to the chief priests, those who oversee the activities in the temple, and to the temple police, whose job it is to enforce obedience. Perhaps Judas will later justify his act as something he has a very good reason to do.

Imagine how Judas's offer thrills the chief priests. Finally they've found the way to capture Jesus when there are no crowds around. *Judas* is their way. They give him money to seal the deal.

Was Judas's act motivated and empowered by the forces of Evil One? Don't we sometimes fear that we too are pawns in some cosmic chess game—not making our own moves but *being* moved by a force greater than ourselves? Do we then give up the game and let happen what will happen? Turn to Jesus. Let him be your Mover. He will win the game.

PRAYER

Jesus, please walk with me. Even from here to eternity, walk with me. Amen.

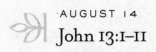

Matthew 26:26–30

While Jesus is eating the Passover meal with his disciples, he speaks and acts out a curious and wonderful thing.

During the meal, bread is broken and cups of wine are served four times between its beginning and its end. Jesus breaks the bread and blesses it, as do all the heads of households, before everyone else begins to eat. But while Jesus distributes the pieces to his disciples, he astonishes them by saying what has never been said before, "Take. Eat. This is my body." Peter almost chokes on the bread. His Lord's *body*? How—?

Next Jesus takes the cup of wine, blesses the cup, raises his eyes in thanksgiving, then passes it around, saying, "This is my blood [*blood?*] of the new covenant [New Testament], poured out for the forgiveness of the sins of many people." Saint Paul adds, "Do this in remembrance of me" (1 Corinthians 11:23–26). Thus, Jesus is establishing a new ritual for his church, ever to remember that Jesus will be with them "until I drink it with you in my Father's kingdom." The Passover meal remembers the exodus. The Lord's Last Supper, eaten *at* Passover, remembers Christ's death and resurrection on behalf of the world.

Even so do we eat the bread of his body and drink the wine of his blood—his salvation—every time we receive and celebrate the feast to come.

PRAYER

> Let us break bread together on our knees.
> Let us drink wine together on our knees. Amen.
>
> —"LET US BREAK BREAD TOGETHER"

AUGUST 14

John 13:1–11

When I was fourteen years old and living in a dormitory, homesick and desperately lonely, I telephoned my father at home and poured out my heart. He said, "Read John. John, the gospel of love." I did and came upon the words, "Having loved his own, he loved them to the end" (John 13:1). The passage made me, a young boy, weep.

Once more Satan initiates Judas's betrayal.

The disciples lie with their left sides on the bolster that surrounds three tables shaped like a *U*. Jesus stands up and performs the role of a servant or a household slave (see 1 Samuel 25:41). He removes his robe and takes up a towel, reminding us of Mary who dried Jesus's feet with her hair. He kneels behind the disciples and begins, one by one, to wash their feet—an act very like a baptism. Last of all he comes to Peter. Peter says, "Don't do that!" What? His exalted Lord should humiliate himself like this?

But Jesus says to Peter, "You still don't understand, do you?"—that to be washed by Jesus is to share in his life. Peter thinks that the washing is a cleansing by water and begs to be cleansed from top to toe: "Not just my feet. My hands and my head too."

Jesus says to his disciples, "You are all clean, but not all of you." He knows what Judas is about to do. But it's noteworthy that Jesus includes Judas too in the foot washing.

PRAYER

Who can stand in your holy place, my Lord? Those who have clean hands and pure hearts. But you've washed me through and through and made me a sharer in your life. Here I am, Lord, sharing both in the infamy of your cross and in your resurrected life. I weep and then I laugh. Amen.

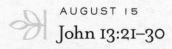

AUGUST 15
John 13:21–30

Jesus is angry at Satan, once more to battle the Prince of Darkness.

The disciple whom Jesus loves reclines by his right side, a position of honor. He lays his head on Jesus's breast and looks up at him. Jesus says, "One of you is going to betray me"—an awful prediction. The beloved disciple asks, "Who, Lord?" Peter says, "Not me, right?" Jesus answers, "I will dip a piece of bread in the sauce and give it to that one"—and gives it to Judas Iscariot, who may yet be brought back into the fold, for he too has shared in this Last Supper.

Jesus now commands both Satan and Judas, "Do what you are about to do. What you're going to do, do it quickly."

Judas leaves the light that is Jesus and goes out into the darkness. Long ago Jesus said, "People love darkness more than the light" (John 3:19). Darkness is a separation from the Lord. To choose darkness is to shut one's mind to the life and the light.

PRAYER

You, Lord, have lit the wick of my lantern. You, Lord, break through my darkness and cancel the night (Psalm 18:28). Always walk before me, my bright and shining star. Amen.

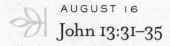

AUGUST 16
John 13:31–35

Judas is gone. To the rest of his disciples, Jesus says, "Now is the time of my glorification, and the Father will be glorified in me." Artists have depicted Christ's glory as a halo around his head. But the root of the Greek word for *glory* can mean "reputation." Soon Christ's rank and his splendor will be known throughout the world.

The new commandment, to love one another, in Latin is *novum mandatum. Novum,* "new" and *mandatum,* "mandate." *Maundy* is a shortened form of *mandatum,* which is where we get the name Maundy Thursday.

What Jesus now says to his disciples he says to the whole Christian church: "Love one another." At this point his commandment to love does not mean love your enemies. It's in Matthew that we hear those words (Matthew 5:43–48), but not in John. Nor does it yet mean to love the whole world. Jesus is speaking about the fellowship of his new family: "Love as I have loved you." How, then, should they love? By washing one another's feet as Jesus washed theirs, by laying down their lives as Jesus lays down his. (This is symbolized by the taking off and the laying down of his robe [John 13:4].)

It is by such loving behavior that the world might recognize to whom the disciples belong, might see the acts of Jesus in their acts.

Always and always, what Jesus says to the disciples, he says to *us*, who are here today.

PRAYER
Your church, Jesus, and the people in your churches are too often divided. Denominations from denominations. Congregations from congregations. People from people. If we lack love, how can the world know you? By the powerful love with which you love us, lead us to love one another. Amen.

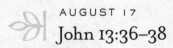

AUGUST 17
John 13:36–38

Good old dumb Peter. He wanted to be fully washed. Now he asks, "Lord, where are you going?"

Well, Jesus is going the way of the cross, and on the cross to die. "You can't follow me now," he says.

Peter says, "Why not?"

Jesus says, "But you will follow me in the future." For now Peter boasts, "No! I'll follow you right now, even if I have to die!" Does Jesus look on Peter with sadness? Or with rebuke? "Peter, Peter, before the rooster crows the morning in, far from dying, you will deny knowing me three times."

Look up John 21:18–19, where Jesus describes the death that Peter will die and where he finally says to Peter, "Follow me."

Mornings—morning after morning—Christians could wake to their persistent iniquities. But neither the curtain of darkness nor the morning wakes us to confession and repentance and a plea for salvation. We go on with our lives thoughtlessly.

PRAYER
Jesus, shout me awake. Make my heart restless until I find my rest in you. Amen.

John 17:20–23

Jesus and his disciples have left the room of their Passover supper and gone out into the dark night of his destruction. As they walk to the Mount of Olives, Jesus prays for his own, those who believe in him now and those who *will* believe by the witness of the faithful. Prays that they all—and we all—may be made one. Prays that the unity he has with the Father will become the unity of every generation until he comes again in glory.

"That they be *completely* one." To know Jesus is to know the Father. *Their* unity is the primal mystery of divine love. Nevertheless, Jesus prays that *that* love should be the mirror of our love. But more than a mirror, it will be what we *experience* of the Father/Son relationship. There can be no unity between you and me without the "we" of the Son of God with God the Father.

PRAYER

A church divided against itself cannot stand. We stumble and break our toes against the rocks of our transgressions, and we fall (as Adam fell). As you took Peter's hand and saved him from drowning, take our hands and pull us out of the swamp we made for ourselves. Take me to you that I, like the disciple whom you loved, might lay my head on your bosom too. Amen.

PART 5

The LONG WALK to the CROSS

Matthew 26:36–46

It's long past midnight when Jesus and his disciples arrive at Gethsemane tired after a long day. Jesus walks with his three privileged disciples into a grove of olive trees with gnarled roots. In this hour Jesus is altogether like us, a human being. He can and he does tremble with anxiety. To Peter and James and John: "Stay here. Sit, watch with me."

Now he moves a little farther away and falls on his face, agonized. "Father, this cup of suffering is too much for me. Remove it." The breath through his nostrils puffs up a little dust. Then he says, "But my will is less than yours." (Our Father, your will be done, on earth as it is in heaven.) Jesus stands and returns to the disciples. They who should have been watching have fallen asleep. "Peter," he says while Peter snores, "you would die with me? You can't even stay awake for me. Pray that you don't enter into temptation." (Lead us not into temptation, but deliver us from evil.)

Once more Jesus falls on his face. His fingers wind though the gnarled roots of the olive tree. "Father, I can't. I can't. . . . But if I have to drink it, your will be done."

He goes slowly back to the disciples. They are leaning against each other, fast asleep.

For the third time Jesus returns to the olive tree and for the third time prays what he prayed before. It is written that his sweat fell from his forehead like great drops of blood (Luke 22:44). Jesus has given himself completely over to his humanity—even as he has given himself over to the stern will of God.

Jesus says to the disciples, "Wake up. See? My betrayer is already halfway up the mount."

PRAYER

But thine is the kingdom and the power and the glory. Amen.

John 18:1–13

In the garden Jesus was flesh and blood. Now he reveals his divinity.

Torches snake up the side of the Mount of Olives—Judas, leading the temple police and a detachment of Roman soldiers with swords and clubs. In the other three gospels, Judas identifies his Lord with a kiss. But in John, Jesus knows why they've come. He stands up straight and says, "Who are you looking for?" They answer, "Jesus, the man raised in Nazareth." Jesus answers, "I AM," and the force of his declaration knocks the strong men to the ground. They get up. Jesus asks the same question. They answer as they did, and his "I AM" blows them off their feet again. Of course, they represent those who live in and love the darkness.

The reason for Judas's betrayal may be that he's a Zealot and thinks that Jesus is taking too long to start his rebellion. Therefore, he's put Jesus in a situation that will force him to release his power and to go into action. But Jesus's only act is pitifully mild. He asks the police to let his disciples go away.

Then Judas thinks that Peter knows what to do. The bluff disciple yanks out a dagger and slices off the ear of a man named Malchus. But Judas is grievously disappointed, for Jesus rejects weapons and chooses (as he told his disciples three times) death.

Now the cup of suffering which Jesus begged his Father to take away becomes a chalice of blood. He does not oppose his arrest. He accepts it willingly. They bind his arms and carry him into Jerusalem to be tried in the court of the high priest.

PRAYER

>Jesus, I will ponder now on your holy passion.
>Let your Spirit me endow with inward meditation.
>Grant that I in love and faith
>>May the image cherish
>Of your suffering, pain and death
>>That I may not perish. Amen.

>—"JESUS, I WILL PONDER NOW"

AUGUST 21.
Matthew 26:57–68

The high priest lives in an elaborate palace with two stories and many rooms. Caiaphas sits as judge behind an elaborately carved table. Jesus has been arraigned in front of the high priest. Scribes (lawyers) and rulers of the Sanhedrin have been rousted out of their beds. Witnesses are deposed. Caiaphas asks them to testify, and they do, but they contradict each other, and Caiaphas dismisses them as brainless fools. Finally, two men step forward. "This Nazarene claims that if the stones of the temple were destroyed, he could build it up again in three days. Who could do such a thing? Only the Messiah. Jesus is an imposter!"

Caiaphas pretends to be a just judge. "Speak," he says to Jesus. "You have the right to answer these charges." But Jesus, calm and dignified, holds his peace.

"Give glory to God," he says. "*Are* you the Messiah?" Now Jesus does speak, though his answer is ambiguous: "You say so." Caiaphas takes that answer for a yes, jumps up, and cries, "Blasphemy!" He tears his clothes, not because of sorrow but because of an angry indignation. By the tearing of his robe, Caiaphas has broken the law of Moses which forbade a priest to do so on pain of death (Leviticus 10:6). Caiaphas rounds on the jury. "How do you find him?" "Guilty!" they thunder. "*Guilty!* Execute him!"

A spiteful jury: some of them spew spit into Jesus's face. Others hit him with their fists as it was prophesied by Isaiah (50:6): "I gave my back to those who struck me." They tie a rag over Jesus's eyes. "You think you're a prophet?" Someone slaps him. "Tell us who slapped you!"

PRAYER

"If anyone strikes you on the right cheek [a backhanded blow], give him your left." We've heard what you taught. We've heard what you expect of us and have tried to figure out how to explain away your real meaning because we thought it an impossible commandment. But here you are, modeling the possibilities of faith. O Jesus, grant us such a faith. Amen.

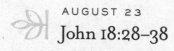

Luke 22:54–62

Peter follows Jesus into the high priest's courtyard. Because the predawn air is chilly, he joins several servants warming themselves before a small fire. The flames flicker on their faces and cast shadows on the ground.

A servant girl eyes Peter, thinking she's seen him before. She whispers to the man beside her, "You know? I'm pretty sure I saw that fellow walking with his teacher." Peter overhears the girl and says, "No. You're mistaken."

Then the man scrutinizes him. "Right you are," he says. Then to Peter, "She's right. You *are* one of Jesus's disciples." But Peter, afraid for his life, says, "You've got it wrong. It couldn't have been me."

Another servant pricks up his ears and says, "You're a Galilean. I can tell by your accent." Peter backs from the fire into the shadows. "In the name of God," he swears, "I have never even *seen* the man!"

Just then Jesus comes out of the palace, bound and flanked by two guards. He pauses to gaze at Peter with very sad eyes. The rooster crows, and Peter is so stricken by guilt that he fairly runs out of the courtyard. He goes into a dark alley and crouches down and sobs. He sobs for the evil he's done to his Lord.

PRAYER

Lord, I know my transgressions. My sin is ever before me. I have sinned against you. I know that by the sorrow in your eyes. Purge me, please, and I will not be guilty when I stand before the universal Judge, your Father and my God. Amen.

John 18:28–38

The morning sun sits like a blister on the eastern horizon, causing the clouds to burn fire-red. The Jewish authorities (not the Jews themselves) bring Jesus to the pavement in front of Pontius Pilate's grand palace and demand that the governor show himself. "Our law forbids us to enter the house of an unclean gentile." Pilate fears an insurrection. Rome would demote him. So he comes out and sits on his judgment bench.

"What do you want?" "This man is a criminal." "Against the empire?" "Against our laws." "Then," says Pilate, "judge him yourselves." The priests and the Pharisees say, "We have. We've sentenced him to death." "Right," says Pilate. "You have the stones to carry out the sentence." They answer, "We don't have the right to put a man to death." Pilate says, "I'll interrogate the man myself," then takes Jesus into his palace.

"Are you the king of the Jews?" Jesus answers a question with a question: "Do you ask this of your own, or did someone tell you to ask it?" Pilate lifts his lip in a sneer. "You think I'm a Jew? *Your* people are handing you over to me. Answer my question!" Jesus looks steadfastly at the governor and says, "My kingdom is not of this world. If it were, my followers would be soldiers, fighting to save. As it is, my kingdom comes from above." The Roman governor's intent is political. "Then you *are* a king." Jesus says, "That's your opinion. I've come to testify to the truth" (the way and the truth and the life).

Pontius Pilate stands up. "Yeah, right," he says. "What is the truth?" The better question would have been: "*Who* is the truth?"

PRAYER

Christ, I have often found my truth in the observable realities of the world. My reality has been my spouse. That's been enough to know. Or my bank account or the rules of the road. Let your Spirit persuade me that you are my Truth and that your love and all your promises are the truths that I can trust. Amen.

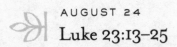

AUGUST 24

Luke 23:13–25

By now a multitude of Jews crowd the pavement. The chief priests and the elders have been moving among them, convincing them that Jesus will bring whole Roman legions down on their heads! "This man must die, one life to save our lives."

When Pilate comes out and takes his judgment seat, with Jesus standing beside him, he announces his verdict: "Not guilty."

The people raise a roaring, "Away with him!"

Pilate remembers the custom that one prisoner could be exchanged for another. He calls for the most brutal murderer in his prison. Surely the people will choose Jesus (the Son of *the* Father) over Barabbas (whose name means "son of *a* father"). But they shout, "Give us Barabbas!" And of Jesus, they cry, "Crucify him! *Crucify* him!"

Pontius Pilate is beginning to give in. "I will have him flogged!"—not with whips but with whips containing steel hooks—"And that should satisfy you."

Nothing can satisfy the hysterical mob. "Kill him! *Crucify* him!"

Pontius Pilate fears a full rebellion. He turns Jesus over to the people, saying, "Do with the man whatever you want to do."

PRAYER

You were the Lamb who was led uncomplaining to your slaughter. You were the Lamb who sacrificed himself to save sinners. You are the Love that holds me close beside you. You are my Jesus. Amen.

AUGUST 25
John 19:16–30

The cross that Jesus carries is actually the crossbeam with a hole drilled into the back of it. The hole will fit into a stout peg in the upright beam. But it is a heavy burden nonetheless.

It's about nine in the morning. Jesus has spent a full day and a night without rest—captured, bound, enduring the high priest's rump court and Pontius Pilate's sardonic questioning and the hateful cries by the same people who welcomed him to Jerusalem with cries of "Hosanna!" Jesus is dead tired.

The Roman soldiers lay him on his back on the crossbeam. They stretch out his arms and drive spikes through the bones that can hold his body up, then heave up the beam with the body of our Lord hanging from it. The hole drops over the peg. The drop jerks Jesus's frame painfully. This morning's schedule calls for three executions. Two other men are crucified, one to his left, one to his right.

Pilate gets in one last dig, posting above Jesus a sign that reads, "Jesus of Nazareth, king of the Jews"—and that in three languages of the day so that *everyone* could read it. Pilate's dig finds a nerve. "Change that!" the chief priests demand. "Say that he *said* he was the king of the Jews." Pilate smiles and says, "No."

A cross doesn't stand too high off the ground. Jesus is able to look almost directly at his beloved disciple and at his broken-hearted mother. (Long ago the old man Simeon said to Mary, "A sword will pierce your heart.")

Now the Lord gives his spiritual family a mother and a brother. To his mother he says, "In place of me, this is your son." And to the disciple whom he loves, he says, "Take care of her. She is your mother."

PRAYER

I could not be there, but your cruel experiences wound me. They break my heart as though I were there. Oh, my Lord. Oh, my Lord. I love you so much. Amen.

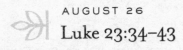

AUGUST 26
Luke 23:34–43

"Father, forgive them. They don't know what they're doing"—don't know whom they're killing. These are Jesus's first words from the cross—a prayer for mercy.

A priest pauses and leers. "Well, look at you now! You said you saved others, right? Prove it! Save *yourself*!"

The criminal hanging on Jesus's left manages to turn his head and lifts his lip in a taunt. His teeth are as black as cinders. "Saved others? Save yourself and me too." The man's jeer is tantamount to blasphemy.

Jesus holds his peace.

The criminal hanging on Jesus's right leans his head forward to look at the other. "Why are you talking like that? Don't you fear the day of God's terrible judgment? We're dying here because we deserve to die. But this man is innocent." He allows his head to fall back against the rough wooden beam, then says, "Jesus, remember me when you come into your kingdom."

The Lord utters a second word of mercy and gives the criminal more than he asked for. "Today [immediately at your death] you will be with me in paradise"—where grows the Tree of Life.

PRAYER

Jesus, remember me when you come into your kingdom. Amen.

AUGUST 27

Luke 23:44–46 and John 19:28–30

When Jesus was a little boy, his mother may have prayed a nighttime prayer with him. It came from Psalm 31:5: "Into your hands, O Lord, we commit our spirits." As Jesus is about to pull the covers of death over himself, he becomes a child again, the Son of his Father, and prays the same words, "Father, into your hands I commend my spirit."

The hour of Jesus's mission on earth is almost done.

This is how a crucified man dies: When his strength fails and when he can no longer hold himself up by his arms, he slumps, his ribs contract, and the breath is forced out of his lungs. He strives to pull himself up again, but soon he sags completely and suffocates to death. In the meantime, the loss of blood creates a terrible thirst.

Jesus says, "I'm thirsty." Someone offers him sour wine, which is likelier to increase his thirst than to stanch it. Yet Jesus drinks and then he murmurs, "It is finished." *All* is finished, his life and the purpose for which he came: salvation for those who believe in him.

His lungs close, and he breathes his last.

PRAYER

O my Lord! How perfect is your love. All, all is finished now. You died the death for us, an atoning sacrifice. Amen.

PART 6

RESURRECTION

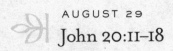

Mark 16:1–8

In those days it was the women and not the men who attended to life's beginnings and its ending. The women bore the children. They washed and swaddled and nursed them. And it was the women, not the men, who saw to the dead.

At dawn on Sunday morning, Mary Magdalene and another Mary and Salome are hurrying to the tomb with spices to anoint Jesus's corpse in order to cover the scent of corruption.

On their way they wonder if they can find a strong man to roll the stone away—but then are astonished. The stone has *already* been rolled away, and the tomb is open. But instead of Jesus's body, there sits a young man whose robe is a blinding white, and the women are terrified. As angels do, this one says, "Don't be afraid. He isn't here. He has arisen from the dead. Go, tell his disciples, and Peter especially, that Jesus is going to Galilee ahead of them, even as he promised" (Mark 14:28).

But the bright man's "don't be afraid" doesn't calm their quaking fear. They can't know that they've just witnessed the explosive glory of the Lord! The women are too frightened to tell anyone at all.

We Christians must never reduce our Easter celebrations to a pretty holiday. Though we look back on the resurrection, we should try to be like the disciples and every Easter be astonished that the Lord lives. Then let our joy and our prayers and our hymns be spontaneous!

PRAYER
People, clap your hands! Shout to God with loud songs of joy, and sing, "Amen!"

AUGUST 29

John 20:11–18

Oh, Mary. Oh, dear Mary, weeping because you have been abandoned. When you stoop to look into the tomb, you see two angels sitting on your Lord's stone platform. They ask why you're crying, and you say, "They've taken my Lord away, and I don't know where to find him." The life of *your* life has been stolen from his tomb, and your heart has died within you. You are like a widow wandering in a wilderness.

His tomb is in the garden outside Jerusalem. Now, through the blur of your tears, you see a man walking toward you. He must be the gardener. You ask, "Where did you take him?" And then you give yourself an impossible task. You tell the man that if he knows where Jesus lies, you will carry his body by yourself.

The man speaks. He says one word. He says your name. He says, "Mary." You know that voice, and all at once your heart is revived. "O my Master!"

Jesus says, "Don't hold on to me now. Don't try to keep me from ascending to my Father."

Mary, how does it feel? How does it feel?—the joy as you rush to the room where the disciples are hiding? I hear your knocking on the door. I hear your cry of good news. And your laughter when you cry out, "I have seen the Lord!" How does such a riotous joy make you feel?

PRAYER

> Joyful, joyful, we adore thee,
> God of glory, Lord of love!
> Hearts unfold like flowers before thee,
> Praising thee, our sun above. Amen.
>
> —"JOYFUL, JOYFUL, WE ADORE THEE"

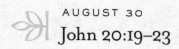

AUGUST 30

John 20:19–23

On that same Sunday, the disciples—both men and women—have locked the door of the room where they're hiding. They are afraid that those who killed Jesus will come for them too.

Jesus appears in the room. When Jesus came walking on the water, they feared it was a ghost until Jesus identified himself with the godly name I AM. Here in John, Jesus says, "Peace be with you," and they're frightened once again. Jesus shows them the scars on his hands and his side and repeats, "Peace be with you"—my peace (John 14:27). And the disciples are filled with joy. Jesus has fulfilled his promise of peace. Now he fulfils his promise of joy (John 16:20).

How long have the disciples misunderstood Christ's words and his purpose on earth? Finally, at his appearance their minds are opened to a true understanding.

Jesus breathes on them—breathes into them a new life. ("I am the way and the truth and the life.") Remember that the Creator breathed into a lump of clay, and it came to life? The word *breath* also means "spirit." Jesus is fulfilling a third promise: to give his disciples the Holy Spirit by breathing on them (John 14:17). By that same Holy Spirit, they will both forgive sins or leave them unforgiven.

Jesus commissioned his disciples to open the eyes of the blind. Even so does he commission us to open eyes blind to the gospel. Those who believe will be on the route to heaven. But those who choose their blindness will remain sightless.

PRAYER

> Holy Spirit, light divine,
> Dawn upon this soul of mine. Amen.

—"HOLY SPIRIT, LIGHT DIVINE"

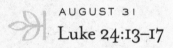

AUGUST 31
Luke 24:13–17

If possible, we should experience our Easters as the disciples experienced theirs.

Their Lord died, and they were more than sad, more than merely mourning. They were devastated. At the death of Jesus, pieces of them had died too. "But we hoped he was the one to redeem Israel." From that day forward, they would live as if they had no life at all.

Now, then, imagine their surprise, their astonishment, and their outright *joy* when Jesus rose and returned to them! How could such a thing be? It should never have happened!

The disciples experienced the first Easter as we do not. They were looking forward. We look backward. Our Easters don't astonish us.

When a father or a mother reads a nighttime book to their child, that child actually lives in the story. When we sit in a theater, watching a movie, we enter *its* time and place, and even its heroes as if we were in them, as if we *were* them. This is how we ought to enter the disciples' skins and experience what they experienced, or how else can our Easters become our first Easters?

PRAYER

Lord, I wasn't there at your crucifixion or at your resurrection. But I want, this Easter, to shout, "Glory! Glory! Glory!" Amen.

SEPTEMBER 1
Luke 24:17–28

Cleopas and a companion (his wife?) are walking from Jerusalem to Emmaus, discussing sad things, when a man joins them and asks, "What's this? What are you talking about?" The two travelers stop, their heads hanging low. "You must be the only one who doesn't know what happened in Jerusalem." The man says, "Tell me about it." And they do.

Their Lord was arrested and handed over to the chief priest and condemned to death. He was dragged out of the city and killed on the cross. And this is why they are sad: "We hoped that he would set Israel free."

The man says, "Let's keep walking." The day is setting. Their shadows stretch before them. The two disciples think that the man beside them is a rabbi, because he uses Moses and the prophets to teach them that the Messiah had to die in order to reveal his glory.

The evening is growing dark when Cleopas says, "Here we are. This is our house."

The man is ready to continue walking, but Cleopas urges him to stay and eat with them. "A kind offer," says the man. "I accept." While the three are eating, the visitor picks up a small loaf of bread. He blesses it and breaks it and gives a piece to each of them. Didn't they remember what Jesus did with bread when he fed the five thousand? Were they there to hear what he said and to see what he did at his Last Supper? Probably not.

In the instant after giving Cleopas and his wife the bread, Jesus vanishes from their sight. "I know," breathes the woman. "Now I know why my heart burned. It was the Lord!"

PRAYER

Lord, I come to your table with bated breath, for you are in the food. You are the food. My sight can't see you, but my faith can. Amen.

SEPTEMBER 2

John 20:24–29

In the past, Thomas said to the disciples, "Let's go with Jesus to Jerusalem"—and maybe to their deaths. Now he hears them say with joy, "We have seen the Lord!"—exactly what Mary Magdalene said to them, words they did not at first believe. Now Thomas doesn't believe what they tell him. He wants empirical proof. He reminds us of what Jesus said to the royal official: "Unless you see signs and wonders, you will not believe" (John 4:48).

Jesus doesn't reappear in the room for a full week. When he *does* reappear, it's not because he pities Thomas. Rather, he's come to demonstrate the true cause of faith. "Peace be with you," he says again. The disciples have already enjoyed that peace. Now it's offered to Thomas too.

I think it's Christ's mercy that grants Thomas his empirical proof. "Put your finger in my hands and your hand in my side."

All at once Thomas's unbelief becomes belief because this is the Lord. He falls down and confesses his faith. "My Lord," he says. But that's not enough to say. He says, "And my God!"

"In the beginning was the Word, and the Word was with God, and the Word *was* God!" (John 1:1). "He came to his own, but his own did not accept him. But to those who received him, who believed in him" (John 1:11–12) . . . This is Thomas, surely.

Our generation can't see what the disciples saw, but we can come to faith by hearing. "Faith comes from what is heard, and what is heard comes through the word of Christ" (Romans 10:17).

PRAYER

O Lord, open our ears to your gospel and our hearts to your "peace be with you." Amen.

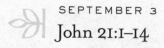
SEPTEMBER 3
John 21:1–14

Jesus told his disciples, including Peter, that he was going before them to Galilee, and he has.

If a seasoned fisherman catches nothing after a night's fishing, he pulls in his net and rows for shore. Even so at daybreak do the seven disciples start to haul in their nets.

A voice calls to them across the water. "Children," he says, "I'm guessing your nets are empty. Am I right?" The disciples see a man standing on the beach. Peter growls, "Yeah, you're right."

"Tell you what," says the man. "Cast your net on the right side of the boat." Peter says, "That fellow's a fool." John says, "Why not? What have we got to lose?" So they cast the net, and in seconds it is heavy with a great shoal of fish.

John says to Peter, "That's Jesus." Peter's been fishing while wearing a loincloth. He wants to jump into the lake. But out of respect for Jesus, he throws on his tunic and *then* jumps in and swims for shore. Because the haul of fish is so heavy, the others row more slowly in.

Jesus's word *children* was a term of intimacy. An even dearer gesture of intimacy is the little fire that Jesus has kindled and the invitation to sit on the ground and eat with him. He grills some of the fish, then says, "Breakfast is ready."

This is the Lord who fed five thousand people with bread and a few fish. At that time it was a miracle. Now it's simple food eaten privately with a little family.

All down the centuries church scholars have tried to make sense of that number 153. Saint Augustine used mathematics to show that it could represent the Trinity, or else that it represented the complete fullness of all the Christians in the church of Jesus Christ.

PRAYER

The small bird sings, What cheer! What cheer! And she sings, Come here, my dear! Come right here. I take nature's song to be like your song, my dear Lord Jesus, and with cheer I do come to you. Amen.

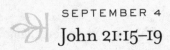

SEPTEMBER 4

John 21:15–19

After breakfast, Jesus says, "Simon, son of John, do you love me more than these?" Without a thought Peter answers, "Yes!" And Jesus says, "Feed my lambs." But Peter's yes isn't enough. Jesus asks the same question a second time, and Peter repeats his assertion with an emphatic, "I do! I do." The Good Shepherd says, "Tend my sheep." Jesus asks his question for the third time, "Do you love me?" Peter remembers his three denials and feels like weeping all over again. It is for this very reason that Jesus has asked three times: so that it connects his sin to what is about to become forgiveness.

It's important to know that Jesus addressed Peter with his full name, Simon, son of John, because he has already addressed Lazarus and Mary by their names, and they came alive. Here, too, Peter is coming to life, to his intimate relationship with his Lord. Earlier Jesus predicted that Peter would die, to which the disciple boasted, "I'll go with you even unto death."

"When you were young, Peter, you used to tie the cincture around your robe and used to go wherever you wanted. But when you are old, someone else will tie the cincture, and someone else will lead you where you don't choose to go. You will stretch out your arms to be crucified."

When Jesus said, "Tend my sheep," he was commissioning the disciple to be the shepherd in place of the Good Shepherd.

The Lord's first words to Peter were, "Follow me." Now that Peter has been prepared to teach and preach and even to die, Jesus says again, "Follow me."

PRAYER

You have called us, Lord, to serve the flocks of your worldwide church. Then let your commission to "follow me" also invest us with the faith and the strength to follow you indeed. Amen.

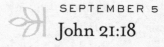
SEPTEMBER 5
John 21:18

A brief explanation of martyrdom.

Often people think that martyrs are those who suffer violent deaths for the sake of the gospel. But the word *martyr* means "witness." It doesn't matter how they die, or whether they die at all. They witness to the life, the death, and the resurrection of Jesus Christ. *That's* what they do.

In his old age, the father of my sister-in-law lay paralyzed and dying in the Philippines. Four times Liza flew half the world round to visit him. The first time she entered his bedroom, he could express his love only by the movement of his eyes. Liza expressed *her* love by crawling in bed beside him.

At her second visitation Liza learned that his skin had ruptured with bedsores. When a nurse came to bandage her father, Liza couldn't watch. She could not look at the running puss and left the room. But the third time she went to her father, Liza's love persuaded her to remove the bandages herself. His bedsores had eaten through his flesh, down to the bones.

Back home Liza described the grisly things she had seen. "Why," she asked me, "is God waiting so long before my father dies and goes home to heaven?" The words I next said were not mine. They were words of the Holy Spirit. "Because he's witnessing, even if you're the only one who sees it."

Her last visit was to bury her father.

When I come to die, Lord, whether in pain or in peace, let my dying testify to your salvation. You are mine and I am yours, and the banner over us is love. Amen.

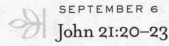

John 21:20–23

Peter points to the disciple whom Jesus loves and says, "What about him?" Peter will die as a martyr. What about John? Will John live to see Christ's second coming? Jesus says, "What is that to you if he remains to my return?" *Remain:* to stay with Jesus, to abide with him, to live with him. "I said it once," Jesus says. "I'll say again: 'Follow me.'"

Peter will follow Jesus by dying a martyr's death. John will follow by remaining as a witness to the gospel because Jesus will do what he wills to do.

After that, it is rumored that John will never die. Later it would become a tradition in the church that Mary, its mother, and John, its brother, lived long lives together in Ephesus.

Friends, keep the faith. Remain in the house of the Holy Spirit. Continue to preach and to model Christ as long as you live and move and breathe.

PRAYER

Praise the Lord! Praise the Lord, O my soul! I will praise you, my Lord, as long as I live, and sing your praises (Psalm 146:1–2). O my God, reign as the king of all creation. Reign all down the generations. Reign forever! Amen.

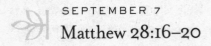

Matthew 28:16–20

Which is the mountain where Jesus meets his disciples? That of his "Sermon on the Mount"? The mount of his transfiguration? Matthew doesn't identify this mount, except to say that Jesus has chosen it. Then let it be a Mount of Spirituality.

False preachers declare that they come with the authority of Jesus's name. But now Jesus bestows on his disciples the true fullness of his authority.

"Teach as I have taught," which is to say, "Keep on healing as I have healed, and preaching about me, for I *am* the gospel." (How beautiful are the feet of those who bring good news [Romans 10:15].) "Baptize as I have baptized—with the Holy Spirit and fire," which is as much as to say, "Let the Spirit burn in the hearts of all the people on earth so that they may become my faithful disciples too." And how are they to baptize? "In the name of the Father and the Son and the Holy Spirit"—for that is the name of the Trinity!

What Jesus now says to his disciples, he says to us: "I will be with you, even unto the end of this world."

PRAYER

God the Father is with me. You, Jesus Christ, are with me. The Holy Spirit is with me. I am your disciple. I work and wash and teach by your authority and am confident that what I do will be done by you. Amen.

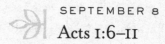

SEPTEMBER 8

Acts 1:6–11

Jesus gathers together his disciples, the men and the women. Something wonderful is about to happen. They are vibrating with anticipation. "Is it time, Lord? Is your kingdom coming now?"

What Jesus said before he says again: "No one knows the times or the seasons. Not even the Son. Only the Father knows. As for you, stay in Jerusalem until the Holy Spirit is poured out on you, then go. Witness to me in Jerusalem." Jesus widens the mission field to "Judea and Samaria." And then as wide as wide is: "To the ends of the earth."

Jesus's feet walked on water. Now his feet walk on air. In the sight of the disciples, he rises. Jesus ascends higher and higher until he vanishes into a cloud and is gone.

The disciples can't stop gaping. Perhaps their hearts will never be able to understand this mystery. But two angels appear before them (are these the same two that Mary Magdalene saw sitting in the tomb?). The angels say, "This is the time. This is the season to go into Jerusalem and to prepare to do what Jesus has appointed you to do."

PRAYER

For everything there is a season and a time for every matter under heaven (Ecclesiastes 3:1). This is our season, and this is our time. Lord Jesus, your season is always the spring, when the grass puts forth its tender shoots, and things are reborn, and we celebrate your resurrection. Amen.

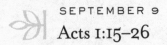

SEPTEMBER 9
Acts 1:15–26

Simon Peter wept and was forgiven. Judas Iscariot believed that his guilt could never be forgiven, and he chose suicide. Peter lived to shepherd his Lord's flock. Judas Iscariot died a most gruesome death, and his absence broke the unity of the twelve apostles.

"Lord," they had asked in the moments before he ascended, "is it now that you will restore the kingdom of Israel?"—Will, they were asking, the twelve tribes of Israel become one again? It takes twelve to make Israel whole. It must take twelve to make this band of the apostles whole, and then it will take twelve to be the gates of the new Jerusalem.

Peter puts himself in charge. He takes a stance before 120 believers and says to them, "We have to select someone to take Judas's place." As if he were an employer stating the qualifications of one he would employ, Peter says, "Someone who has traveled with Jesus from the beginning of his ministry to the end, when we saw him taken up into heaven. And someone who can witness to the resurrection and to the gospel."

Two men are selected, one named Justus and one named Matthias. The first thing the apostles do is to ask the Lord to make the hard decision: "You know the hearts of everyone." Then they cast lots; that is, each name is inscribed on a pebble. The pebbles are shaken in a jar until one falls out. It is "Matthias." This is the Lord's doing.

PRAYER

We are not twelve. Your church is a billion twelves, and your body is made whole in us. Oh, what a sound we sing in the universe. Even the galaxies hear your name! Amen.

PART 7

The
APOSTLES

Acts 2:1–13

On the day of his ascension, Jesus instructed his disciples to stay in Jerusalem until the Holy Spirit was poured out on them. That was fifty days ago.

Jerusalem is thronged with thousands upon thousands of Jews who have come from many nations to celebrate the Feast of Weeks, the ingathering of the harvest. Twelve men would have been lost among so many people—except that the sound of a windstorm (but no wind and no storm) rushes down from heaven to the house where the apostles are. Tongue-like flames suddenly appear above each one's head. As in the beginning, when the Spirit of God blasted across the waters of chaos, so now the Holy Spirit breaks into the universe, to Judea, to the city of Jerusalem, and then out of the mouths of the twelve.

And this is the sign of the Spirit's coming, that Babel is being reversed!—Babel, where God scattered the language of those who thought they could build their way to heaven. Shattered the language into many. Here in Jerusalem the apostles gather the scattered languages by speaking words that *everyone* understands!

Some people are thunderstruck. "What—what's happening?" Others snarl, "They're drunk."

A Christian should never think the Holy Spirit wants a personal relationship with him or her alone. Nor that the spiritual gifts belong to her or him alone. They are to be shared with the whole Christian community. Her singing, his scholarship, my writing, your gift of healing—these are for the upbuilding of the church. And the speaking in tongues is not for one's own ecstatic experience but for the greater good of the church (1 Corinthians 14:4–5).

PRAYER

Holy Spirit, touch my tongue that I may witness to Christ and his resurrection and that I may utter the glory of God. Amen.

Acts 2:14–24

All throughout his ministry, Jesus was building a family, a community which is now complete. His church will arise on every continent.

It is Pentecost when Christ's new church is baptized with the Holy Spirit and with fire.

Peter preaches about God's deeds of power on behalf of all the disciples.

Some cry, "Hey, man! You're *drunk*!"

"Do I slur my words? It's nine o'clock in the morning! Listen to me, and listen to the prophet!" Peter quotes Joel: "God declares that in these latter days he will pour out his Spirit on all flesh." (See Joel 2:28–32.) Peter continues by accusing many Israelites of crucifying the Lord. "But God raised him and set him free from the bonds of death."

Guilt twists their hearts. "What should we do?" "Repent." (Penitence is always followed by mercy.) "Be baptized in the name of Jesus Christ, and your sins will be forgiven." They did indeed repent and followed the apostles to the Jordan, where three thousand souls were added to the church.

Before he died, a friend of mine, a missionary among the Maasai in Africa, did on a single day baptize two thousand people. This is true.

PRAYER

Lord, have mercy on those who don't know you, people scattered to the four corners of the earth who are like sheep without a shepherd. Send them gospel messengers to gather in the lost. Amen.

Acts 2:43–47

The characteristics of the Christian community are radically different from the practices of the general society. Christians meet together as a *single* people. There can be no competition. The church would splinter if it found rank or wealth or certain gifts more important than unity, more important than holding all things in common. The wealthy share with the needy, and those who have food with those who are hungry until all are equal to all. Jesus prayed: "That they may be perfectly one" (John 17:23).

The Jewish Christians continue to worship in the temple. At home they break bread as Christ broke bread at his Last Supper. The "real" world admires these believers, unaware that the Christian's world is the real one.

Common worship, common practice, common good, and common witness—these should be what we are today. But the church is splintered. We see great gulfs between the rich and the struggling. Denominations divorce themselves from other dominations because one believes that the other teaches a false interpretation of the Bible. Even within the same congregation, one will hold a grudge against another.

PRAYER

Lord, have mercy on us. Christ, have mercy on us. Lord, have mercy on us. Amen.

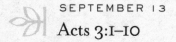

SEPTEMBER 13
Acts 3:1–10

If this beggar had, say, a clubfoot, he could walk on a crutch. But he is altogether lame and must be carried to a place outside the temple. As far as Jerusalem is concerned, his infirmity makes him unclean, and he can't enter the temple. Beggars come shortly before three o'clock midafternoon. This is the hour of prayer when devout Jews are likely to give alms.

As devout Jews themselves, Peter and John are mounting the steps to the temple. As they pass him, the crippled man taps his begging bowl. The two apostles pause. Peter makes the encounter very personal by looking directly into the man's eyes and telling him likewise to look at him. The beggar does. It's little enough to do for a few coins.

Peter says, "I don't have any money." The beggar's expectations are disappointed. Peter continues, saying, "But what I do have, I'll give you, not in your bowl but in your body." Jesus once healed a paralytic by his words alone (Matthew 9:2–8). Now Peter, by his words alone, heals the crippled beggar: "In the name of Jesus, stand up and walk." Not only does the beggar walk. He jumps and praises God! The unclean beggar has been made clean, and the outcast enters the temple.

A sign and a wonder! Of course the Jews who have come to pray are amazed. But Luke doesn't tell us whether or not they understood what "in the name of Jesus" means.

PRAYER

Jesus says to us what he said to the paralytic: "Your sins are forgiven" (Matthew 9:2), and we are received into the company of his family. Our hearts leap up for joy! Amen.

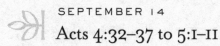

SEPTEMBER 14

Acts 4:32–37 to 5:1–11

Because Barnabas respects the practice of the Christian community, God favors him. He's a Jew who came from Cyprus to Jerusalem to be baptized. Immediately, he shares all the money he got when he sold his properties in Cyprus.

Ananias and Sapphira also share their money—but only in part. They have the freedom to keep some of it for themselves. Their sin is that they lie to Peter. Once more God and Satan have joined in the cosmic struggle for the souls of a man and a woman.

Jesus knows a person's secret thoughts. Peter can do the same. When Ananias brings to Peter a pouch full of denarii, Peter asks, "Is this the whole of what you have?" Ananias answers, "The whole of it." But Peter knows better. He says, "You have deceived not only me but the Holy Spirit too." These words are Ananias's sentence. He drops dead at Peter's feet.

Sapphira has colluded with her husband. Ignorant of his punishment, she too brings only a portion of the money. She too tells Peter that this is the whole of it, that there is nothing more. And she too drops dead like a sack of flour. Their bodies are carried away and buried.

The Christian who believes in the Holy Spirit should not deceive. Our humble generosity levels the playing field. The poor and those who are outcast become our equals, raised to the level of us all. The faithful Christian works for justice in an unjust world, and the whole community is blessed by the spirit of Jesus.

PRAYER

Humble me, my Lord. Teach me to tell the truth, even if it's a confession of my negligence and my pretending to be good. Jesus, you are the Truth. Teach me to know myself truly. Amen.

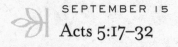

SEPTEMBER 15
Acts 5:17–32

Watch and see how the apostles' ministry duplicates the Lord's.

Peter preaches the gospel, bringing many people to the faith. They are filled with the Holy Spirit. The high priest himself is filled with jealousy. He gathers a council and appoints it to act as a jury, then demands a verdict. The council sentences the two apostles to be imprisoned, and so they are. But during the night, an angel of the Lord throws open the cell door and tells them to continue preaching the gospel in the temple.

Again, for reasons of his own, the high priest wants to confront this Peter and that John. He tells the captain of the temple police to send men to haul them out of prison. The police find the prison locked. They lift their torches. The cell is absolutely empty. They return to the high priest and their captain, and report what they saw and what they did not see. The captain is afraid that his career is finished.

One of the policemen goes to his post at the temple, then rushes back to the high priest: "The men are preaching in the temple!"

Once again the apostles are standing in the presence of the high priest while Peter tells him the story of Jesus and his death. "*You,*" Peter accuses him. "You lynched him!" Premeditated murder! The high priest is afraid. "You want to bring this man's blood down on our heads?"

Mercy can follow accusations, if it is accepted. Peter says, "But the Savior is always ready to give Israel repentance and forgiveness."

PRAYER

What is my prison? Fears that my colleagues might learn that I'm a Christian? Self-doubt? Afraid to pray in public? Hiding my candle under a bushel? I repent. I seek your forgiveness. Amen.

SEPTEMBER 16
Acts 6:8–15

The apostles perform wonders among the people in Jerusalem. Others who were converted to Christianity have received the same gift. By God's grace Stephen also performs wonders. Therefore, the highest council in Jerusalem calls him to explain himself. But they can't undermine the wisdom of Stephen's words. What they can't do aloud, they start to do in whispers. They move among the nonbelievers, persuading them that Stephen blasphemed both the law and God. The subterfuge works. Stephen is captured and brought before the council, where witnesses accuse him of teaching false words against the Messiah. Often and often the disciples of the Lord live the life and die the death that Jesus did before he rose. "This man," the witnesses testify, "this Stephen keeps teaching that *his* Messiah claimed he could destroy the temple together with the laws of Moses."

At his transfiguration Jesus shone with a white and radiant divinity. Now Stephen's face shines as bright as an angel's. Let those who have eyes to see, see.

Christians, Jesus is *our* temple, the temple that was destroyed on Golgotha and in three days built up again. We ought not to think that the doctrines of our church are the only true doctrines in Christianity. Don't put your trust in pastors, however righteous is their preaching. Don't even believe in the Bible itself. Believe in the risen Word *taught* in the Bible. Believe in Jesus.

Christ, wherever you go, I will follow your light. Moses's laws have given way to your laws. Help me to obey your commandment to love you with all my heart and my strength and my mind. Amen.

SEPTEMBER 17
Psalm 23

Stephen's martyrdom, his sojourn in the valley of death, will feel as though he were lying beside an unruffled water, and his faith will still his soul. God's love will enlighten the shadows that cover him. God will be his lantern. The Lord will go before him like a shepherd. His rod will keep Stephen on the right path. His staff will catch Stephen ever if he should fall. The Lord's two sheepdogs, one named Goodness and the other named Mercy, will protect him through the last days of his earthly life and will lead him to the house of the Lord, where he will dwell forever.

PRAYER

Jesus, you have set a table before me here below—your bread and your wine—which will become for me a feast in heaven. Amen.

SEPTEMBER 18
Acts 7:51–8:1

Jesus said, "Blessed are those who are persecuted because of righteousness, for theirs is the kingdom of heaven."

Stephen delivers a stinging indictment against the council ruled by Caiaphas: "Stiff-necked! Enemies of the Holy Spirit! Betrayers and murders!" Though the council is enraged, Stephen lifts his eyes to heaven. He sees the glory of God and is granted peace for his ending. "Look," he says, "I see the heavens opened and my Jesus clothed with the holiness and the authority of God." This is more than the council can stand.

They drag Stephen out of the city and throw him down a hill, where he lies with a luminous tranquility. A first accuser heaves up a heavy stone and drops it down on him. Stone after stone breaks his arms and his legs and his ribs. Stephen prays, "Lord Jesus, receive my spirit"—into your hands, O Lord, I commend my spirit. Stephen prays the prayer that Jesus prayed from the cross: "Father, forgive them." A final stone cracks his skull.

The early Christian church watched as its bishop Polycarp was tied to a post in a Roman amphitheater and set on fire. The fire burned his ropes, but not him. Its flames encompassed him like the billowing sail of a ship. The soldiers ran to him to bind him up again, but Polycarp promised to stay right where he was, and a Roman sword pierced him through and through.

PRAYER

Lord, let your martyrs be our models. Amen.

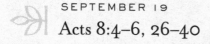

SEPTEMBER 19

Acts 8:4–6, 26–40

The high officials serving in pagan palaces are mostly eunuchs. The law of the Jews considers them unclean and forbids them to enter the temple. Therefore, this dark-skinned Ethiopian must have worshipped in an outer court. He is a seeker after God. While riding home in his chariot, he's reading a passage from the book of Isaiah (53:7–8).

This Philip is not the apostle. He's one of the seven who were chosen to serve.

What is about to happen is ordained by God.

An angel tells Philip where he must go, and the Spirit tells him what he must do.

No one in these days reads in one's mind silently. Philip hears the Ethiopian eunuch's words and asks, "Do you understand what you're reading?" "I can't," the man answers. "Not without help." Philip says, "Let me teach you." The Ethiopian invites him into his chariot. Philip reads aloud the passage from Isaiah, then the God-seeker asks, "Tell me, does the prophet talk about himself or about someone else?" Then Philip opens his mouth and says what he's been sent to say. He fills the Ethiopian's mind and his heart with the gospel of the Messiah. So powerful are Philip's words that the Ethiopian burns with desire to be a Christian. And this is how one begins. "Look," he says. "Here's water. Baptize me." Philip baptizes him, then vanishes.

This is the power of our witness and the accomplishment of our preaching the gospel: to fill the souls of those who have no faith with faith and to promise the promises of God.

PRAYER

Open my eyes, O Lord, to those whom the world, and even Christians, considers outcasts and unclean. Open my ears to their deepest yearnings, and open my mouth to proclaim your word. Amen.

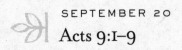

SEPTEMBER 20
Acts 9:1–9

Saul (Saul is his Aramaic name, and Paul is his Greek name)—is a young zealot fiercely devoted to the God of Israel and therefore hostile to anyone who perverts the name of his Lord.

Because Philip and others have spread the gospel even as far as Syria, Saul learns of Christians living in Damascus—followers of the "way" (and the truth and the life). Caiaphas grants him letters of introduction to the leaders of the Jews in Damascus, and Saul, intent on arresting and even murdering Christians, mounts his mule and rides more than a hundred miles from Jerusalem toward Syria's capital city.

Not far from Damascus, a blinding light—a *strobe* light—strikes Saul from the back of his mule. An imperial voice speaks from heaven, calling Saul by his name (it's *personal!*)—"Saul, Saul, why are you persecuting me?" "Sir," Saul answers, "who are you?" "I am Jesus." Jesus? Jesus is his church? And it is against him that Saul is breathing threats? Suddenly, the Saul who was strong is weak, and the man who disobeyed the Lord of the Christians now obeys, and Christ begins to commission him for the ministry. "Go into Damascus, where I'll tell you what I want you to do."

That "blinding light" has blinded Saul—a sign that it was Jesus indeed who spoke to him.

His companions aren't blind, except to the presence of the Lord. Saul does not remount his mule but is led by hand into Damascus, where, as one now devoted to Christ the Lord, he fasts for three days.

PRAYER

I came to faith by hearing your gospel, my Lord, and by searching the Scriptures. And I have obeyed your command to leave my home and "go" into big cities, to "go" to the places where I am stranger. Take me by the hand and lead me. Amen.

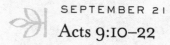

SEPTEMBER 21
Acts 9:10–22

Moses balked because he thought himself unworthy. Isaiah and Jeremiah also balked at the Lord God's command to prophesy. Now Ananias, a disciple in Damascus, balks not because he's unworthy, but because he doesn't like what the Lord commands him to do. "Ananias." "Here I am, listening" (see 1 Samuel 1:10). "Go to the house where a blind man named Saul is praying and lay your hands on him" (a sign of consecration). Ananias says, "Why? I know that fellow. He's been persecuting your people in Jerusalem, and now he's here, planning to do the same in Damascus." But the Lord says, "I have chosen him to preach my name among the gentiles."

Note: just as Jesus told his disciples to preach first in Jerusalem and then to the gentiles (Philip, to the Ethiopian eunuch), so now, through Saul, the gospel is preached to the nations abroad. Ananias obeys and finds Saul in the house of a man named Judas.

Since the Lord has chosen Saul, Ananias calls him "Brother," and when he lays his hands on him, flakes fall from Saul's eyes, and he can see. Three days sightless, as though with Jesus in the tomb, and on the third day sighted, as though raised from the dead.

Immediately, the Holy Spirit rushes into him. Saul breaks his fast, regains his strength, and is baptized. "You are mine."

Saul's tongue is loosed, and he starts to proclaim that Jesus is the Anointed One, the Son of God.

We Christians shouldn't think that conversions today must be as dramatic as Saul's was. Conversions may be as sudden as an altar call or else a slow learning by studying and hearing the gospel. In either case, we shouldn't doubt their new faith. Rather, we simply observe the changes, for their works do follow them. We welcome them into our Christian community. In love we call him "brother" or her "sister" because we are one.

PRAYER

Breathe on my heart, O Spirit of God. Open my eyes. Loose my tongue that I may speak the truth of Jesus among the nations. Amen.

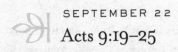

SEPTEMBER 22

Acts 9:19–25

While he's in Damascus, Saul preaches in the synagogues, saying that Jesus is the Son of God (see Psalm 2:7). The persecutor will soon become the persecuted.

Saul increases in power. The Jews who hold fast to the laws of Moses are incensed by his interpretation of Scripture. Not for the first time in Saul's career do his enemies plan to kill him.

But the Christian Jews help him to escape by night. Saul climbs into a large basket and then is lowered by ropes over the wall of Damascus. He lives to preach another day.

Ours are the ropes of the Holy Spirit. *We* escape the Devil's plan to steal our souls. We are lowered over the wall of the Evil One both by the power of the Holy Spirit and by our trust in Jesus. And what then? Then we are called to preach the gospel, to model the gospel, to *be* the gospel among our neighbors and our coworkers and the unbelieving people who live in our cities. "Have no fear, my children. I will not leave you orphaned."

Relieve me of my fears, O Lord. Grant me power to preach your Word. I have no greater purpose in my life than to walk with you. Amen.

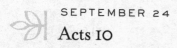

SEPTEMBER 23
Acts 12:1–5

It is said of James, the fisherman, the son of Zebedee, that he prays daily on his knees in the temple and that his prayers last so long that his knees become as leathery as a camel's. The people of Jerusalem are more and more inclining to his ministry and more and more giving themselves to Jesus.

At this time Herod Agrippa I (not the Herod who ruled when Jesus walked the earth) thinks he might lose control over the Jews in Palestine. To please them and to keep them in his fold, Herod acts harshly. His reign is marked by violence and caprice.

Herod Agrippa has James arrested, accusing him of fomenting a rebellion. And, to finalize the legalistic Jews' attachment to him, he has James beheaded.

James, then, is the first of Christ's apostles to be martyred.

PRAYER
> For all the saints who from their labors rest,
> Who thee by faith before the world confessed,
> Thy name, O Jesus, be forever blessed.
> Alleluia and amen.

—"FOR ALL THE SAINTS"

SEPTEMBER 24
Acts 10

God communicates with the early church by visions and by his voice.

Simon Peter is praying on a roof in the city of Joppa—the house belongs to a tanner—when the Lord opens his mind to a vision. A wide picnic blanket floats down from heaven, and the Lord directs him to break the law by eating the unclean creatures inside the blanket. Impossible as it seems, here are beasts without cloven hoofs and vultures that feed on dead flesh (see Leviticus 11:13–19) and reptiles that move along the ground (see Leviticus 11:29–38). "Kill these," says the Lord. "Grill them and eat." Peter denies the Lord three times now as three times before. "I can't do that." But the Lord is changing the old laws into new laws of his own. "What was unclean I have made clean." The vision vanishes. While Peter's trying to make sense of the vision, three men knock on the door below. The Holy Spirit snaps Peter out of his thoughts and tells him to go downstairs and meet the men and to "go with them to their master in Caesarea."

Their master is a Roman centurion named Cornelius, a truth-seeker among the Jews.

The centurion's family, his servants, and all his household have been waiting at home. Peter enters the house. Cornelius, who is not yet a believer, makes the mistake of kneeling down before Peter. "Don't do that," Peter says. "I'm a man. Worship only the Lord Jesus Christ." Then the apostle preaches the good news to those who are otherwise unclean. During Peter's sermon, the Holy Spirit falls on Cornelius and his household, and those who were unclean are made clean; those who didn't believe in Jesus now believe, and are baptized.

"God shows no partiality." But sometimes *we* do. Whom do we think we are better than? Liberals? Conservatives? Jews, Muslims, Lutherans, females, people of other races? The "unclean"?

PRAYER
Lord, in your sight I am not higher than anyone else, but if I live as if I am, cut me down to size. Amen.

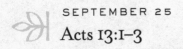

SEPTEMBER 25
Acts 13:1–3

Not long after Jesus ascended into heaven, the church began to develop a pattern of worship.

On the Lord's day they gather in a Christian house with food for the supper to come. Worship begins with prayer. One of them sits on a stool and teaches while the rest of the assembly listens intently. After the teaching they sing. Sometimes, in the thrill of the moment, someone may make up a new song: "Praise the Lord! Praise, all you servants of the Lord!" Another might shout spontaneously, "In the name of Jesus!" And people are likely to answer, "Amen! Amen!" Then the worshippers sit down. The leader passes the bread around, saying, "The body of Christ" and then "the blood of Christ," and everyone starts eating.

(Paul has harsh words for those who abuse the meal [1 Corinthians 11:29 and following].)

On this particular Sunday, an elderly prophetess rises and moves over to Paul and Barnabas, who came from the island of Cyprus. The woman speaks in a cracking voice, saying, "The Spirit of God has given me a word." She lays her hands on both men's heads and blesses them and says, "The Lord has set you apart to preach in foreign lands." After prayers and fasting, Paul and Barnabas kiss the others farewell and take their leave.

After a while Paul will send a letter to the Christians in Rome: "Paul, a servant of Jesus Christ, called to be an apostle, set apart for the gospel of God" and "Some of us have been called to sing, others to be teachers or physicians or nurses or philanthropists"—or, babysitters, statesmen, athletes. Even so do we serve the church and give glory to God.

PRAYER

O Lord, keep us from glorifying ourselves, and help us to give glory only unto you. Amen.

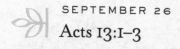

SEPTEMBER 26
Acts 13:1–3

I spent eighteen years serving an inner-city, African American church. During that time I invited a pastor from Zimbabwe to preach to the congregation. Faria Gambiza's earlobes had been pierced, and the hole stretched wide open, as was the custom of his tribe. After worship I asked him how he became a Christian.

He told me that when he was a boy there came a missionary to his village. Faria's father, as did many people in the Bible, wanted to hear more and maybe to believe in the missionary's God. "First," said the missionary, "you have to divorce all your wives except one." This was something Faria's father would not do because a divorced woman would never find another husband and would be left to raise her children and to work her little plot of land alone.

Now, what about Faria?

Faria was a young man when another missionary, kinder and more cheerful, appeared. This one began by saying, "What, Mr. Gambiza, do you believe to be true?" Faria recounted a creation story somewhat different from Genesis, yet the missionary said, "Yes. That's true. But," he said, "the Creator did one more thing. He sent his Son into Africa and into the whole world to save us from our sins." God has a *Son*? "We call him our Savior."

I had become Faria's friend because he'd come to America to earn his doctorate in theology.

As for us, we shouldn't demand that others obey our laws and follow *our* ways. Whatever our motives, it'll sound like scolding. First love them, then find what we have in common, accept it, then add God's new thing.

PRAYER

I will not rail against the sins of other people. I will call them to you with the same gentleness and compassion by which you called me. Amen.

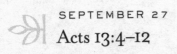

SEPTEMBER 27

Acts 13:4–12

Paul and Barnabas set sail for Cyprus. They then cross the island to Paphos, its capital city. The Roman proconsul Sergius Paulus invites them into his palace. He's a thoughtful man who wants to hear more about the word of God.

One of the proconsul's advisers, a magician named Elymas, feels threatened because these preachers have invaded his territory. He's afraid that he will lose his political influence. Elymas is a con artist, a man who declares himself to be a dreamer and an interpreter of dreams, pretends to be a prophet of his god. Paul fixes his eyes on this man and says, "You son of the Devil!" The cosmic struggle between good and evil, between God and Satan, will not cease until the end of time.

The Lord God acts. He blinds the eyes of the one who proclaims to be a seer, hoping that he will repent. Sergius Paulus is astonished by the miracle and immediately believes in the Lord Jesus.

During my own ministry in the inner city, I visited a young man lying facedown on the floor of his jail cell. Junie Piper had fallen into a black depression. I visited him again and again, always repeating the parable of the prodigal son and the waiting father, who represents God the Father. One day I found Junie clean and sitting up. He said to me, "I love you" and then asked for my blessing.

PRAYER

Jesus, help me to distinguish between good and evil, between those who would blind me by calling their evil good and those whose goodness is open for all to see. Amen.

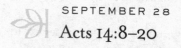

SEPTEMBER 28
Acts 14:8–20

Paul and Barnabas are proclaiming the good news in the city of Lystra. Because of the apostle's eloquence, a man who has never walked in his life listens intently. Paul perceives faith in this man and cries aloud, "Stand up!" The man *springs* up, and the crowd who saw the transformation shouts, "The gods are walking among us!" They called the stalwart Barnabas "Zeus," and Paul, the swift messenger of the gods, "Hermes." When the priest of Zeus hears their wild acclamations, he prepares two oxen to be sacrificed. He festoons the oxen with laurels and wreaths of flowers. As soon as Paul and Barnabas realize what's about to happen, they tear their clothes as a public display of protest.

Paul shouts, "We are not gods! There is but one God, the Creator, who sends you rain and who gives you every good thing!"

Now a group of hardline Jews enters Lystra, breathing threats against the Christians there. In the hearing of Lystra's citizens, they rail against Paul and Barnabas: "Liars! Frauds *pretending* to be gods!" So outraged are the citizens and the priest of Zeus at such trickery that they stone Paul. They drag him out of the city and leave him for dead. The disciples of Christ find Paul unconscious and lying in a ditch. They salve his wounds and bandage them and help him up to his feet, then Paul and Barnabas and the disciples escape from Lystra and head for Derbe.

PRAYER

The stones of gossip fall on me, O Lord, killing my reputation, which is the same as killing me. Stones of scorn shatter my labors on your behalf. The world dismisses me as a "do-gooder" whose efforts to find justice for the lower classes is impeded because those who scorn me are set in their ways. Give me courage. Grant me peace in my endeavors. Amen.

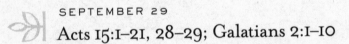

SEPTEMBER 29

Acts 15:1–21, 28–29; Galatians 2:1–10

Decades after the birth of Christ, three groups of Christians assemble in Jerusalem to debate a thorny problem. Paul, Barnabas, and Titus form one group, the apostles another, and the other is made up of Jewish Christians who continue to obey the laws of Moses. Their problem concerns circumcision. Paul is certain that his gentile converts have been set free of such laws. They need not be circumcised. But the other Christian Jews are just as certain that *every* believer should be circumcised.

Paul and Peter come to an understanding: Peter will preach to the circumcised, and Paul to the uncircumcised gentiles. Both Paul and Peter are in Antioch when the church in Jerusalem sends a letter requiring the converted gentiles to obey a number of the Mosaic laws:

"Don't eat meat the pagans have offered to idols. As for clean animals, drain their blood before you eat. Fornication is absolutely forbidden!" Oh, what a low opinion these Christian Jews have of the gentiles. Fornicate? Really?

Should we today divide our ministries?—Hispanics preaching to Hispanics, African Americans to African Americans, rock-ribbed pastors preaching only to rock-ribbed congregations? It has been said that the hour of worship is the most segregated hour of the week.

There is no bigotry more dangerous than that of a person who is totally unaware of his or her bigotry. ("Some of my best friends are black.") How important it is that we examine ourselves. Even though I served an African American parish, it took me five years before one of my members lovingly revealed to me that my intolerance was woven into my very nature.

PRAYER
Christ, however painful it may be, open my eyes to the prejudice within me. Cleanse me of my secret faults. Amen.

 SEPTEMBER 30
Galatians 2:11–14

Paul can be obstinate, cantankerous, and inflexible, always ready to wage a war of words with anyone he thinks is misguided—such as that blowhard, Peter.

The two apostles are in Antioch, sitting and eating with gentiles, sharing in the celebration of the Lord's Supper, when a delegation of hardline Christian Jews comes and accuses them of breaking the law: "Eat not with them, because their works are unclean!" Peter draws back. Paul says that Peter caves because he's afraid to be censured.

Paul goes on the attack. "You hypocrite! You're distorting the very truth of the gospel!" He's angry at Peter and sad for Barnabas, who has taken his stand by Peter.

Who, then, is truly in the wrong? Peter might very well have acted out of concern for the Christians in Jerusalem, to protect them from the persecutions of the zealous high priests and Pharisees. Paul meant to keep his gentile Christians in the faith. It's a toss-up.

PRAYER

My motives are hard to discern. Am I acting proudly on my own behalf (look at how good I am!), or am I acting humbly on your behalf? I can be my own worst enemy. Separate me, Lord, from myself so that my worser self repents and my better self rises up renewed. Amen.

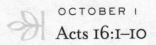

OCTOBER 1
Acts 16:1–10

Perhaps it was when Paul and Barnabas first preached in Lystra that the apostle brought to faith a young man named Timothy. Because he was born of a Greek father and a Jewish mother, Timothy is at ease in both worlds. His father died an early death, after which his mother Eunice and his grandmother Lois raised him. Neither was strictly pious. Timothy wasn't circumcised. For many reasons, as well as the possibility of an apostolic council in Jerusalem, Paul chose to have Timothy circumcised.

Paul revisits his scattered churches. In Galatia he falls sick, and there the Galatian Christians care for him. Some say his eyes are severely infected.

Paul and Timothy and another companion named Silas travel west to Troas, planning to sail across the Aegean Sea to evangelize the Greeks. But the Holy Spirit blocks them until Paul receives a vision of a man standing on the Macedonian coast, begging him to come over. The three sail the Aegean, landing at Neapolis, the port city of Philippi.

We ought to learn Saint Paul's wisdom in selecting Timothy. When we interview people for ministry positions, we should, of course, read their résumés and ask about their experience and their skills. But far more important it is to search their inward hearts. Are they faithful? Do they love Jesus?

*Friend, be my Timothy and I'll be yours, and Christ will see us through.
Jesus, see us through. Amen.*

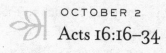

OCTOBER 2
Acts 16:16–34

Certain Roman Philippians earn a good deal of cash by having their
slave girl tell fortunes, which she does by means of an evil spirit living
within her. When Paul exorcises the demon in the name of Jesus, the
girl's owners lose their income. They go to the city magistrates and
charge Paul and Silas with causing chaos in the city. The charges stick.
The magistrates order Paul and Silas to be stripped, flogged, thrown in
prison, and to have their feet locked in stocks. They can't move. They
can't lie down or sleep.

Yet the two men sing hymns with loud and fearless voices. At midnight the Lord God causes a violent earthquake. The chains break. The
wooden stocks crack into kindling sticks, and all the prison doors fly
open. The jailor, who was knocked to the ground, gets up, wild-eyed. His
prisoners have escaped! There's nothing left but to kill himself before
the magistrates do.

Paul knows what the jailer's thinking. "Wait!" he shouts. "We're
here. We're all still here!" To the jailer's ears, Paul's words have the force
of Zeus. The poor man lights a torch and rushes to find Paul still sitting
in the cell. The jailer pleads with Paul, "How can I be saved from this
disaster?" Paul says, "Save your life?" "Yes, yes, my life!" "You mean your
bodily life, but I mean your soul. Believe in Jesus Christ, and you will
be saved."

There follows what so often follows a conversion. Come what may,
the jailer and his whole family are baptized.

PRAYER
*O sing to the Lord a new song. Earth, sing to the Lord. O Christians all
around the world, tell of his salvation from day to day! (Psalm 96:1). Amen.*

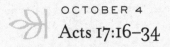

Acts 17:1–15

Wherever he goes, Paul leaves newborn Christians behind, as well as his angry Jewish opponents. So it was in Philippi, and so, now, it is in Thessalonica, where he preaches in the synagogue through three Sabbaths. "Jesus of Nazareth is the true Messiah. He suffered and died to save us—all according to God's plan." Some receive his testimony with joy. Others do a slow burn. In *their* reading of the Law and the Prophets, the glorious Messiah comes in power, not in weakness, to rule and not to suffer, and to die? Blasphemy! They go out and raise a riot in the city. "That man is turning the world upside down! Who can stand upright in such a turmoil?"

That night Paul and Silas and Timothy slip out from Thessalonica. By dawn they're walking the streets of Berea.

Then Paul is in Athens, writing to his baby Thessalonian church, "I grew weary of my relentless opponents and so made a decision to spend some time alone in Athens. Timothy remains with you to strengthen and encourage you to stand true in your faith" (1 Thessalonians 3:1–2).

PRAYER
You came lowly, riding on the little foal of a donkey, your feet dragging in the dust. Paul was right. You had to suffer and die. O Lord, let me proclaim that sad word first in order to prepare people for the joy of the glory yet to come. Amen.

OCTOBER 4
Acts 17:16–34

Athenian intellectuals debate in public on Mars Hill, and Paul is always ready to join a debate. He has strolled through the city. There was much to admire ("the glory that was Greece") and much to aggravate him: shrines, so many shrines, devoted to their pagan gods. Alight. Now Paul has something to say to the intellectuals.

Some murmur, "Babble, babble, babble." Others call him a "seed-picker" from foreign religions. And still others are keen to debate this philosopher.

Paul begins to address the Athenians in this manner: "I can see that you are more pious than people in other cities because you worship a god you don't even know. Let me tell you of the God you *should* know, the God who created the entire universe, the God whose hands formed humankind." So far, think the Athenians, so good. But Paul goes on to urge them to turn away from gods made by human hands. "The true God has excused your ignorance until now. But I've come to teach you about his Son, who came and suffered and died and rose to life again."

That is too much for the intellectuals. What? A man can rise from the dead?

Ears that will not hear. Paul leaves them unto themselves. They may die, but they will not be raised again.

PRAYER

There was a time when I thought I knew you, my God. But I didn't. I was only going through the rituals. In graduate school I thought of you as a God who cared nothing for the world or for me. But then I felt as if I were alone in a starless universe. I needed someone. I needed you, and you came to me. Amen.

OCTOBER 5
1 Thessalonians 3:6–10; 4:13–18

Timothy brings good news to Athens. The Thessalonian church has put down deep roots. Paul immediately writes to its members a letter of sincere gratitude. Their faith encouraged him during his persecutions, he writes.

But he has to answer a traumatic question. People are dying before Christ's return. The Thessalonians fear that these brothers and sisters won't be able to enter the kingdom. Paul writes, "Don't grieve as non-believers grieve. We are a people of hope! We, who will be alive when Jesus comes again, won't ascend before our sleeping friends do." And then Paul promises the Thessalonians that "God will come with a cry of command" (as if he were a captain calling his troops together). "His archangels will sound their trumpets. Then those who sleep in Jesus will rise first, and we will follow them into the clouds, all of us to meet our God in the air!"

Paul pauses, then writes, "Whenever you stand beside a grave, comfort one another with these words."

PRAYER

> God be with you till we meet again,
> By good counsel guide, uphold you,
> With a shepherd's care enfold you.
> God be with you till we meet again.

—"GOD BE WITH YOU TILL WE MEET AGAIN"

This is my prayer. And you, whom I hold so dearly, let it be yours too. Amen.

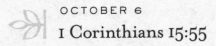

OCTOBER 6

1 Corinthians 15:55

When God created light, he created the first day and the first night: he created *time*. Therefore, God exists outside of time. It was his Son who entered our world of time at his incarnation and who now sits beside his Father in heaven.

When we die, we will be (in a twinkling!) with the Father and the Son, which means that we too will be outside of time. Some say we'll be waiting for our dear ones to come and join us. (How long, O Lord? How long?) But I think a different thought. If heaven is timeless, there'll be no waiting at all. It will seem to us that our friends have entered heaven at exactly the same time as we do. A single *tick*, and there we are, praising God together.

Heaven will be what it will be. We can describe it only in parables. But this I know: we will be with Jesus.

Jesus, you are with me now. And in your now, you are at my baptism. And in your eternal now, you are standing, waiting for me, at the door of my death. Amen.

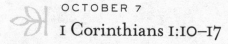

OCTOBER 7
1 Corinthians 1:10–17

Paul spent eighteen months in Corinth, establishing and enlarging a church there. After he met and befriended two of the Christians whom Claudius Caesar had driven out of Rome, Aquila and his wife, Priscilla, Paul left Corinth and sailed to Ephesus, where, as always, he proclaimed the name of Jesus as the Messiah.

Six months after his arrival, a Corinthian businesswoman named Chloe sends Paul a letter with bad news. She's worried about her church and describes the errors and the dangers now embroiling it: Rivalry. Backbiting. Dissention.

Paul fires a letter to Corinth, demanding that it be read aloud before an assembly in the house of Titus Justus. He intends to shame them into repentance.

"Factions, is it?" he writes. "And each fraction has its own slogan? Some of you say, 'I'm Paul's!' and others, 'I'm Apollos's!' and others, 'I belong to Peter,' and still others—oh, for heaven's sake!—say, 'I am Christ's!' Which of you claims Christ for yourself? We *all* belong to Christ the Crucified! Or do some of you think you have his bleeding feet, while others of you think you have his bleeding hands? You are so divided that it's as if you've chopped off the hands and feet of your church! But Christ prayed that we all should be *one*! What do you have to say for yourselves?—not to me. To Jesus."

What if someone asked the same of us today? How would we answer? "I'm a Lutheran." "I'm a Baptist, not like Catholics, who pray to saints." Or "I'm a Catholic, not like Protestants, who reject the pope." What stubborn fools we are! We *all* believe in the same Savior.

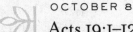

OCTOBER 8

Acts 19:1–12 and Ephesians 3:1–2; 5:1–5

In Ephesus Paul has thrown himself body and soul into teaching and preaching and performing miracles, converting many Ephesians and building up the church. He cautions the new Christians not to fornicate, not to be greedy, not to indulge in obscenities or silly or vulgar talk.

"The days are evil," he says. "The Prince of Darkness seeks to devour your souls. But Christ is your light. *Live* in the light! Let the Spirit of God fill your souls with his light and his life! You may have good reasons to be angry—I certainly have. Be angry, but don't sin. If you're angry at your brother or sister, reconcile yourselves before you go to bed. The Devil sings at night."

The more that Paul's exhortations are successful, the more do his enemies despise him. Near the end of two years in Ephesus, they seize him and throw him into prison.

Do we backbite other Christians? Or bed others without a second thought? Or mumble obscenities against the cop who just gave us a ticket? Or at the driver who cut us off in traffic? Then we must remember the breadth and the length and the height and the depth of the love we have in Christ Jesus.

PRAYER

But you, dear Jesus, have built a precious house for my soul. Thank you. Amen.

Philippians 2:1–12

Still sitting in his Ephesian cell Paul receives word that a conflict exists between two leading Philippian women.

"Reconcile with one another," he writes. "Be of the same mind which you have in Christ Jesus." The apostle then quotes a hymn which the Philippians sang when he was with them, hoping that the repetition will call them to account.

Even before God uttered the world into being, Jesus shared in the personhood and the dignity of the Father. Yet, for our salvation, the Son of God became the flesh-and-blood Son of Man. He "made himself in human likeness" and was born like us, limited human beings (Philippians 2:7). How great was his love and how beautiful his sacrifice, for he died as all humans must die, but his death saved us.

In Paul's day people believed that the world was divided into three parts: a heaven above, an earth in the middle, and, below, a place for the dead. Jesus descended from heaven to earth, and then still farther into the underworld (Ephesians 4:9). But then he rose from the dead and ascended through the earth into heaven, where he resumed his exalted glory with the Father. Let everyone on the middle-earth worship him and praise his name, for he is Lord of all! "Make peace, my daughters," writes Paul. "Kneel down. Worship the one God in whom you both have put your faith."

Likewise, let none of us think we should be exalted for our good and superior works. We might think it right when our pastor calls us up in front of the congregation to give us an award, a plaque or something. But James wrote in his book, "Humble yourselves before the Lord, and [then] he will lift you up" (4:10).

PRAYER

Just as I am without one plea, I come, I come, O Lord, to thee. Amen.

Philemon

Paul writes to one whom he'd brought to faith, a man named Philemon. Philemon's slave, Onesimus, ran away from his master and ended his journey with Paul in prison. (In those days slavery did not have the shame that it has today for some slaves.)

"When I pray, my dear friend, I always thank God because you've kept refreshing the saints where you are. I write now concerning Onesimus. He has served me well, and I have converted him to believe in the Lord Jesus Christ. He is like a son to me, and I am like his father. Philemon, I am sending him back to you, appealing to you to receive him like a brother." Paul writes this with his quill and ink.

It's interesting that Onesimus's name means "useful," because Paul speaks of him as having been useful to him in prison and can, at his return, be useful to Philemon.

Though Paul is in authority, he will not impose it on his friend and partner. Rather, he asks for the man's consent. Philemon should not ask Onesimus to pay a reparation or punish him for running away. "Just as you think of me as your partner, receive him as you would receive me." Earlier, Paul wrote to the Colossians, "Masters, treat your slaves justly and fairly" (4:1).

Sometimes Christian authorities will deal with the problems in their churches according to some law. But a Christlike approach calls for a spirit of persuasiveness. It should be done with divine grace.

Let us, then, manifest the love of the Lord by inviting friends to our houses for a regular (weekly?) fellowship and Bible study and prayer, for we all are uniformly children of the heavenly Father. The living rooms in our houses can light the church universal on fire.

PRAYER

What a fellowship, what a divine joy it is to meet in a house to read Scripture and to pray and to sing a hymn—have "church." Let it be, Lord. Let it be. Amen.

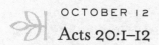

Romans 15:22–33

Paul turns his attention to the church in Rome, which consists of a hundred believers in a city of a million. When the church was still a small sprout, Aquila and Priscilla told him about the faithful there. Paul hopes to visit Rome one day. He says so in the last part of his letter. He's a Roman citizen, after all. But circumstances constrain him. He won't go. Not yet. Not till six years later.

For now Paul worries about his trip to Jerusalem. In Judea he's known as the man who betrayed the laws of Moses. What if even the Jewish Christians reject him, both because of his cantankerous personality and because of his teachings?

"My way is dangerous," he writes to the Romans. "Pray for me."

One of the members of my congregation is serving a twenty-year sentence in a state prison. I pray for him, and my prayer is answered not by his early release but by the peace in which he lives till his release. My niece (my friend, my aging grandfather, my colleague) lies on her deathbed. I pray for her healing, and my prayer is answered not by her survival but by the mercy of God that takes her to himself in heaven. I pray, and I pray, and my faith understands and accepts whatever the Lord decides.

PRAYER
Our Father, let your will be done, on earth as it is in heaven. Amen.

Acts 20:1–12

Finally, Paul is ready to make his pilgrimage to the Holy City. But the plan is thwarted even before it begins. His enemies are plotting his death. Instead of sailing directly to Palestine, Paul takes the slower route overland through Macedonia, sending his seven companions ahead to Troas to prepare for his arrival. Finally, he and Luke are free to make passage to Troas.

After a week's stay, Paul gathers the church in a third-floor room where he then speaks a long farewell. He has to leave Troas in the morning. His speech and his instructions last past midnight. A young fellow named Eutychus ("Lucky") has been sitting on the sill of an open window. The room has become stuffy and warmed by the people's bodies. Eutychus leans his head against the window frame and soon nods off to sleep. Suddenly, his feet fly up, and he drops eighteen feet to the flagstones below. Adrenaline fires the people's nerves. They rush down and out into the darkness and find the poor fellow dead. Then Paul, without a fuss, touches the lad and says, "There's life in him." Then it's back upstairs, Eutychus and all, where Paul celebrates the Lord's Supper and continues teaching till dawn.

There is the Negro spiritual that says, "Let us break bread together on our knees," and we do. Together. Jesus is present. He sanctifies our togetherness. We are the church at worship, and this is our beauty: that we represent the church universal.

PRAYER

I kneel at your table, Lord. I alone, and yet not alone, for I am the "we" of every believer in the world — even if they aren't here, for we are all members of your body, the church. Amen.

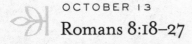

OCTOBER 13
Romans 8:18–27

After her ejection from Eden, Eve bore her infant in pain (Genesis 3:16). Rebekah's twins struggled painfully in her womb. Rachel died in childbirth. These women groaned in their deliveries. Now all creation is pregnant and moaning in labor pains. "And we too," writes the apostle Paul to the Christians in Rome, "sob while waiting for Jesus to reveal his glory." But a Christian's suffering has hope at its core. And if a Christian is beaten into weakness and bewilderment and an inability to pray, the Holy Spirit helps them, praying on the Christian's behalf—not with words but with groans too deep for words.

That same hope rests in *our* cores too. Sometimes we yearn desperately to pray but can't. Despair may have darkened our souls. Grief may have taken the words out of our mouths, and our hearts are silent. Then let us *be* silent. That's enough to do, because the Holy Spirit murmurs our needs to Jesus.

PRAYER

> Are we weak and heavy-laden,
> Cumbered with a load of care?
> Precious Savior, be our refuge—
> Take it to the Lord in prayer. Amen.
>
> —"WHAT A FRIEND WE HAVE IN JESUS"

OCTOBER 14
Romans 8:31–39

My inoperable lung cancer has developed a growing mass of fibrotic tissue which is slowly overtaking my lungs, more and more restricting my breathing. In the end it'll kill me. Yet I've made peace with my inevitable death. God is for me. He gave his Son over to death, then raised him up again. My dying is only a prelude to my rising. As long as I live, nothing separates me, or will ever separate me, from the love of my Savior. Neither hardship nor distress, neither death nor life nor angels nor Satan nor the courts of worldly powers, nothing now and nothing to come, neither the heights of the stars nor the depths of hell can separate me from the love of Jesus Christ, my Lord.

I am Christ's and he is mine, and I am sailing to the shores of my heavenly home.

PRAYER

Though you have been called mighty and dreadful, Death, you are not! You can't kill me. When my one short sleep is past, Jesus will wake me unto eternity, to whom is my every "Amen."

Acts 20:17–38

Paul's in a hurry. He wants to get to Jerusalem before Pentecost. He bypasses Ephesus, perhaps because of the malice that awaits him there. He asks the Ephesians to meet him in the city of Miletus, and they do. Paul rehearses his ministry, talking about his sufferings and his testimony to Christ and Christ's resurrection. Then he speaks in his pastoral role, preparing the leaders of the Ephesians to serve the church as he has done among them. Paul says, "Shepherd the church, for it is the flock of God. But watch out! False teachers will attack your sheep like ravening wolves. And worse than that, some of your own people will break from the Good Shepherd's flock by betraying him and joining the wolves' attack." And then, "You will see me no more."

Paul concludes his speech with a prayer while the Ephesians weep warm tears. After the amen, they embrace him and kiss him. Only God knows what will happen to him in Jerusalem.

In Jeremiah 23:4, God promised to send to Israel shepherds of his own. The word *shepherd* is also the word "pastor." Paul's preaching urges *our* church leaders to pastor as he pastored. Preach as Paul preached: the cross, the tomb, and the resurrection. Don't preach with eloquence in order to be praised by the flock, nor else to compromise the gospel by making it fit the passing fads of society. Though we preach humbly, it may yet be with the eloquence that springs from a devout faith.

PRAYER

Our Father, appoint faithful men and women to lead their congregations with tenderness and truth. Let them count it a joy to spend and to be spent for the sake of your dear Son. Grant them your bountiful grace and your heavenly benediction. Amen.

Acts 21:26–36; 23:12

Paul arrives outside Jerusalem in time to celebrate Pentecost—he and several gentile companions. They purify themselves by fasting and by making the sacrifice of having their heads shaved. Now that they've been cleansed, they can enter the temple.

Paul's intense and highly emotional personality has always allowed Paul to make fast friends and hateful enemies. He and his friends enter the inner court of the temple. His enemies, likely from Ephesus, are outraged: "Unclean Greeks in the Holy Place? Blasphemy!"

They foment a riot in the streets. A gang drags Paul out of the temple and begins to beat him. When the Roman tribune, Claudius Lysias, hears of the savagery, he takes four soldiers and charges into the mob. "You will *not* abuse any man under my governance!" The mob backs off, afraid that they're about to be arrested. But Claudius orders his soldiers to "bind that man with two chains!" When the rock-ribbed leaders of the Jews hear this, they cry, "Kill him! Kill him!" So forceful is the press of the people that Paul has to be carried bodily to the barracks.

Not long afterward, forty fanatics take an oath to eat nothing and to drink nothing until Paul has been put to death.

This passage can lay a heavy judgment on our world today. Religious violence is absolutely condemned: Muslims against Christians. Christians against Muslims. Terrorists imprisoned or executed. Murderers in America sentenced to life in prison or given the needle. O my Christian friends, let us pray for our broken world.

PRAYER
O Lord God, your flocks are tearing themselves apart. Put a stop to our belligerence. Be the shepherd who brings peace. Amen.

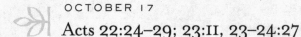

Acts 22:24–29; 23:11, 23–24:27

God's plan is Paul's destiny. He will in the end go to Rome. But for now...

The Roman tribune interrogates Paul in the barracks. Paul must have done something wrong, but Claudius Lysias is a pagan who doesn't understand what the Jewish leaders are so angry about. He has Paul flogged, a military practice used to force the truth out of a criminal, and the whip *does* get a truth, but not the one the tribune expected. "I," says Paul, "am a Roman citizen." The tribune rubs his chin and says, "I paid a fortune for my citizenship." Paul says, "I was born to it."

Forty men are prepared to ambush Paul, and Claudius has found a way to get himself out of this mess. He commands a full cohort of soldiers to take Paul by night north to Caesarea and to deliver him to Felix, the Roman governor of Palestine. Claudius writes, "I rescued this man, a Roman, from a sect of Jews who planned to kill him. I've sent him to you for a proper judgment."

Paul defends himself before the governor as innocent. And more than innocent, he is a prophet of the crucified Christ. Paul is an educated man and articulate and reasonable.

Felix postpones a final judgment, perhaps because his wife wants to hear more about this Jesus. But a second reason is the likelier one: that Felix hopes for a bribe, but none is forthcoming. Paul's imprisonment lasts until Felix dies two years later, and Festus takes over the governorship. He knows that the charges against Paul are false. Nevertheless, he keeps him still in prison.

If you ever feel imprisoned by doubts or hesitations or by fears of failure, appeal to the Lord to banish the bars of your cells. "I will save," says our Savior.

PRAYER

Jesus, I want to be your servant. Set me free, and send me wherever you want me to go. Amen.

Psalm 139:1–18

Lord, there's nothing you don't know about me. You know my daily habits and my mind. Even before I can find the words to express my thoughts, you know what I'm going to say. On the other hand, because I am a creature formed by your hands, I will never be able to plumb the depth of your mysteries, you who exist in the infinities beyond the universe, outside of time and space.

Where can I go from your Spirit? If I fly on the wings of the morning and land on the uttermost shores of the sea, you will be there, holding my hand. You wove me together in my mother's womb (knit one, purl two). O Lord, you have created me as a fearful and wonderful creature. Such knowledge is too deep for me.

Even at my ending, you will be there. And for all my days between the first day and my last, I will praise you.

PRAYER

Jesus, let me go to bed without the fear of darkness or of death. Let your angel's wings protect me while I sleep. Even though I can't find the words to praise you or to pray rightly, you know them, and you answer what I cannot say. O my Redeemer, I rest my faith in your love. Amen.

Again, read Psalm 139:1–18

Some scholars interpret the word *flee* as "escape." I won't argue with that. But I'll add the psalmist's faith that God is everywhere present. "Where can I go from your Spirit?" Not up into the highest of high heaven. Not down into Sheol, the black cave of chaos and death.

The Lord bears his bright torch to dispel the darkness.

Today we repeat the benediction: "The LORD make his face shine on you and be gracious to you" (Numbers 6:25). I think about our four children, my wife's and mine. They are scattered—Joseph in Minneapolis, Matthew in Atlanta, Mary in eastern Michigan, and Talitha in Washington, DC. I may be their earthly father, but God is the supreme Father of us all. And I thank God because, though they are far away from us, they are in the hands of Jesus, protected from the Evil One, and beloved. And the Lord will always lead them in the way everlasting.

PRAYER

My life, past and present and future, I have entrusted to you, Christ Jesus. I will never be put to shame because you lead me by your torch—a light for the gentiles, and for the glory of your church. Amen.

OCTOBER 20
Psalm 139:19 and Psalm 140

In spite of the comfort in Psalm 139:1–18, verse 19 and the whole of Psalm 40 beg for protection. Skim the passages in Acts found in the October 16 and 17 devotions, where evildoers battered the apostle Paul and cried out, "Kill him!" Now the psalmist prays for God to defend him (or her) from those who would work violence. It has always been so (Psalm 11:5).

Already, with Satan's temptation of Jesus, we've studied the galactic battle between the black prince of the world and the king of heaven. It continues. It will not end until the Devil is thrown into the lake of fire.

Three of the four words in the Hebrew text (verse three in your translation) begin with a *Sh*, the sound a snake makes when it crawls through the underbrush. Wickedness plots to kill the psalmist. "Guard me, O Lord. Save me from the grasps of the corrupted—the violent, the proud, the arrogant."

The Lord is present. He is sovereign. He is just, saving the poor and the upright, those who do not depend on themselves for life, but on the Lord.

In Paul's letter to the Romans, he writes that people "are all under the power of sin" (3:9). That *all* includes us too. Many of us glorify violence. Children, women, and those who are dominated by others suffer abuse. Violence will never be overcome by violence. If we want peace, we must work for justice.

It's me, Christ Jesus, who is confessing my sins. It's me, praying for your loving kindness. It's me who believes in the forgiveness you worked out on the cross. Amen.

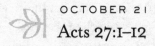

OCTOBER 21
Acts 27:1–12

In Caesarea, Paul and his companions board a merchant vessel with 276 passengers and sailors. And the pilot puts out to sea. It'll be a dangerous voyage. Sometime in October the Mediterranean's shipping lanes will close before the winter storms bear down.

The pilot puts in at the port of Sidon. By the time the ship sets sail again, the wind is blowing, heaving up great swells. The pilot navigates on the leeward sides of islands and then tacks into the wind and then drops anchor on the island of Crete in the port of Fair Havens. But only for a short while. This is no place to while out the winter, and the captain is hot to plow the waves of Rome. He commands the pilot to set sail. Soon gale-force winds will raise tremendous, dangerous breakers. Paul predicts a shipwreck. No one pays attention. The crew tries to furl the sail, but the canvas sail rips apart.

So what, my Christian friends? Are we so set on achieving some worldly goal that we would ignore the warnings of our parents? Or the cautions of friends? Or of people more experienced than we are? The wisdom of the wise knows that a failure can destroy us and pitch us into the troughs of anger or despair or jealousy, or else cause us to withdraw from the world altogether. We ought never to trust in ourselves, but hope in God, our captain, our pilot, the Creator of heaven and earth *and the seas*, he who is forever faithful.

PRAYER

Jesus, Savior, pilot me over life's tempestuous sea. Be my chart and compass. Blow me by your gentle love into your safe harbor. Amen.

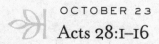

Acts 27:13–38

Wild winds shear the sea, driving the helpless ship to the tops of foaming billows, then dropping it into deep, watery troughs. Paul shouts that God will save them. Nonetheless, the sailors prepare to survive the tempest. They throw a drag anchor over the stern of the ship to keep the bow facing into the wind. No good. Their efforts aren't enough. The crew throws the ship's cargo overboard—jars heavy with grain, barrels of beer, casks of wine, cartons of hardtack bread. Not long and they jettison the rigging. But the sea pounds the planks of the vessel. The passengers fly into a blind panic, and the sailors are no help. Again Paul yells louder than the shrieking wind: "Last night an angel of God stood beside me and promised me that the God whom I worship will bring us all safely to Rome!"

The sailors break their backs pulling at the oars. For two full weeks the violent tempest prevails. Days are as dark as nights. On the fourteenth day, in spite of the storm, the captain hears?—hears a thunderous crashing of waves. Land! The crew hopes to bring the boat ashore in one piece. But the hull hits a hard reef and breaks in two. Paul cries to the passengers and the crew to swim to the beach or to cling to broken planks. Two hundred and seventy-six people carpet the water, every one of them falling exhausted on the beach of the island of Malta, less than sixty miles from Syracuse, Sicily.

Our own Maltas save us. Our Jesus, nailed to two wooden planks and then rising from the drowning seas—*he* saves us.

PRAYER

I am a sailor lost at sea and panicking because I am close to drowning in my iniquities. But you are my captain, and yours is the vessel that saves my life. No, you are the life that saves my life. Amen.

Acts 28:1–16

From six to ten on Saturday nights, my wife and I feed homeless men and give them mattresses to sleep on through the night. Some of these are recovering alcoholics. Many are looking for work. We should never blame the lost, the least, and the last for shaming themselves nor think that they are too simple to know God or to see the Lord reflected in us. We pray with them. We sit and talk with them.

The people of Malta immediately serve the ship-wrecked with a kind hospitality. As pagans, they may be the "lost." But they kindle a little fire so the survivors can dry wet clothing. Paul drops firewood on the fire. Suddenly, a snake is driven out of its den and strikes Paul's hand with its poisonous fangs. The islanders expect his body to bloat, his tongue to turn black, and him to die a painful death. Nothing like that happens. The apostle goes back to work unharmed. The pagans say, "It's a sign that this man is a god."

Paul is not a god; neither was it he who performed the miracle. *God* is God. In the days that follow, he witnesses to the gospel, and those who were lost are found.

PRAYER

The song of the Negro spiritual is,

> One day when I was lost
> (At sea and tempest-tossed)
> Christ died upon the cross.
> I know it was the blood for me. Amen.
>
> —"I KNOW IT WAS THE BLOOD"

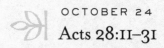

OCTOBER 24
Acts 28:11–31

After Paul and his companions have spent three months on Malta, the centurion who's been guarding Paul books passage on an Egyptian vessel bound for Italy.

Before Christ was taken up into the clouds, he commissioned his disciples to be witnesses "even to the ends of the earth." Rome and the Roman Empire can be called one of the ends of the earth.

Although Paul remains a prisoner, he is honored and respected as a citizen of Rome. The centurion rents a room for Paul to use while he waits to be brought before the imperial tribunal. The centurion posts just one ordinary soldier to guard Paul. Furthermore, the members of the church in Rome visit him frequently. The apostle has finally made good on his promise and has journeyed here to visit them.

Paul's bold and passionate preaching confirms them in the faith. Even the gentiles come to him, and his insistent voice penetrates many a heart. Soon both the gentiles and the Christians are praying together and singing hymns and worshipping the Son of the Most High God.

This is where Luke ends the account he's been writing for Theophilus, whose name means "friend of God." Luke ends on a high note. Likely he knows nothing about Paul's martyrdom.

But endless is our own Christian mission. Though Christianity girdles the world, there are still countless souls who haven't yet heard the Word. "Go out," said Jesus, "into *all* the world. And lo, I am always with you, even to the end of time."

PRAYER

We pray, we sing, we worship you, Lord Jesus, for you have pierced our hearts with the lance of your love. Amen.

PART 8

The EPISTLES of PAUL

Philippians 1:19–26

Today most people take it for granted that each individual consists of two separate parts, a body and a soul. The body dies and rots. The soul continues on. But this division has come down to us from Greek philosophers. From Genesis to the book of Revelation, the Bible knows nothing of such a notion. For Paul, the body and soul are indivisible—the human being whole. Preaching and believing are one in the same, exalting the name of Jesus.

Paul writes to the Philippians from his imprisonment. This church he seems to love the most. "I long to die and be with Christ," he writes. "There is nothing better than that. But a close second is to remain with you and *for* you, rejoicing in the progress of your faith. Which should I choose? Ah, but the Lord has chosen for me. I must continue my ministry." Yes, God will act for the benefit of the Philippians.

And he is in control of our destinies. Sometimes we think his control is to save us from disasters or too much pain. "Why," we cry, "are these things happening to me?" But that isn't the right question. Rather, ask, "What is God's purpose for me in my circumstances?"

PRAYER

Put me to what you will. Rank me with whom you will. Put me to doing, to suffering. Put me to your work, or to be laid aside for you, exalted for you or brought low for you. To be full, or empty. Let me have all things. Let me be empty. Amen.

—METHODIST COVENANT SERVICE

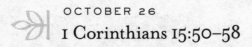

I Corinthians 15:50–58

A grain of wheat that has been planted in the ground and dies, it soon emerges—stem and leaf and the full ear—radically changed. It isn't what it was. Even so, when Christians are sown and rot in the earth, they spring up like nothing they ever were before, in a twinkling, at the trumpet's last blast. They arise as new creations.

"Listen!" Paul writes to the Corinthian church. "What is flesh and blood can't inherit the kingdom of heaven. But," he writes, "listen to this mystery. We will all be changed! We will put off our perishable clothes and put on the imperishable; we will put off our mortal flesh for immortality!" Then the apostle quotes a passage from Hosea (13:14) but with a twist. Hosea prophesied that God would not have compassion on his people. But Paul proclaims God's triumph:

> "O death, where is your victory?
>   O death, where is your sting?"

The Father's grace will be poured out on *all* of us. Do not fear your death, whether sooner or later, whether at home or in the hospital or under hospice care. When we die, Death shall die! It cannot sting us.

PRAYER

From the joyful faith of a Negro spiritual.

> My Lord, what a morning;
> My Lord, what a morning;
> My Lord, what a morning
> When the stars begin to fall.
>
> You will hear the trumpet sound
> To wake the nations underground—
> Looking to my Lord's right hand
> When the stars begin to fall. Amen.

—"MY LORD, WHAT A MORNING"

OCTOBER 27

1 Corinthians 6:12–20

Often a Corinthian pagan would practice prostitution. Paul condemns all fornication. But he is downright angry to hear that a Christian has bedded his stepmother. (See chapter 5:1 following.)

He writes to the church in Corinth, "You have been set free from the laws of Moses, but that doesn't mean you can do whatever you want. Don't you know that your bodies were made to procreate, not to fornicate? You are not your own. You belong to God! He redeemed you. He purchased you from your slave masters with the coins of his blood."

Paul writes, "The Creator said that a man and a woman become one flesh [Genesis 2:24]. The bridegroom Christ has married you. You are one with him. But if you go into a prostitute, you become one with *her* body! Listen to me! Your bodies are temples in which the Holy Spirit lives." The temple in Jerusalem must be kept clean and pure and holy. "Therefore," Paul encourages the Corinthians, "let your bodies glorify God!"

Most people today would laugh at the idea that they're not free to make their own decisions. And why not? No one else controls them. Even Christians may think *we* chose *Jesus* to be our personal Lord and Savior. We can, indeed, make lesser choices—which car to buy; how to schedule our time; whom we pick to be our friends; which dress, this one or that one? But Jesus chose us! Our *lives* belong to him.

PRAYER

Twenty-four hours a day, seven days a week, I have given my life over to mundane things, looking to be glorified by the smiles and the approval and the praise of my friends and other important people. At the same time I withhold the glory I ought to be giving you. Set me free of myself, and bind me to you. Amen.

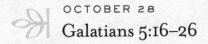

OCTOBER 28
Galatians 5:16–26

The cosmic war between God and the forces of darkness has not yet ended. But the Holy Spirit will prevail in the end. Therefore, "Be led by the Spirit."

Paul thanked the Galatians for nursing him when he was sick. Now he instructs them in the difference between the works of the flesh and the fruits of the Spirit. The first are "obvious" because they are enacted in the visible world.

Paul begins his list with three examples of fleshly desires. Then come the magic, sorcery, fortune-telling of the priests of idols. The third part of the list, Paul finds most fearsome among the Galatians, the dissensions and offenses that fracture the unity of their church: jealousies, arguments. Finally, he completes his list with examples of loose living.

But the Holy Spirit bears a single fruit with many benefits. (See John 15:1–2.) The first of these is love, and the last (against that "loose living") is self-control. This harvest of the fruit is what binds each individual and the entire church in Christian unity. Surely every one of us will strive to bear Christ's fruit together. We take our marching orders from the Spirit of Jesus Christ.

And how is this possible? We have by a mystery participated in Christ's crucifixion, his death, and his resurrection.

"We have all been," Paul writes to the Romans, "baptized into Christ, baptized into his death and buried with him so that as Christ was raised from the dead, we too will be raised to walk in the newness of life" (6:3–4).

PRAYER

Jesus, when I was baptized, I was given a new name: "Child of God." From that day to this, I've always kept my baptismal certificate hanging on a wall in my house. But whether I do so or not, my name is written on my forehead for all to see and as a remembrance for me. Amen.

OCTOBER 29
1 Corinthians 12:1–11

"Jesus is Lord!" is the first creed of the early church. When Christians rise up—*spout* up—from the baptismal waters (see v. 13), they cry, "Jesus is Lord!" *My* Lord. And they do so by the inbreathing of the Holy Spirit.

In Greek the word *gift* can also be translated "charisma." The Holy Spirit makes believers charismatic.

But Paul is aware of the divisions in the Corinthian church. They abuse the Lord's Supper, the rich eating sumptuously, the poor eating poorly. Some claim their gift to be superior to the gifts of others. Paul scolds the Corinthians for their sinful separations.

Though one is given wisdom, another knowledge, another prophecy, and to others various manifestations of faith and so forth—all these come from the same God.

I'm an author, my wife a spiritual leader and healer, my friend Mike Carson a discerner of spirits. To Pastor Gibson-Even has been given the spirit of wisdom, and to my grandpa Storck, knowledge.

I suggest that you spend some time making a list of those whose gifts have served you too.

PRAYER

Come, Holy Spirit. Help each of us first to know and then to do the gifts you've given us. Amen.

OCTOBER 30
1 Corinthians 12:12–31

I wonder whether Paul intends his description of the one body (Christ's church on earth) to be amusing. Think of a single eyeball bouncing *(boing, boing!)* down a hill (verse 17).

The dusty foot pities itself because it isn't part of the body—but think of a body without a foot. Or the head announces itself to be sufficient in itself, that it can do right fine without feet. Paul scolds such boasting because it was *God* who designed the body just as it is.

"How often," Paul complains, "will I have to rebuke you for your dissentions? How long will you weary me by ignoring what I've taught you? Listen! Pay attention! When one member of Christ's body suffers, the whole body should suffer too!"

This is the reason so many members of our congregations attend the funeral of one who died. We unite ourselves to the grieving family. This is why we pray for the members who are sick and for those who rejoice at a birth, a wedding, a graduation.

What should we say about today's churches that make speaking in tongues proof of having the Holy Spirit?

But "strive for the greatest gift, which I will set before you now" (1 Corinthians 12:31).

PRAYER

Though you've given us different gifts by the Holy Spirit, you've given us all one purpose: to be witness to your gospel. None of us can think of ourselves as better than other members of our congregations. Give us minds like your mind and teach us the most excellent gift of all: to love. Amen.

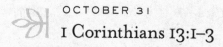

OCTOBER 31
1 Corinthians 13:1–3

In the beginning God was love. In the beginning there was no object to be loved nor a person to be loved. God himself, he *is* love. Then he created human beings and shed his love on them. Our love always needs an object, a someone: spouses, family, friends—and God.

But to love *ourselves* is blasphemous because we're trying to *be* God, to love as he does, without an object. If that's the case, says Paul, all his gifts are trash. Corinth is famous for its great brass gongs. Paul's preaching is powerful. He has turned countless souls to the Messiah. But without love, he wouldn't have converted one single soul. He'd have planted no churches at all. He has the gifts of knowledge and prophecy. More than anyone else, he's begun to penetrate the divine mysteries. And if he had a faith so powerful that he could command the mountains to move from this place to that but yet do these things without love, he'd be a flat failure in the eyes of God and of the world. Paul is willing to die for Jesus's sake. But without love, even that great and final sacrifice would turn his body into dust. Dead is just dead.

When I ask young couples to choose a text for their wedding ceremony, they'll often pick 1 Corinthians 13. Standing at the altar, they'll look into each other's eyes and vow to love each other as long as they live. But the love that Paul writes about springs *not* from romantic love, nor does it come from the couples' infatuation with each other. It is the love that God bestows on them, the love that embraces everyone else. By *that* love they model the love of Jesus.

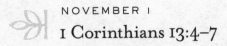

NOVEMBER 1

1 Corinthians 13:4–7

Paul writes, "Even if I am endowed with many gifts of the Spirit, even if my piety gives alms, and even if I'm willing to die but don't love with a Christlike love, my head and my heart are hollow."

Now he defines the qualities of a perfect love: it waits patiently, waits with kindness and mercy. But it isn't love if it is jealous or arrogant or ill-mannered or does just what it wants to do or if it keeps score of the wrongs done to it.

But!

Now Paul identifies what might seem to us impossible. Love loves all things—that is, embraces *everything*. Love endures all things, such as the irritabilities and the complaints of the beloved. It believes all things, though the beloved repeats and repeats promises it fails to keep. It hopes all things; that is, it looks to the future when the beloved purifies its faults by repentance and prayer. And love *can* hope because it is founded on the faithfulness of God. Then Paul ends his fourfold list as he started it. But now our endurance encompasses every tribulation and every error, every prejudice, every transgression, and every attack of those whom love continues to love.

We walk by faith and not by sight (2 Corinthians 5:7). We should therefore not judge another by what we see externally, but internally by the spiritual eyes of Christ.

My friends, what seems impossible to us is possible in Christ Jesus (Luke 1:37; Matthew 19:26). Christians, have patience, then, even as the Lord has been patient with his people throughout the Old Testament.

PRAYER

I am a human. I fall far short of loving as you love. O Lord Jesus, do the impossible. By your goodness and by your mercy, grant me to love according to the characteristics set out by the apostle Paul. Amen.

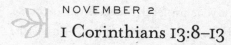

NOVEMBER 2
1 Corinthians 13:8–13

Now is now. We live within the limits of time. The limitless, eternal future belongs to the future, when Christ will descend in all his glory with his angels. In these verses Paul writes of the present, convinced that Jesus will keep his promise: "Come, Lord Jesus. Come."

Every gift of the Holy Spirit will come to an end: prophecies, tongues, knowledge, all of them that are bound to the Now, and all of them incomplete. Everything, *everything* will cease, even the faith within the hearts of human beings, because God's faithfulness will be all in all.

The mirrors that Paul knows are made of polished bronze or silver circles. When they become scratched and hazy with use, the image reflected grows "dim." So it is for us. All is blurred. But at the end of time and the beginning of time eternal, when reflections would fail us, we will see face to face.

And three gifts will be perfected in heaven: faith, made complete by God's faithfulness; hope that will find what it hopes for now; and love, God's love for us and our love for God will go on forever and forever.

PRAYER

Lord Jesus, stir up my faith. Grant me the hope of that great cloud of witnesses (Hebrews 12:1). As for love, it is the greatest gift of all the gifts. Amen.

2 Corinthians 2:5–11

One of the members of the church at Corinth, whatever he or she may have done, has cut Paul to the quick, causing him a pain still fresh in his memory—and if Paul, then the whole congregation is pained. For the offense, the congregation thinks it has a right to punish the offender. But Paul gives the church a different counsel.

"It's enough. Forgive him [her] as God has forgiven you. Console him as God consoles you [2 Corinthians 1:3–5]. Ease his sorrow so that his sorrows don't swamp him. Confirm your love for the man." It may, of course, be women like Euodia and Syntyche (Philippians 4:2–3). Paul then tells the Corinthians that his instructions are something of a test. "If you prove to be obedient, then I too am ready to forgive. But if you keep punishing him, if you cast him out, then Satan has had his way with you. But we know Satan's schemes. And we know the One who overrules him. Cling to Jesus."

Today we ought to fall on our knees before the Lord and confess that we have been unforgiving, in various ways punishing anyone who has offended us (tit for tat). We must do that first—seek God's forgiveness so we too can forgive.

PRAYER

There's no doubt about it. I have offended you, Lord, whether by choice or by habit. Then search my heart. Help me to search myself in order to know my offenses. Daily I beg your forgiveness. Daily I rise renewed. Amen.

2 Corinthians 4:7–15; 6:4–10

Paul's theme is power through weakness.

God's grand treasure God chooses to put in breakable clay pots, in the standing clay of human flesh.

Paul writes that what he suffers in his body witnesses to the suffering and the death of Jesus Christ, who also preserves him.

Though he has—as we've seen throughout his ministry—been brought to trial and imprisoned, his spirit has never been broken. Though confounded, never hopeless. Persecuted in city after city, but not abandoned by the Lord. Wounded, whipped, beaten bloody, but, by God, never yet killed.

And this is the good effect of Paul's bodily witness: that the Corinthians may have life. That they may find their lives in Jesus.

Our willingness to suffer disgrace and ill will and indignities without blaming our persecutors reveals both the death of Jesus and his dear love for us. That is our witness.

While Martin Luther King Jr. was protesting racial discrimination in Chicago in 1966, I was a young twenty-two-year-old. I watched as a man in the crowd threw a stone that hit King's head and knocked him to the ground. He stood up and kept on marching. In King I saw both the death of Jesus and the life that overcomes.

PRAYER

I am mortal. The pastor draws with his finger a cross of ashes on my forehead: "Remember, thou art dust, and to dust thou shalt return." But your death for me is life in me. Amen.

NOVEMBER 5

2 Corinthians 9:1–8, 13 and Deuteronomy 14:22

The generous gift that the Corinthians have "promised" is to support other churches with gifts of money, not as though they were compelled to do it, but gladly. Today we calculate our own giving according to Deuteronomy: 10 percent of our entire income—the tithe. Paul writes that the blessing a cheerful giver receives is the love of God. Deuteronomy offers those who tithe liberally that God will bless all the work of their hands.

That blessing is emphatically not money or prosperity. It is the joy God gives the givers in all the work they do. I'm afraid most of us never think of that joy. We may give ungrudgingly, but we mostly think of it as a duty.

Our tithe, Thanne's and mine, consists of a tenth of our income before it's been reduced by taxes. But our true joy comes at Christmastime, when we're able to donate the greater portion of our savings to people and charities. Thanne makes a list of these, then we sit at the dining room table and calculate how much to give each one.

We recommend it.

PRAYER
Let my hands be your hands, O Lord. Amen.

NOVEMBER 6
Galatians 3:27–28

When the early Christians baptize, the people go down naked, and after coming up, they are clothed in a new, white garment, which signifies that they've put off their old life and put on a new. To be baptized into Christ means to be clothed in his love and to be unified with him in the love of the Father. Then everyone is one. There is no distinction between one and another.

In the past, Jews set themselves apart from gentiles. Now they are both together the people of God. In the past, a social hierarchy maintained an absolute division between slaves and slave owners, between the shackled and the free. But now they are one family, brothers and sisters together. In the past, males dominated females, and women were made to serve men. But now there is no divergence at all—no more gender distinctions, because males and females have become the same. They have both been baptized and have both been dressed in the garments of the one Lord Jesus Christ.

How do Christians identify themselves today? I am an American and not an immigrant. I'm a car mechanic. I teach in the university. I am married. I am not married. I have children. I can't have children. I am a Catholic. I'm a Southern Baptist. Our churches have nothing to do with each other.

No, there ought not to be distinction between us, because we are all one in Christ. *That* is the ground of our single identity.

NOVEMBER 7
1 Corinthians 3:16–17

In the Old Testament, God dwelt among his people in the Most Holy Place of Solomon's Temple. In the New Testament, God the Father dwells in and makes himself manifest in the temple of his Son. Now Paul adds one more temple: the bodies of those who believe.

Solomon's Temple was destroyed by the Babylonians. Christ was destroyed by the leaders of the Jews and the Romans. What now? asks the apostle. "Will you too destroy the temple in which lives the Holy Spirit, by defiling it? Corrupting it?"—such as the man who lies with his father's wife (1 Corinthians 5:1).

Paul warns the Corinthians with the harshest measures: "If you ruin your bodies, God will ruin you! But as long as you live a holy life, the Holy One will live in you."

You shall be holy, for I, the Lord your God, am holy (Leviticus 19:2).

If we dishonor our bodies, we dishonor Christ, who dwells in us (John 17:20–22). Dishonor: unwashed bodies; ingesting anything that hurts the body, such as too much sugar or too many potato chips, drugs, alcohol (alcoholism is a disease, but Alcoholics Anonymous can lead to sobriety); too little exercise; refusing to see a doctor even though sick and getting sicker; ignoring good advice. We should welcome the Holy Spirit, then let the Holy Spirit guide us in all our ways.

Ephesians 2:1–10 and Romans 5:1–11

The ruler of the air, Satan, the Prince of Darkness, works to turn human souls from obedience to disobedience, and so to kill those who live by the passions and the desires of the flesh.

But even while people are dying in their transgressions, the God of mercy, the God of love, elevates us (Paul includes himself) to a life in Christ. This is by grace and not by our own works! "While we were weak," Paul writes, "while we were ungodly sinners and God's enemies, his Son died for us. We have been rescued from the wrath to come. Do we want to boast? Then boast in the Lord Jesus Christ, who recreated us to be his own."

As it was for the Ephesians, so it is for us. We need not worry. Our faith is secure. Because Christ's death has justified us and glorified us. Our faces shine with the light of the love of Jesus.

PRAYER

Satan seeks my soul. He entices me with the pleasures of this world, and I'm drawn to those fleshly things that draw me to my death. I turned away from you because you offered me no such pleasures. But you never turned away from me! Your rich grace has saved me from myself, and I rest securely in the palm of your hand. Amen.

Ephesians 6:10–17

Not always is the Devil a cunning tempter. He, the dark force on earth, is also a warrior fighting full-out. Paul warns the Ephesians to prepare to battle the spirit of this age with the Spirit of God, whose armor is likewise spiritual.

His marching orders: "Free your legs by tucking the hem of your tunic up under the belt of truth. The liar lies. The truth can vanquish him. Protect your chest and your heart with the breastplate of God's impenetrable righteousness. Wear studs on your boots. Announce the gospel of Peace." When speaking of shields, Paul doesn't mean small, round shields, but the full-length shields of the Roman legions, constructed of wood and covered with rawhide. "If one of the flaming arrows of Satan's blasphemy should lodge in a soldier's shield, he will throw it down and become vulnerable to Satan's spear. But you have the shield of faith! You can break his spear asunder. And protect your head [which represents the head of the body of Christ] by donning the helmet of salvation, and his victory will be yours."

If we truly seek to live holy lives, we will be attacked (yes, by the Devil) and find ourselves confronted on all sides with the sharp spears of the sins of this world, the flaming arrows of society's rejection, the ignorance of human hearts. Nonetheless, we are able to continue proclaiming the gospel of peace and thereby opening hearts to Jesus's words of salvation.

PRAYER

> Rise! To arms! With prayer employ you,
> O Christians, lest the foe destroy you,
> For Satan has designed your fall.
> Wield God's Word, a weapon glorious.
> Against each foe you'll be victorious.
> Our God has set you over all.
>
> —"RISE! TO ARMS! WITH PRAYER EMPLOY YOU"

This is my song. This is my cry. Amen.

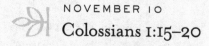

NOVEMBER 10
Colossians 1:15–20

Sing with Paul the new hymn he includes in his epistle to the Colossians:

> He is the image of the invisible God,
> The firstborn of all creation
> For in him were all things created
> In heaven and on earth,
> Things visible and invisible.

Marvel at the supremacy of the Lord in whom we believe.

Everything that wasn't, *is*: the cosmos, the whirling galaxies, stars and angels, and this—the unseen is made seeable in Jesus! He has authority over thrones and rulers, whether threatening or benign. He oversees our going out and our coming in.

And just as Jesus was the means and the goal of creation, so is he the means and the goal of reconciliation. Peace, peace! By the blood of the Redeemer's cross, be at peace.

Earth and heaven and everything in between are the Lord's. And we are his. His authority reigns supreme, and he who is King has made us kings.

PRAYER

I stand amazed before your glory. Wherever I walk, I walk beneath your powerful grandeur. You watch over my going forth in the morning and my coming in at the close of the day. Such love renders me speechless. I haven't the words to thank you. Read them in my heart. Amen.

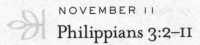

NOVEMBER 11
Philippians 3:2–11

Dogs are scavengers. They skulk. People kick them out of the way. Jews will call a filthy foreigner a dog. Paul uses the epithet to scorn those who demand circumcision according to the law. (See Galatians 5:12, where he wishes that the circumcising knife would slip and castrate the one being circumcised.)

Paul boasts, "We are circumcision itself!"—though he could, if he wanted, boast in his Hebrew credentials: born in the tribe of Benjamin, the son whom Jacob in his old age loved the most; a zealot highly praised for persecuting Christians; a Pharisee who kept the laws of Moses blamelessly. All of these he calls obedience to (the law) the flesh, which has nothing to do with the freedom of the Holy Spirit.

Paul has happily trashed his old credentials in order to be found in Christ, not because he was righteous according to the law, but because he has been made righteous by faith in the righteousness of Christ.

"Trash" is how we cover up what Paul really says: "Feces. Dung. Excrement."

Once more he repeats the value of sharing in Christ's sufferings. He will by that share in Christ's resurrection.

Know this, my friends: to put our faith completely in Jesus is to abandon trust in *anything* else! Were we born to privilege or wealth or on the right side of the tracks or to the dominate race or in an educated family or to parents with good names? Trash it all. Jesus is our priceless treasure.

PRAYER

Abide in me, my Lord, that I may abide in you. Amen.

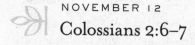

NOVEMBER 12
Colossians 2:6–7

I believe in God, the Father Almighty, Creator of heaven and earth. He created me and still preserves my body and my soul.

I believe in the Holy Spirit, who has called me through the gospel and watches over my faith so that it will grow stronger and stronger.

And since Jesus is my strength and my Savior, I am able to walk according to his commandment to love one another as he has loved us (John 13:34). I walk according to the gospel which my teachers taught me. My taproot runs deep in the ground of my Lord, by which he nourishes me as though I were his beautiful apple tree. And my faith is always being built up like a church whose steeple reaches to his high throne. And my worship rings with loud thanksgivings as though I were a cathedral bell that keeps on tolling.

This is our Christian confession. This is our creed.

PRAYER

I talk the talk, O Lord. Let me also walk the walk. Help me to become what you are and what you have always been. I believe in you. You are the root of my nourishment and the source of my love. Amen.

1 Timothy 1:12–18

To Timothy:

I slandered Jesus. I persecuted those who believed in him. Nevertheless, I, even I, received his mercy. He strengthened me. By and with his overflowing grace, he accounted me to be faithful and granted me to serve as his apostle.

Paul's love for Timothy is expressed by calling him "my child." "My dear son," Paul writes, "I've taught you according to the prophecies about you." Timothy has been given the authority to preach, not from Paul but from God, who made himself known through the prophecies.

"I've been found worthy to preach to lost sinners the salvation of the Lord. I am an example of his patience. As God said to Moses, 'I am slow to anger.'

"Timothy, fight the good fight free from the world's distractions. Our fight is not against people but against the spiritual forces of evil. Strength and faith will prevail!"

And we also are called to fight that good fight, to empty our minds of mundane things. But if we continue to chase the pleasures of the world, proud of our actions (even of our "Christian" endeavors), our spirits will be vulnerable to the Devil, who roams about, seeking whom to devour. But if we fill our minds with faith in the Holy Spirit, nothing can destroy us.

PRAYER

Lord Jesus, so strengthen the faith of your sons and your daughters that we will in the end conquer the Devil and his fire-eyed angels. Amen.

I Timothy 3:1–7

Bishop can be translated "overseer," one who manages a church. *Family* in this passage means both the church over which one has oversight as well as that one's family. He is a paterfamilias with authority or she a materfamilias with the same authority.

Paul instructs Timothy in the characteristics of a good bishop. For "above reproach," a bishop must be respectable in order to make his or her church respected by society. Must lead with good sense, mother wit. Must be hospitable, receiving a traveler with a gracious welcome, offering bed and board. (Inns were often dangerous, their beds infested with fleas.) There are bishops who rule by force, bishops whose rule is compromised by alcohol. Bishops who are greedy both for money and for a higher position in the church, climbing the episcopal ladder, as it were. Must have one wife throughout his career, never divorcing a wife to marry another. A recent convert should not be given the authority of a bishop. Inexperience makes for a foolish leader, one who could become proud of his high office, taking care of himself more than caring for the Lord's people. Furthermore, he will be vulnerable to Satan's temptations.

These same principles apply to us today—not only to pastors but also to anyone responsible for communicating the gospel: Sunday school teachers, hospice caregivers, parents, those who visit the sick, and those who pray for the afflicted. We should reread Paul's instructions one by one, seeking to know how they apply to us.

PRAYER

Lord Jesus, I fail to follow Paul's description of a bishop. Be my bishop. Amen.

1 Timothy 4:1–16

"Let no one despise your youth." Timothy is no longer a young man. He's worked with Paul for fifteen years. Paul is thinking of the time when Timothy first began to work with him.

The apostle reminds Timothy of the two paths in which those whom he teaches can walk. The first is according to deceitful spirits and demons, hypocrites, liars, old wives' tales, and the Devil, who brands their consciences with red-hot irons as masters brand the foreheads of their slaves. That is to say, many of the taught will forsake the teachings.

The second path consists of self-discipline and faith and bodily purity, loving those who are taught, always convincing them of the Savior's grace. Paul reminds Timothy that his gift comes from the Holy Spirit through prophecy and by his consecration when the elders laid their hands on him. "Timothy, devote yourself to the things you teach. Practice them, or they may wither. Rather, submerge yourself in them, and they will flourish."

We too are free to choose between the two pathways, each with its profound consequence. To speak the gospel but not to live it, to pretend to love (someone in our families or communities, the outcast, the poor without safety nets, those borne down by unjust systems) and yet not *truly* loving—this will be judged by Christ (Matthew 25:31–46). Or else to enact the gospel in spite of the difficulties, to love as Jesus loved, to labor for justice, and to serve our Lord as he served the Father—those who do these will be called "my faithful servants. Come, inherit the kingdom of God." (See Matthew 25.)

PRAYER
Lord, grant me the grace and the guidance to choose as you have chosen. Amen.

Philippians 4:4–7

Paul is held prisoner in Rome while writing to his church in Philippi. Near the end of the letter, he writes a farewell—but in no wise with sadness.

"Rejoice in the Lord!" This has been Paul's theme throughout the epistle. "Rejoice! He is not far off." Psalm 145:18 is for the Philippians as much as it is for us. "The LORD is near to all who call on him, to all who call on him in truth."

Today Christians cry, "Maranatha!" Come, Lord Jesus. He is coming. He has come and yet has always been here. That's why Paul writes, "Don't be anxious. Pray with thanksgiving, and the peace of Jesus will protect your hearts and your minds from hopelessness and every spiritual trouble."

Who would Paul be if he didn't take every opportunity to instruct his churches? He wouldn't be Paul. Therefore, some fatherly advice: "Pay close attention to things that are true, things that are honorable, just, pure, pleasing, worthy of praise, and the peace of God will embrace you now and forever. My dear ones, farewell."

Are we too able to experience Paul's profound joy? Do we think "happiness" is "joy"? It's the thought of a foolish and thought*less* generation. Happiness vanishes with the first signs of trouble, but joy *endures* trouble, can even arise *from* the most painful troubles.

"Farewell. Farewell."

PRAYER

I've got the joy, joy, joy, joy deep in my heart, deep in my heart today. Amen.

PART 9

JAMES, PETER, JOHN, and HEBREWS

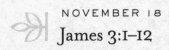

James 1:1–18

James, the brother of Jesus, not the son of Zebedee, is a servant and a teacher. He never elevates himself to the status of the apostles. Yet, like them, he cares for the Jewish Christians scattered around the empire and suffering various trials. "Endure," he writes. "Your tribulations are meant to test your faith. In fact, consider it a joy to be tested, because by it you're growing into full adulthood, learning that in God you lack nothing at all because his generosity gives you everything you need."

If, in the Hebrew churches, there are both rich and poor, and if, as Paul wrote, the rich are neglecting the poor, the poor should console themselves. James can be as winsome as Paul and also as harsh as Paul. "Under the scorching sun of God's judgment, the stems and the stalks of the double-minded rich will wither and die, while the flowers of the poor will flourish and become the radiant, God-given crowns of life."

Do our congregations include the needy? They do indeed. And do the rest of us treat them as our equals? (But they put nothing in the plate. They come to church in threadbare clothes, do they have jobs?—it's *their* fault that they live the way they do.) But we are called to imitate Jesus, to care for them as if they were (well, they *are*) our elders and we their servants.

PRAYER

Lord, I have said to my soul, "I've prospered [invested money to get more money] so much that I will build bigger barns." But you have turned your spotlight on me and have found me wanting. God, I can't abide your light. It shines on my pride. All I can do is humble myself and confess and fall on your mercy. Amen.

James 3:1–12

Again James pulls no punches. His are gut punches. He does not accept excuses.

"Watch what you say!" he writes. "Control your tongue, or it will control you!" He makes these punishing comparisons: that a small bit in a horse's mouth can make the beast go where the rider wants to go, and a little rudder in an ocean-going vessel can be turned into the direction where the pilot wants to go. Likewise, the small tongue dominates the whole body! The tongue can be the match that ignites the fires of hell. But James's instruction isn't only for the people in his day, for he calls those to whom he writes "my brothers and sisters."

People have always tamed God's creatures, but who can tame the two-forked tongue that has a poisonous bite? It blesses God and curses those in the image of God. (See 1 Corinthians 12:3–4.) The tongue is a perversion of nature! A stream of water can't be both sweet and brackish at once. Nor can a fig tree bear olives, nor a grapevine figs. But the tongue? Blessings and blasphemies. Powers and perils.

C. S. Lewis once wrote that if we try to create (to speak into existence) what God created with his spoken word, we will produce unnatural monsters. I write fiction. Long ago I wrote a story that I thought wonderfully artistic but which my wife called bad. I tried to prove her otherwise by showing her my precise language and my effective metaphors. No, "bad because it's immoral." Apparently an author must not dabble in immorality. I hadn't learned from Lewis's caution. I had created a monster.

PRAYER

O God, the author of creation, grant me always to write and to speak the truth. Your Son, our Lord, is the Truth. Amen.

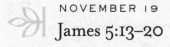

NOVEMBER 19

James 5:13–20

"Is anyone sick?"

Perhaps James has heard of a woman in one of his churches who is running a dangerously high fever, vomiting, suffering a diarrhea that is depleting her bodily fluids. Some may have tried to treat her diarrhea with rue, but if rue is swallowed, it becomes a poison.

Whatever the case, James writes, "Let the church elders pray for her and anoint her with oil." James knows that olive oil's value is in the warm hands of those who massage the sick one. And those who apply it should do so in the name of the Lord so that it will heal both the body and the soul.

Then *we* should sing songs of praise, for God hears our prayers. The prayers of the righteous, the prayers of the Christians who support us, are effective and powerful and trustworthy.

PRAYER

Our prayers, Lord, are for the families who mourn the death of one they loved, for parents with difficult or troubled children, for those who have lost their jobs, for the young men and women trying to make their ways in a difficult world, for our pastors, for the members of our own families, for (add the names for whom you are praying). Amen.

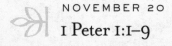

NOVEMBER 20

1 Peter 1:1–9

Not long before he dies, Peter writes from Rome to the Christians in Asia Minor. Perhaps Sylvanus is translating the fisherman's Aramaic into an elegant Greek prose.

Peter's word *peace* translates the Hebrew word *shalom*, which doesn't mean mere peacefulness (the absence of war). It means wholeness and health and well-being. Christians have been born anew, as Paul writes in Romans 6:4: "We've been buried with Christ by baptism into his death and raised (born anew) with him." Earthly life is fraught with its toils and snares. Yet Christians live in the conviction that God has stored up in heaven (keeps, as it were, in the heavenly bank) the imperishable treasures they will receive at the end of time.

"Now faith is the assurance of things hoped for, the assurance of things not seen" (Hebrews 11:1). "Rejoice!" writes Peter. "You live in the faith that you have already received, the salvation of your souls!"

It is the same for us as it was in Peter's time. We live in a tension between the now and the hereafter. We have the strength to endure the present and a joyful hope in the future when Christ will reappear in glory to glorify us. "Therefore my heart is glad and my tongue rejoices" (Psalm 16:9).

PRAYER

> Through many toils and snares
> I have already come.
> 'Tis grace has brought me safe thus far,
> And grace will lead me home. Amen.
>
> —"AMAZING GRACE"

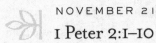

NOVEMBER 21
1 Peter 2:1–10

Once again Peter uses the image of a new birth. Infants drink the milk of their nursing mothers. Christians are nursed with the milk of the Holy Spirit. "Taste and see that the LORD is good" (Psalm 34:8).

God said to the children of Israel, "You shall be my treasured possession, a priestly kingdom, and a holy nation." (See Exodus 19:6.) Likewise, Peter writes to the congregations, "You are a chosen race, a royal priesthood, a holy nation, God's own people. As priests, then, offer spiritual sacrifices pleasing to God."

Jesus is the cornerstone on which believers are being built into spiritual houses. They *are* God's houses. Houses are temples. Priests sacrifice in temples. Unbelievers, on the other hand, break their feet and crack their skulls on the Christ-rock.

Every one of us is a stranger and pilgrim on earth. While we walk through unbelieving nations to our heavenly kingdom, we must walk honorably, and some of the citizens of the nations who see us might glorify God on the day of judgment.

PRAYER

I offer myself as a living sacrifice to you, just as your Son offered himself as a sacrifice for me. I take my priesthood seriously, praying for my fellow Christians and yet calling those who stray back to the path of righteousness. Let me be your voice, O Lord. Amen.

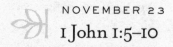

1 Peter 5:6–11

Christian humility comes from the grace of God, and mortification from Jesus, who mortified himself for us. We shouldn't think that these gifts are less than good, because they reveal our sins. Then we can confess and rejoice in the unmerited forgiveness of our Lord Jesus. Be humble now to be exalted later.

A lingering anxiety can become a terror unless it is cast on God's broad shoulders and his generous heart. But watch out! The war isn't over. Great Satan still prowls the earth to enter human souls and to turn them into his servants. But there is God, there is a law, there is an enemy, and there is victory in the eternal glory.

An evil force still prowls our world. Perhaps the Devil's most cunning trick is to persuade us that he doesn't exist. Be watchful because vigilance is necessary to pry the Devil from his hiding places. And God will make us perfect in every respect, repairing us (as fishermen repair their nets), and will strengthen us to endure our troubles for the glory to come.

PRAYER

My Lord, you have raised me up. Now give me ears to answer your call. Amen.

1 John 1:5–10

"The LORD is my light and my salvation—whom shall I fear?" (Psalm 27:1). "In your light we see light" (Psalm 36:9). John writes, "Walk in the light." Christians (John includes himself) who say they are right with God while walking in darkness are liars. Worse, if we say we have no sin, our lies would make God seem to be a liar too!

Then walk in the light of Christ, and we'll see ourselves as we truly are—transgressors. No longer will we try to conceal our sins but will confess them openly because we know that the blood of Jesus has cleansed our souls and made us righteous as he is righteous.

A survey of Christians in the American Midwest revealed these statistics: 98 percent of the people believe in personal sin. And 57 percent think all humankind is sinful. Only 33 percent said that people commit mistakes, but that they aren't sinful in themselves. As my mother used to say, "Read it [these statistics] and weep."

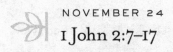

NOVEMBER 24
1 John 2:7–17

The commandment to love one another is as old as Moses. "Love God. Love your neighbor as yourself." But the times are changing. The Light of the World is getting ready to come back into the world. Under these circumstances, the old commandment is new and urgent.

John teaches his "dear children" how to test the truth of their faith. "If any of you proudly says, 'I am a child of the light' while hating your sisters or brothers, there is no light in you. You are children of the darkness, creatures skulking through the midnight shadows, and you have failed the test." On the other hand, "If you love your brothers and sisters as Jesus loves you, you've passed the test and can with humility say, 'I abide in Jesus'"—who is the light that shines in the darkness and who defeats it (the gospel of John 1:4–5). "Rejoice!"

We ought to scan Christendom. Better yet, scan our own churches, and do so with a steadfast, patient, and truth-seeking eye. Without a doubt we'll see many people of the selfless habits of loving. At the same time we will no doubt see signs of hatred, however much the hater tries to conceal them with a false backslap and a hearty handshake or with smarmy smiles and a too, too sweet voice. They live among us, both those who love and those who hate. Let's scan *ourselves* to see whether we love or hate. Then repent, or else glorify God and praise him with our whole beings.

PRAYER

The light of your eye is an unblinking spotlight on my soul. I cover my face and I pray, Have mercy on me, a sinner. Amen.

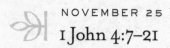

NOVEMBER 25
1 John 4:7–21

I might say, "I love God. I have accepted Jesus in my heart; *I* have done this thing!"—and cannot, therefore, be saved because I love pride, and the truth is not in me. Jesus is the truth. *He* loves. He saves us and seeks to save the whole world. Only by his love are we able to love, and the proof of that is our love for one another (John 13:34–35). If we don't love those we can see, how can we love the God we cannot see?

Beloved, don't fear the day of judgment. Don't fear the door of your death, because God casts out fear. God *is* love. And we will stand before the judge's bench with boldness and confidence.

A journalist in China watched a Catholic nun as she washed the stinking, gangrenous sores of soldiers. The journalist said, "I wouldn't do that for a million dollars." The nun said, "Neither would I"—because it is Jesus who washes our wounds (John 13:1–11). We ought to be like that nun who served and loved in the name of Jesus.

PRAYER

I love you, Lord, because you heard my cries. You heard me when I was in the depths. You heard the voice of my supplications. There is forgiveness in you, and I revere you (Psalm 130:1–2, 4). Amen.

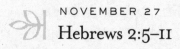

NOVEMBER 26
Hebrews 1:1–4

The author of the letter to the Hebrews writes a letter to the Christian churches in Rome. This is after the apostles have all gone to their rewards.

Long ago the Lord God spoke through the prophets. They heard his voice. They witnessed his mighty acts and saw visions and dreamed dreams. Today God speaks to us through a Son in whose glory we see the Father's glory. Christ is the Word that uttered the universe into existence. By his power he preserves the Milky Way and all the stars sprinkled across the heavens, preserves this turning earth and everything on it. He is the priest at the altar who purifies the souls of sinners and now sits enthroned at the right hand of God (Luke 22:69). Christ the King is higher than the angels, higher than the cherubim who guard the seat of mercy, than the seraphim who come so close to the love of God that they burst into flames.

It's wrong to sentimentalize the Son of God as though he were my sweet, sweet Jesus and my personal angel. He loves me. That's true. And he's my Savior. Also true. But his love is a force! So powerful that it burns Christian hearts, and their souls burst into flame.

PRAYER
I know what I am, a chief of sinners. But I also know and believe you came into the world to save me (1 Timothy 1:15). I have received your mercy. To you, the immortal and the invisible, I will give honor and glory forevermore. Amen.

NOVEMBER 27
Hebrews 2:5–11

Angels may be superior beings. They may be the messengers and the servants of God. Yet God gave the dominion of the world to us (Psalm 8). And this is a stunning wonder: that for a little while, the Father made his Son a little lower than the angels! They are spiritual. Jesus became flesh. They do not die. Jesus shed his blood on the cross and died that we may rise and now has been crowned the King of Majesty in glory and honor, and we may be called his brothers and sisters—he, the Son of God, and we, God's children. God is the Father of us all.

The writer to the Hebrews is a pastor who offers both instruction and encouragement to the churches suffering in Asia. Nero, blaming Christians for the fire that consumed Rome, began to kill them by lions, by fire, by the most horrific means.

Nonetheless, the Christians were cheerful! Jesus was the pioneer that went before them. Not only did he show the way. He *was* the way, and on his path they walked through horrors to their salvation.

PRAYER

I am not ashamed of you, Lord, because you are not ashamed of me, though I have often strayed from your path. But you bought me with your precious blood and brought me back to you, and I am heaven bound! Amen.

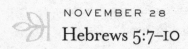

NOVEMBER 28
Hebrews 5:7–10

In the Jerusalem temple, a high priest offers up prayers for the people and sacrifices on their behalf. Jesus, their High Priest, he understood their griefs and their sorrows and took them upon himself.

While he was in human form, writes the author of Hebrews, Jesus *howled* his fervent prayers, his eyes streaming tears of anguish, begging God to save him from death. "Father, if it's your will, take this cup of suffering from me!" That was Thursday night. On Friday, in the thick darkness of a storm in the middle of the day, he cried, "My God! My God, why have you forsaken me?" In that black hour God was silent. Yet on Sunday the Father did save his Son from death. Jesus is the author and the finisher of our pilgrim faith. He is the High Priest who sacrificed himself on our altars.

Our own prayers may be met with silence, yet we can trust that they have been heard. Someone might say that the answer was to grant us a calm courage in the face of trials. But I think it's enough for us simply to believe that God has heard us.

I wonder whether the minister who is not burdened—or even anguished—by the ministry should be called a pastor, a shepherd.

There's a church in Ohio, which, when interviewing various people to minister to its congregation, doesn't think about their candidates' discomfort at the task set before them—except, maybe, the grandmother who knows what good can come from suffering. If the interviewees should confess themselves unworthy, who would continue the questioning? Who would elect unworthiness? Rather, the congregation judges the candidates according to the reports of past congregations and to their credentials.

PRAYER

Lord, send us pastors who have experience of the suffering of your suffering. Their sense of their own unworthiness will find their worthiness in you, and their passion will make them compassionate. Amen.

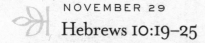

NOVEMBER 29
Hebrews 10:19–25

Faith, hope, and love.

When Christ died on Calvary, the temple curtain was torn in two, opening the way to the Most Holy Place, where people could meet the person of the Godhead (Mark 15:38). Likewise, Jesus's flesh was torn apart, opening a living way from sin to triumph.

Faith: We can approach God with "true heart"—with conviction and sincerity. Moses sprinkled the blood of a sacrificed animal on the altar (Leviticus 9:18). Even so has Jesus sprinkled our hearts clean of a guilty conscience and washed us with pure water, the waters of baptism. Peter writes in his first letter: "Baptism now saves you. It is not a washing of the body but an appeal to God for a good conscience" (1 Peter 3:21).

Hope: Believers can hold fast to hope, which is the sure and steadfast anchor of our souls. Don't waver. Be tenacious!

Love: We should pester those sisters and brothers who have become indifferent to the faith or neglectful of the Christian community, worshipping with lackluster spirit or not worshipping at all. We ought to encourage one another so that the whole community is prepared for the day to come.

One of the most effective preachers in Chicago visited one of its leading citizens on an ice-cold day. They sat before a fireplace where burning coals lay on the grate. The citizen said to the preacher, "I can be as good a Christian outside the church as sitting inside it." The preacher didn't say anything. He took a poker and separated one coal from the others. They watched as it smoked and smoldered and died.

The man said, "Okay, I get it."

PRAYER
And the greatest of these is love. Amen.

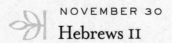

NOVEMBER 30
Hebrews 11

If we could *see* what lies in the future, if we could *see* the gates of Jerusalem, that wouldn't require faith. Faith believes in what *can't* be seen. Before the writer plunges into example after example of those who believed, sight unseen, he refers to creation, where the invisible word of God created a right visible universe.

Now comes a troop of people whose eyes saw nothing, but who believed nevertheless.

Abel made an offering which the invisible God accepted and who accounted his faith as righteous. He died, yet his faith still says, "Have faith." Enoch's faith so pleased the invisible God that he took him from this world without experiencing death. And we know Noah's story.

Abraham obeyed the Lord when he sent that old man from his known home to a land unknown. And he believed in the impossible promise of God that his stick-and-bones body and Sarah's dried-up womb would bear a baby who would bear as many babies as the stars.

The writer to the Hebrews can't stop! Moses, the Israelites, Rahab, Gideon, Samson, Jephthah, David and Samuel and the prophets, the many who were tortured and murdered.

All these heroes knew that they were strangers on earth and pilgrims wandering the wilderness, always holding the hope of a better country. They never saw the fulfillment of God's promises, but faith assured them that the promises would be fulfilled at the end.

PRAYER

> Faith of our fathers, living still
> In spite of dungeons, fire, and sword.
> Oh, how our hearts beat wild with joy
> Whenever we hear that glorious word.
> Faith of our fathers, holy faith,
> We will be true to you till death. Amen.
>
> —"FAITH OF OUR FATHERS"

The Book of
REVELATION

ABOUT REVELATION

Before we start studying Revelation, it's important to know that John is not the source of the book. Rather, it comes from the God who loves us and reveals himself not to frighten us but to comfort us. Let great Satan and his demons be frightened. Their ends will be violent and absolute.

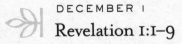

DECEMBER 1

Revelation 1:1–9

God, the Is and the Was and the To Be, has saved Christians by the blood of his Son and made them priests, as Peter wrote in his letter—priests to serve him. God is the Alpha (who created all things) and the Omega (who will at the end bring golden Jerusalem down to earth).

Patmos lies some forty miles off the coast of Asia Minor, is ten miles long and six miles wide, and Mount Elias is its highest point. Rome exiles its prisoners to this tiny island, and yet John is able to send letters to the Asian churches by the packet boat that carries food and supplies to and letters from.

Though we ourselves may not recognize the islands that separate our churches from society, we ought to, or else we might mix our beliefs with its bland, too-easy beliefs: "I don't like organized religion, but I'm spiritual." Or "My God is in the vistas of forests and canyons and the snow-crowned mountains." Or "I see his hand in the changing of the seasons. In stunning sunsets. And, oh, in the marvelous human brain!" Someone else might say, "George was such a good man. I know he's in heaven now"—as if mere goodness were enough to scoot poor George off to heaven.

And what about us? In spite of the pleasant, "spiritual" generalities of those around us, we fix our faith on the one Lord Jesus Christ, who is coming with the clouds.

God the Father, the Beginning and the End, the Origin and the Conclusion of everything that was and is and ever will be, you are faithful. Draw my faith to you. Amen.

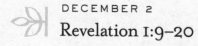

DECEMBER 2
Revelation 1:9–20

John's reference to persecution may refer to the Roman Emperor Domitian, who demands that his subjects worship *him* as their Lord and God.

Our brother John hears a voice that sounds like a thundering mountain cataract, commanding him to write his visions on scrolls and send them to seven churches. First he *hears* and then he *sees* the splendidly radiant Son of Man, who wears the purple robe of the King of Kings. The sash over his shoulder is made of molten gold; his eyes shoot fire. He holds seven stars in his right hand and is surrounded by seven lampstands. His tongue is a two-edged sword which, when swung one way, will fight the dragon and, swung the other way, will be the salvation of his people. The face of the Son of Man is so blindingly white that John falls down as if he's been struck dead. But the splendid Christ touches him, and the voice that was a cataract now speaks a consoling word. "Don't be afraid. I was dead and am alive eternally. I want you to write what will be shown you in your vision. Record them for the seven churches in Asia. They are the seven lampstands. And the stars in my hand are the seven angels that minister to the churches."

If we could allow ourselves to experience God's omnipotence, it would blow us away with such fear that our spirits would fall down. We would cover our eyes against the pain. But the first commandment is the word of a protecting Lord: "You shall fear God above all things." We fall, but Christ revives us by his touch and comforts us and sets us to work: "Write . . . speak these things. Become the things you see, for they are trustworthy and true."

We are your eighth church, Lord—countless churches that girdle the world, and your stars, your angels, do continually sing the good news about your gospel, about you. Oh, let us always sing along with them. Amen.

DECEMBER 3
Revelation 2; 3:19–22

Each of John's seven letters to the seven churches are made up of three parts. The first praises them. The second tells them what Christ has against them. The third part promises the churches that they will triumph. The Son of Man has this against the people at Thyatira: that they eat unclean food and fornicate. The word *fornicate* is a metaphor for having social intercourse with non-Christians and possibly even worshipping with them. Although the sin of the Laodiceans seems innocuous (lukewarm), Christ's judgment is anything but: "I will spew you out of my mouth. But repent and you too will conquer."

He has spoken sternly to the angels of the churches. Now he speaks tenderly, lovingly. He stands outside the door, knocking to be let in. And if the faithful open the door, they will be given a foretaste of the feast that is to come. "Taste and see that the LORD is good" (Psalm 34:8).

Matthew 7:7 reverses the image with a promise no less loving: "Ask and it will be given to you; seek and you will find; knock and the door will be opened to you."

We are the fortunate. We are the blessed, standing in the doorway which is our Lord, and we are given to taste the hidden manna of Christ's body and the wine of his blood.

PRAYER
Our Father in heaven, give us today your daily bread. Nourish our souls. Deliver us from the Evil One. Amen.

DECEMBER 4
Revelation 4:3–5:14

Sitting on the throne in limitless heaven is the mighty, the omniscient, and the omnipotent God. Around that throne are four living creatures, each with six wings as had the seraphim Isaiah saw in the temple, and twenty-four elders on twenty-four thrones, each with a crown of gold. When the creatures burst into song, the elders fall down and worship, singing the worth, the honor, and the glory of the Creator.

He holds in his right hand a scroll sealed with seven seals. An angel cries, "Who is worthy to open the scroll of destiny?" Because no one is found worthy, John begins to cry. But then the elders and the creatures and ten thousand times ten thousand angel hosts break into a new song: "Worthy is the Lamb that was slain [Christ on Calvary]. Worthy is he to crack open the seven seals!" There can be no greater praise than that which all creation sings!

In the book of Revelation, God will savage the great beast who is called the dragon, the ancient serpent, the devil of deceptions, Satan (Revelation 12:9)—but he does so for the sake of his people. The Lamb loves those who believe in him.

We're inclined to think of lambs as meek and lowly. But *this* lamb will be aggressive, the Lion of Judah, the lineage of David, who, as a young lad, slaughtered a lion, the lion that is the Devil.

PRAYER

Crown him with many crowns,
The Lamb upon his throne.
Hark! The heavenly anthem drowns
All music but its own.

Awake, my soul, and sing
Of him who died for thee,
And hail him as thy matchless King
Throughout eternity. Amen.

—"CROWN HIM WITH MANY CROWNS"

Revelation 6:1–11

The number seven indicates completeness, that a sequence has been fulfilled.

A seal is the wax that closes the scroll and is imprinted with the owner's signet ring. When the Lamb opens the first four seals, four horses and their riders gallop forth. The first horse is white (as Christ the Lamb is white). The second is as red as warfare, its rider given a sword of destruction. The third horse is black.

Its rider holds balancing scales in his hand. In normal times a quart of grain sold for pennies. But in the time of drought and famine, sellers on the black market could sell food for eight to sixteen times the normal price.

The pelt of the fourth horse is as sickly pale as the flesh of a corpse. The rider's name is Death, and the realm of the dead follows him.

At the breaking of the fifth seal, John sees under God's heavenly altar those who have been martyred for witnessing to the Word of God. They cry out, "How long, O Lord? How long before you avenge us?" (See Psalm 94:3: "How long will the wicked, how long will the wicked exult over us?") The Lord gives them the white robes that acknowledge their purity and says, "Be patient until the time comes when your brothers and sisters and all who are mine will also have been martyred."

As for us, we are called on to watch and wait and witness to the gospel. *Witness* is the English word for *martyr*.

PRAYER

For the present, my faith in the purity you've given me and my hope for a final vindication are fixed on you, Lord, because you will in the future conquer death and will crown me in your kingdom. Amen.

Revelation 11:3–14

God's two witnesses, Moses and Elijah, are not robed like that angel in white. They wear the sackcloth of mourning and are given the power to prophesy. And they do for three and a half years until the great beast, the enemy of the Lamb, rises from the bottomless pit and makes war on them. The beast kills them both and debases their bodies by leaving them to rot in the city streets. "Jerusalem," says Jesus, "Jerusalem, the city that kills the prophets and stones those who are sent to you." (See Matthew 23:37.)

For three and a half days the people on earth jeer at the prophets' decaying bodies. But then the Creator breathes the breath of life into their nostrils, and their cheeks flush pink with health. They stand upright, and all who jeered are struck with terror. A voice that sounds like the blast of a trumpet cries, "Come up!" And Moses and Elijah go up in a white cloud just as Jesus made his heavenly ascent into a white cloud. And as it happened at his death (Matthew 27:51), an earthquake jerks the surface of the earth as if it were a rug yanked back.

"Woe," the eagle cried as it flew through midheaven. "Woe, woe, woe to the inhabitants of the earth!" (Revelation 8:13).

The second woe has come to pass, and a third is yet to be. But the eagle is one of the four creatures that stand before the cosmic throne of God. It is *God* who controls the destiny of the universe—to crush evil for the sake of his people. The book of Revelation is always a book of mercy.

Some today think they can calculate the times and the years and the specific details of the prophecies in Revelation. But who truly knows the meaning of those "thousand years"? Well, there are Christians who *think* they know yet have had to revise their calculations over and over again. "Christ will come at the last battle in Armageddon. He will come when all the Jews have gathered again in the Holy Land. I've seen the signs. It's coming soon."

PRAYER

I know nothing about times or seasons or details. Only you know, not even your Son. Therefore, I wait on you. Amen.

Revelation 12:1–9

A celestial woman is crying out with labor pains. Call her the queen of heaven. Her clothing is as dazzling as the sun. She stands on Sister Moon and wears a tiara of twelve stars. At the same time, Satan, that fiery dragon, waits with open jaws to swallow down the babe as soon as it's born. The dragon's seven horns and his seven crowns signify the bloody force with which he rules the universe. His massive tail sweeps a third of the stars from the heavens to earth, stars that are his demons prepared for war.

But Satan fails. At the instant of the tiny boy's birth, he is snatched up and given a place in heaven. This child is the Messiah. Think of Herod's effort to kill the two-year-old Jesus. The queen of heaven escapes into the wilderness, where God sustains her for three and a half years.

The archangel Michael and his hosts of angels wage war against the dragon and his demons. It is a cosmic conflict in which Michael triumphs and Satan is thrown out of heaven forever.

Comfort! Comfort! John's vision continues to speak comfort to Christians. We are secure in the Messiah. The world's wickedness will attack us, but it can't destroy us. Walk strong! Talk boldly!

PRAYER

The wilderness in which I walk, though the sun beats down, is not a desert. God sustains me. Here the whole church lives both nourished and secure. The evil of the world may rule for an eon but will be defeated in the end, and I endure under the cover of your love. Amen.

Revelation 12:17; 13:1–8, 11–18

Satan stands on the shore of the sea of crashing chaos and calls forth a beast in his own image. Its wound is a perversion of the wound of the Lamb. When nations and languages and the people of the earth see that Satan has given his authority to the beast, they worship the raging

Satan, whose beast blasphemes both God and his saints in heaven, while God withholds his hand until, as he promised, all those yet to be martyred have been martyred.

The first beast swam out of the sea. The second beast arises out of the abyss in the earth. The first beast caused people to worship Satan. The second causes them also to worship the first beast. Its signs (and its wonders) are corruptions of Jesus's signs and wonders. The first beast churned the sea. Christ calmed the sea.

And the second beast brands with his own name the foreheads of those who worship Satan. The name is a number—666. Readers of Revelation have never ceased trying to figure out what this number means. Seven is the number of completion. *Three* sevens signify a pure and complete perfection, and nothing more need be said than that. The number six, on the other hand, falls short of completion, and three sixes might see perfection, but it will always and ever be out of reach.

Sometimes the church of Christ tries to protect itself from the turmoil of the world by building walls, not of faith but of caution and moderation and a self-preserving silence. But it should be going forth to challenge the attitudes of the powerful and the unjust and the harmful legalisms of the state. Jesus sacrificed himself for us. That should inspire us to sacrifice ourselves on behalf of justice and the setting free of the oppressed, the taking in of strangers and comforting them with the gospel of our Lord Jesus Christ.

PRAYER

> A mighty fortress is our God,
> A sword and shield victorious.
> He breaks the cruel oppressor's rod
> And wins salvation glorious. Amen.
>
> —"A MIGHTY FORTRESS IS OUR GOD"

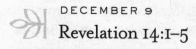

DECEMBER 9
Revelation 14:1–5

The mark of the beast? Rather, the mark of the Lamb!

In Isaiah 2:2–4 the prophet announced that God would appear on

Mount Zion to instruct Israel to walk in his paths. For me, one of the most yearning and beautiful passages in Scripture is Isaiah's prophecy: "They will beat their swords into plowshares and their spears into pruning hooks. Nation will not take up sword against nation, nor will they train for war anymore." What was good in that day is now the very height of excellence.

One hundred forty-four thousand from the tribes of Israel (Revelation 7:4) stream up the mount to the Lamb, who stands on its summit. The spotless multitudes of martyrs follow. These are they who bear on their foreheads the names of the Lamb and of his Father. They sing a new song of an indescribable beauty. Theirs is the music of the spheres.

"Oh, sing to the Lord a new song! Sing to the Lord, all the earth. Bless his name! Tell of his salvation!" (Psalm 96:1–2). The saints know the words of their choral song. To us they will remain a mystery until we sing the song in heaven.

PRAYER

Lamb of God, who takes away the sin of the world, have mercy on us, mercy, mercy on us, and grant us your peace. Amen.

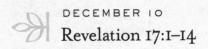

DECEMBER 10
Revelation 17:1–14

What is the great whore? She is Babylon. What is Babylon? The city that sits on seven hills—Rome.

Believers are clothed in the white of purity. The whore is dressed and jeweled in crimson luxury. Painted lips. Rouged cheeks. A lascivious, smoldering "come hither" look in her eyes. And kings have indeed come and fornicated with her and have drunk from her cup of blasphemies. The name written on her forehead is "Mystery! Babylon the great! The mother of prostitutes! She who gives birth to abominations on the earth!"

The beast on which the woman rides is the same as the beast that Satan called out of the wild and fathomless sea. God's title is the Is, the Was, and the To Be. The beast's title is an awful parody of that: the Was, the Is

Not, and the Will Be Destroyed. Like the sea beast and like Satan before it, this one has ten horns of an earthly power, the power of the Roman Empire, and the seven heads of Roman emperors, some of whom have already died (the Was), one whose authority has been undercut by one of the members of his court (the Is Not), and Nero, about whom it has been said that he would rise again, only to fall into perdition (the Will Be Destroyed).

Though these with the whore of Babylon make war on the Lamb (Comfort! Comfort ye!), the Lamb will conquer.

PRAYER

Worldly luxuries entice me, Lord. I study the Bible regularly but often spend more time reading detective books or Harlequin novels. Or else I'll page through magazines that advertise things I'll buy for my own pleasure. Snatch me out of the world to see your excellent things to come. Amen.

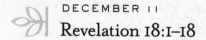

DECEMBER 11
Revelation 18:1–18

With a voice like a mighty cathedral bell, an angel tolls the funeral of Babylon: "Fallen, fallen is great Babylon!" Demons haunt the city. The kings of the earth and its merchants—those who have enriched themselves on her resources—now lament her fall because they too are falling into destitution. Babylon, which is Rome, and Rome, which is ridden by the purple-robed whore, have been stripped naked, and her painted body is revealed as a loathsome hag.

Over and over again the book of Revelation contrasts God's wrath for hell's beasts with his mercy for believers. "Come out of the city so that you won't be plagued by her plagues." The great whore thinks she's superior to God. "I am the queen of heaven! I will never suffer grief." Dream on, Babylon, until the fire burns you to ashes.

I wonder: Are we like those who are at ease in Zion? Satan is a liar. He makes our lives complacent. "Alas for those who lie on beds of ivory" (Amos 6:1, 4)—on beds of self-satisfaction. Wake up! Wake up, for night is flying.

The world is evil. Lord, save me from its plagues. In mercy don't judge me according to my sins, but clothe me in a pure, white robe, as you yourself are pure. Amen.

DECEMBER 12
Revelation 19:1–12

Again God exchanges his cruel judgment for his grace to those he loves.

The martyrs whom John saw under the altar cried out, "How long, O Lord?" Now their cry is shown its vindication. With joy the heavenly hosts sing, "Hallelujah! Glory to God!" because his justice is true. The whore and her fornicators are bound for the fires of hell, while the blood of the martyrs is avenged.

"Hallelujah! For God Almighty reigns!"

The bride who marries the Lamb contrasts the whore who fornicates. The bride wears pure white linen in contrast to the whore's polluted purple and red garment.

For the second time in Revelation, John is told to write these things in his letters to the church. "You are invited to eat the marriage feast with Christ the bridegroom."

When Christians share the Lord's Supper, they're given a foretaste of the feast to come.

Hallelujah! Rejoice!

PRAYER

My song is: Praise the Lord. Praise the Lord, O my soul! I will sing praises to you as long as I live. Amen.

DECEMBER 13
Revelation 21:1–8

Everyone dies the first death from which everyone will wake. But the wicked die the second death, which will last forever.

Babylon, great Babylon, has been abolished. Jerusalem, the new

Jerusalem, descends from heaven as a bride bejeweled to meet her groom. Finally, all is well. A voice so loud that all the new earth can hear it sings a chant of blessing. There'll be no more crying, no more pain, no more tears of sadness or longing for relief. These things have passed away. "Behold! I make all things new!" Death is swallowed up by victory! "It is finished," says the glorious Lord, even as the Lord incarnate said at the end of his work on earth. "I," God says, "am the *A* and the *Z*." Once the waters of the bottomless abyss vomited up the blaspheming beast. Now God refreshes the redeemed with the waters of life. All who polluted themselves on the old earth have been shut out of the new Jerusalem to suffer the flames of hellfire.

But we, we will live in the mansions of Christ forever. Rejoice! Your light has come!

PRAYER

Blessing and honor and glory and might be to you, O Lamb of God, forever and forever. Amen.

DECEMBER 14
Revelation 21:9–27

An angel carries John up the summit of the cosmic mountain to view the radiant glory of the new Jerusalem. A monumental wall with three gates on every side, to the east, the north, the south, and the west. The gates are pearls etched with the names of the twelve tribes of Israel. The wall itself has twelve foundations, on each of which are written the names of the twelve apostles. In Jerusalem the Old and the New Testaments are joined together, and what was denied to the heroes of the Bible is finally granted to the citizens of the city: to see God face to face.

New Jerusalem is an enormous cube. So was the Most Holy Place in Solomon's Temple, where God dwelt among his people. There is no temple here, for the Almighty and the Lamb *are* its temple, no longer hidden in darkness but everywhere brilliantly present. Jerusalem is made of gold as clear as crystal. The streets are gold, and those who walk them—their names have been written in the Book of Life.

Where are we? Do we express our faith and worship in our own temple-churches, or else within our houses? Do we worship by means of religious television shows? Do we box God? But he doesn't dwell in temples. He is everywhere, the temple of our High Priest, Jesus Christ. Let's get up and wash ourselves and put on clean clothes and go out to live our faith in public places.

PRAYER

A city gate made of one big pearl? I can't imagine it. But I might understand it if I think of the pearl of great price—the kingdom of heaven. I must sell everything I have and everything I am. As you sold yourself to the smiters, Lord, help me to do the same. Amen.

DECEMBER 15
Revelation 22:1–5

How lovely is this impossibly divided tree, planted on either side of the river of life and producing twelve kinds of fruit for the twelve months of the year. And how wonderful are its healing leaves. They can make a poultice to be laid on the wounds of the nations. No sun or moon or lamps are needed in the new Jerusalem, for Christ, the Light of the World, shines on it. Pagans worship the sun. God's children worship the Son of God, whose divine name is written on their foreheads.

We are that river of life. We are the four rivers that flowed from the garden of Eden. But we must flow among the people of our present nations, bringing them the healing of the gospel, preaching to them the holiness of our living God, for the world is distinctly *un*well. It fears the black night wherein nightmares are inhabited by ghosts and beasts and the scythe of death.

Shine, Christians! Be the light of the Light of the World. Jesus is the life and the light of all people. The darkness cannot overcome him (John 1:4–5).

PRAYER

No more nightmares. My dreams are flooded with your brilliant light. I bend my knees and cry, "Holy! Holy!" Amen.

Revelation 22:3–5

"I am coming soon." Prepare for the day of Christ's return as though Christ will appear tomorrow to take us home. Pack your faith in suitcases. Polish your shoes. Dress your souls in garments pure and white, and wait with the conviction of his coming.

John's letter to the churches is nearly at its end. He writes about his final vision wherein he worships the angel who has shown him and has explained to him the meanings of the things he's seen and heard. Once he was a little lower than the angels. Now he and all believers are equal to them. "Get up," says the angel. "We both serve the same God."

Daniel was told to roll up the scroll of his prophecies and to seal it so that it couldn't be opened until the end of time. John, on the other hand, is told *not* to seal his book, "For the end is almost upon us." No, his prophecies must be left open so that the people of the earth—then as now—may read it and repent and be newly born.

Many of us tend to skip the book of Revelation. We can't make sense of its mysteries, or so we suppose. Or else we *do* pay attention to the book, imposing on it our own notions, making its symbolical thousand years into actual years by which we can determine the when and the what of the things to come.

PRAYER
With my eyes wide open, I read the book of your mysteries, my Lord. Faith doesn't need explanations. It lives and moves, trusting in your love. Amen.

Revelation 22:6–11

"Trustworthy and true" are John's visions. Trustworthy and true are the words he has heard. Trustworthy and true is the Lord God, the king of heaven and earth. Therefore, fight the good fight until the victory is won, always looking forward to the rewards we will receive in the heaven of heavens.

In the meantime, we will place our faith in Christ's assurance: "I am coming soon."

Blessed—this is the second to last beatitude of the whole Bible. "Blessed are those who love me and keep my commandments."

The psalmist (Psalm 8:6) praises the Sovereign God for giving his people dominion over everything he created. Never forget that though he is sometimes silent, God makes himself known in all the works of his hands: the deer that can spring sixteen feet at a jump, the rustling in the leaves of the trees, the rivers and the streams that twinkle in his light. We may be fragile, but we are not weak. We may be shabby witnesses, but we witness to the gospel.

PRAYER

Make worthy my unworthiness, Lord. You are my staff and stay. Whom shall I fear? Amen.

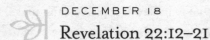

DECEMBER 18
Revelation 22:12–21

For the consolation of the churches that are suffering under Rome's bootheels, John keeps emphasizing Christ's promise, "I am coming soon!"

Isaiah wrote, "Though your sins are like scarlet, they shall be as white as snow" (Isaiah 1:18). With the Bible's last beatitude, John calls "blessed" those who wash their clothes in the red blood of the white Lamb, for the Tree of Life is theirs. To drink from the crystal waters of life is also theirs. This is the first time in John's book that Jesus identifies himself by name: "It is I, Jesus, who sent my angel to you. I, the bright Morning Star." To him a chorus of voices cry, "Come! Come! Come!" Yes, and he *shall* come in all his glory.

Some have interpreted John's warning neither to add nor to take away from the prophecies in his book to mean the *whole* book of the Bible. They say that the Bible is historically accurate in every respect and that those who would change its facts into symbols or mere un-Christlike parables will be cursed. But John is speaking about his book only.

How dearly, now, does John conclude his letter. Christ confirms that "I am coming soon." And then this prayer: "Amen. Come, Lord Jesus."

And then this benediction: "The grace of our Lord Jesus Christ be with all the saints. Amen."

PRAYER
Amen and amen.

PART II

CHRISTMAS AGAIN

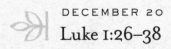

Luke 3:1–16

John the Baptist has said to the crowd that came to the Jordan to be baptized by him, "Be the trees that bear fruit worthy of repentance."

The people are puzzled. "Fruit?" they ask. "What does that mean? And what do you want us to do?"

John's response is as simple as what a mother might instruct her children, something the people can understand, something Jesus himself will say (Luke 6:29–31). "If in a bitter winter you see someone who has no coat, give him yours. Share your food with any Lazarus you see begging at a rich man's door." Likewise does he speak to tax collectors, and likewise to soldiers. And likewise to us.

It's right and proper to serve Jesus in our Sunday worship. But do we serve him by going into the inner city to serve the poor? And what about money? It's right and proper to put money in the collection plate. But do we also buy clothes for the indigent?

PRAYER

Lord, you've taught me not to practice piety by giving alms in public but to give alms in secret. I confess it: too often have I sought the approval of others by allowing them to notice the (false) humility by which I spend myself on good works. But you spent your life to give me life. Take me to your bosom and forgive me. Amen.

Luke 1:26–38

The Canaanites tell this disturbing folktale: if a jealous angel should appear to a young woman on the night of her betrothal, beware! It's a sign that the she-demon will kill the man she's soon to marry.

Could this be one of the reasons why Gabriel's appearance to Mary troubles her? Gabriel (his name means "God is my hero") is quick to allay her fears: "Hush, child. Mary, let your heart be calm. I've come with good news." Ah, then he hasn't come to harm the man she loves. The angel Gabriel says, "God told me to tell you that he has chosen you above all other women. In nine months you will bear a healthy and holy baby boy."

Mary can be calm. But Mary can also be bold and outspoken. "You're wrong, sir. I'm a virgin. I have not and will not lie with any man till Joseph and I are married."

Gabriel says, "A virgin you are, and a virgin you will be, even to the time you've delivered the babe. Nothing is impossible with God. Tonight the Holy Spirit will plant the seed in your womb, and your infant will be called the Son of the Most High God. He will reign, as did his ancestor King David reign, over Israel. But your boy's kingdom will last forever."

Straightway the Virgin Mary's boldness of speech becomes the boldness of faith: "I will be the handmaiden of the Lord."

Likewise, let the women of our age be the Lord's maidservants, and the men his menservants, and let us serve as Mary served—obediently.

PRAYER
I am weak, but you are mighty. My faith is fragile, but your faithfulness is powerful. Help me, my Lord, to believe in your promises, for they shall be fulfilled. Amen.

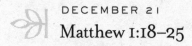

DECEMBER 21
Matthew 1:18–25

Luke records as many as five songs about and around the birth of Jesus. Matthew records another.

Joseph notices that Mary's belly has begun to pooch. She's pregnant, but not by him! Therefore, he's obligated to divorce her—a true sadness because he loves her. A public divorce will humiliate her. Mary will walk in shame the streets of Nazareth.

It's then that Gabriel appears to Joseph in a dream to tell him what is and what is not.

"Go to Mary's house, and take her as your wife. No man has bedded her. Believe this, that she is by the Holy Spirit great with child."

Then the archangel sings a song with the words of the prophet Isaiah:

> A virgin will conceive
> And bear a son,
> And they shall name him
> Immanuel.

Gabriel says to Joseph, "Name the baby Jesus." In Hebrew that name is *Yeshua*: "God helps," which means "God saves his people from their sins." And his name will be Immanuel because the Savior is, and will always be, with us.

Joseph will do more than the archangel requests. He will adopt Mary's baby as his own.

And we? We sing to the Lord a new song (Psalm 149:1). We praise his name with dancing and melodies on our instruments (v. 3).

PRAYER

Ah, Jesus, our Morning Star, arise above the horizon. Shed your light on our dark December night. Grant us dreams of bathrobes and slippers and apples and cookies. Amen.

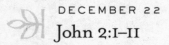

DECEMBER 22
John 2:1–11

A wedding can be an extravagant, week-long celebration, with musicians and jugglers and every entertainment imaginable, with catered food and quantities of flowing wine. The bride and the groom sit under a canopy on an elevated platform, watching the party as though they were a lord and a lady.

But Mary and Joseph's is a simple affair. They live in the little village of Nazareth. They haven't the money to spend on something luxurious. Joseph and his men process through the town from his house, while Mary and her friends process from her house until both processions meet and go together back to Joseph's house, where the wedding is consecrated. Friends and relatives attend. Someone plucks a harp while Mary sings.

Men tell jokes and women laugh, and perhaps their joy outshines the joy of the wealthy, for the Lord God himself directs this marriage.

Today a wedding can cost in the tens of thousands of dollars. "Because," a bride might say, "this will be my only chance to live like a queen."

Thanne and I held our wedding reception in an elementary school's gymnasium. Our meal was cooked by the women of the congregation. Who needs—well, we didn't need—more than that?

PRAYER

Christ, you are our food and our wine. You are the true Bridegroom (Matthew 25:1), and we will sit at the feast of the Lamb. Amen.

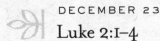
DECEMBER 23
Luke 2:1–4

Before Jesus is born, Caesar Augustus is the most powerful man on earth. His empire covers the world from Gaul in the west and into Asia in the east. Roman taxes can drain a Judean family of all its money. Whether Joseph feels forced to do Caesar's bidding, or else because he is a genuinely obedient man, he puts his bride on a donkey and travels the eighty miles to Bethlehem.

Joseph is a quiet and righteous man. All throughout the four gospels, Mary speaks. But from Joseph not a word is heard. His carpenter's arms are well muscled, yet he treats Mary tenderly and is quick to see and to serve her needs. A thimble and thread? Here they are. A cradle? Joseph builds it of polished oak.

He wears a leather cap. His workman's apron is covered with sawdust.

Wood-shavings cling to his beard.

In two days we will celebrate Christmas. Joseph, I admire you.

PRAYER

With quietness and confidence, I lay me down to sleep. Christ, you reign in heaven. The day after tomorrow I will wake and honor your lowly birth. Amen.

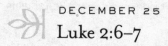

DECEMBER 24
Matthew 21:1–11

Children waved palm branches and sang, "Hosanna!" when Jesus entered Jerusalem riding a donkey so low that his sandals dragged the dust. As for tonight, the children will sit with us in the dark church, holding candles, and the whole sanctuary will look as if a thousand stars have come down to earth. And we will sing "Silent Night."

Grandma will dab her tears with a hankie. Old men will bow their heads, remembering their childhoods, when all the world was simple and good and the Christmas tree was lit with candles on its boughs. Behind us a great grandpa will sing the hymn in German, *"Stille nacht, heilige nacht."*

And who will blame the little children for squirming in their seats? Tomorrow morning Christmas Day will dawn.

PRAYER
So let your angels hover over us tonight. Let their wings cover us like canopies. Let them tune their voices to sing "Gloria!" tomorrow. Amen.

DECEMBER 25
Luke 2:6–7

This morning our children fly out of their beds. They creep to the Christmas tree. Presents! Presents! Mother says, "Save the wrapping paper." The littlest child yells, "Look what I got!" The adults smile and nod and think to themselves, "Look what *we've* got," meaning their children, meaning their families, meaning a time of peace in this hectic world.

Jesus is here in our houses. Of course he is. His name is Immanuel.

Somewhere Christians are singing "From Heaven Above to Earth I Come":

> Ah, dearest Jesus, holy child,
> Make thee a bed, soft, undefiled,
> Within my heart that it may be
> A quiet chamber kept for thee.

Love is the greatest present. Jesus loves us and we love him, and our hearts leap up, and we drink, and we are half-drunk with gladness.

PRAYER
We are the hosts and the holy ones. We are the stars in heaven, singing, "Glory to God in the heavens, and peace to his people on earth!" Amen.

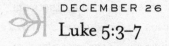

DECEMBER 26
Luke 5:3–7

Canadians call the twenty-sixth of December "Boxing Day"—a tradition which began years ago, the giving of boxes of gifts to the merchants in a city.

In our house it wasn't the giving of boxes on Boxing Day but Christmas stockings hung in the living room, each containing a little toy and each with our names sewn into the fabric. I am the eldest of seven. When we woke on the twenty-sixth, we'd jump out of our beds and dash into the living room.

I've never known what caused my little brother to cry. He was four that year. "What's the matter?" I asked. He didn't answer but huddled in a corner, looking for all the world like a lost and lonely lamb.

Jesus loves little lambs. If one of seven, or even one of a hundred, has wandered off and put herself in danger, Jesus will find her. Jesus will wipe away her tears, then lift her to his shoulders and carry her home, and the whole flock, the whole family, will rejoice.

While my brother was sobbing, our father hoisted him into a hug, and he was consoled. Dad lowered the boy onto the sofa and sat down beside him. Dad took his pipe from a side table, stuffed its bowl with tobacco, lit it with a match, and blew smoke rings, and my little brother giggled, which, you know, is a form of joy.

PRAYER
Lord Jesus, I will invite all my friends to come to my house for a party. We will cut your birthday cake and raise a toast to you, for you are our brother, and we love you. Amen.

Luke 2:41–47

Judean boys were considered children until their thirteenth birthdays. Jesus was twelve, one year short of his majority, when his parents left Jerusalem to travel north toward Nazareth, always supposing that he was somewhere else, chatting with his friends and laughing at their jokes.

But at the end of the day, when everyone pitched their tents and called their families together for a meal, Jesus was nowhere to be found.

I think that every parent can sympathize with Jesus's parents, panicked that their child was lost and maybe hurt, or worse, dying. All that night Mary and Joseph rushed back to Jerusalem, looking for Jesus on the way. By morning they were searching in the city. Where could he be? Why, in the temple courts, sitting under Solomon's Colonnade and listening to the rabbis and asking penetrating questions.

When they finally learned where to find him, Mary was at first relieved, and then vexed. "How could you do this to us?" she scolded. "You're turning my brown hair grey!"

For the first time in his life, Jesus called God "my Father." In his thirteenth year, Jesus began to go about his Father's business.

These days we've been looking backward to the birth of the Lord. Now we must look forward to his ministry, which empowers us to minister too. Haul hay in a good spirit. That is Jesus's work. Launder the bedsheets, thanking the Lord for giving us a daily purpose. That is his work. Tell his stories to the children. Serve widows and orphans. Model the Lord in all we do. That also is Jesus's work.

PRAYER

Make my hands your hands. Make my mind as humble as yours. Give my heart a love like your love, and nothing I do will fail. Amen.

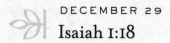

Matthew 2:16–18

It has been a long tradition of the Catholic Church to call the twenty-eighth day of December "Childermas." It commemorates the deaths of the Holy Innocents under King Herod and might be said to remember the innocent suffering and death of Christ. It's a hard thing to think about that event—especially now, when it interrupts our Christmas joy. Yet it must be remembered, because lives of happiness are always interrupted by trouble.

Mary wept at the foot of the cross. She was like Rachel of old, lamenting, *wailing*, and unconsoled because her child was no more.

How could we ever forget, my wife and I, the time when one of our children, having grown into a young man, took his own path, resentful of us?

Christ didn't die in his second year. He died in his thirties. But we must ever remember that he rose to life on the third day.

Likewise, after our son had hit the bottom, had fallen—like the prodigal son—into his own kind of death, he could do nothing but return home. Home was exactly the right place to be, because our love raised him to new life. Even today he hugs us, and I smell the soap that washed him, and he whispers in our ears, "I love you."

PRAYER
Love is love, whether from you, Lord, or yours by the deeds of those who love us with your love. Amen.

Isaiah 1:18

Bells, bells, ring out the old!

We can compare this past year to the snow heaped up along our streets, grimy with salt and blackened by the mud-sludge splashed up by the tires of our cars—snow filthy on its surface and filthy underneath.

These are the sins we've committed through the last twelve months. They require examination.

Do we plan to make New Year's resolutions? How *can* we when we're still polluted and resentful? Every resolution would be self-serving. First we need to resolve the sins committed during this past year and to confess them, believing in God's mercy.

I've found that the most beneficial way to have my crimson transgressions purified is to confess them to my pastor or a most devout Christian. Speaking them aloud puts them out in the air between us. This is the first stage of forgiveness. And if my confessor has stout faith, he or she will not condemn me but will listen without any judgment at all. Neither will the King judge me when he comes in glory.

Bells, bells, ring in the new!

Now we can compare the coming year to snow—fresh snow, newly fallen snow, snow pillow-white. Then a sincere New Year's resolution can, with the help of God, be kept.

PRAYER

Jesus, you have remembered me with your holy promises (Psalm 105:42), and I have received them with a grateful heart. Amen.

DECEMBER 30
Isaiah 62:10–12

Oh, what wonderful things the Lord God has in store for us! "Go through, go through the gates." At midnight tomorrow we will go through the gate of God's providence. "Prepare a way for my people." *We* are God's people! A fresh new year, the new year about to be born, must have a name: its number that counts back to the birth of Jesus. And we are given new names too, names that signify the love of God: A Holy People Redeemed by the Lord, and Sought Out, and Not Forsaken.

How will we today prepare to celebrate New Year's Eve tomorrow? Buying sprigs of mistletoe, with its green leaves and its white berries? Chestnuts and a nutcracker? Pointy party hats and cardboard horns to beep the new year in? Mix eggnog? We'll get ready to sing "*Auld Lang Syne*." We'll plan to watch the ball drop in Times Square. Maybe the old folks plan to be in bed.

All for fun. All to the good.

But even a party ought not to neglect the good things God has in store for us and what he will continue to do. "*Auld Lang Syne*" is appropriate. But the better song is "Every time I feel the Spirit moving in my heart, I will pray."

PRAYER

Jesus, it's you who prepared for us the road from earth to heaven. And you gave me the name Child of God. Amen.

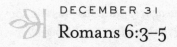

DECEMBER 31
Romans 6:3–5

Evening. Time to have a party!

A friend of mine places on his dining room table a simple wooden cross surrounded by nuts and mugs and two pitchers of eggnog. He will beep and beep the new year in and, yes, at midnight will watch that starry moon descending on Times Square. But he will also keep glancing at the empty resurrection cross on his dining room table, thinking not only about the coming new year but also about salvation ever new.

People picture the new year as a chubby baby with silly little wings and a sash over its shoulder, and on that sash the four-digit number of its name. I don't picture the new year like that. I picture the ascending Christ.

As for the old year, we shouldn't picture it as Mr. Death, black-robed, black-hooded, faceless, and holding the scythe he'll swing when someone's time has come. No, the better picture, though it contains a death too, is that of Jesus on his cross—and of our own deaths, for we have been baptized into his death and buried with him (Romans 6:3–4). Thus, the old and dying year.

But here comes the new year of the resurrection!

Put on your party hats! Beep! Kiss under sprigs of mistletoe! Kiss each other with holy kisses! Winter soon will pass away. The sun will rise higher and higher like a watchman in the sky. And we are already rising higher and higher.

Sing to the Lord a new song! (Isaiah 42:10). Sing "How Great Thou Art." Sing "Christ is the King! O Friends, Rejoice!" And sing loudly "Glory! Glory! Hallelujah!"

Then wake up tomorrow, wild with joy!

PRAYER

Jesus, your love is my chariot. And your four mane-flaming horses (the gospel writers) are galloping me heavenward. Amen! And amen.

My friends, my readers, how glad I am to have shared these last twelve months with you. I've always thought of you as my traveling companions over the high roads and the low roads too. We began with faith, and faith has seen us through.